Speaking my Soul: Race, Life and Language is a fascinating account of a life that started in colonial British Guiana (now Guyana) but was transformed by emigration to the United States in the turbulent late 1960s. Arriving here as a college student challenges Rickford to the core. The embracing Black Power movement presents him with a chance to discover a self essentially misled in British Guiana; seizing that chance, he exorcises some of the main colonialist demons, especially those involving the privilege of possessing a "light" skin color that is often a barrier between him, and others like him, and the black masses. Finding in the study of sociolinguistics a field of inquiry that reinforces his new self-perception, he becomes an expert above all on the dignity and integrity of "Black English." In a crucial way, this is an act of love, and love is a crucial feature here: above all, love of family and love of academia but also love of the masses of people everywhere. This is a notable, instructive story of a remarkable life and career.

—**Arnold Rampersad**, author of
biographies of *Jackie Robinson*, *Langston Hughes* and *Ralph Ellison* and co-author of
Arthur Ashe: Days of Grace, a Memoir

In this remarkable and compelling story about love, family, poetry, language, education, activism and the evolution of identity and acceptance, John R. Rickford illuminates the transatlantic ties that bind Caribbean, African and African American cultures, and the complexities of race that informed his own journey from Guyana to the United States.

—**Tracey L. Weldon**, author of *Middle Class African American English*

Rickford is not just one of the first scholars of color to study modern sociolinguistics. His model as an educator, family member and friend has made our profession more humble, kinder and more caring. He is a transformative figure who has written a captivating account of his journey from a single bedroom with nine kids in Guyana to the leader of the sociolinguistic world. A riveting, inspirational account!

—**Walt Wolfram**, author of *Dialects and American English*, *Appalachian English* and *Talkin' Tar Heel*

T0383722

Speaking my Soul: Race, Life and Language is such a moving memoir—at once a highly personal family story, and yet one with insights that make this book also an invaluable contribution to Black Studies, Diasporic Studies, and the emerging field of Critical Mixed Race Studies. Rickford's intimate family account of his own complex racial heritage, paired with an insider's view of a field of research that he himself shaped, is a wholly engrossing read. The divine irony that this world-renowned pioneer in sociolinguistics temporarily lost his speech after a stroke makes this memoir an even more poignant reflection on life and language.

—**Michelle Elam**, author of *The Souls of Mixed Folk* and editor of *The Cambridge Companion to James Baldwin*

[I]t is Rickford's humanity that shines through these pages, showing how diversity is one of the world's most valuable resources, how diversity arises from the chances and challenges of ordinary people's lives and how academic study, far from meaning elite confinement in an ivory tower, can show how knowledge is not only power but enrichment of everybody's lives.

—**Michael Mitchell**, University of Warwick, UK

Dr. John Rickford is the heart of Black language and linguistics scholarship because of what you see and feel in *Speaking my Soul* from the very beginning: family and friends. I am glad John made his way from Guyana to the United States and developed his "Black complex" that led him to expand our knowledge and understanding of Black languages and Black lives. The homage to his award-winning book co-authored with his son only serves to enshrine him as the heart and soul for those of us who do (Black) language. And though he may have often been the "runt of the litter" in various instances in his life, he is definitely our rock. Thank you for speaking to my soul.

—**Sonja L. Lanehart**, University of Arizona, USA, author of *Sista, Speak! Black Women Kinfolk Talk About Language and Literacy* and editor of *The Oxford Handbook of African American Language*

This moving and honest memoir is crucial to understanding the wider reaches of identity in a multi-racial former British colony, and by extension, to the much-discussed question of identity in today's instantly connected global world. Having himself in 2019 suffered an unexpected stroke (an illness that had killed his father), Rickford was motivated to further explore his family tree ... This leads Rickford to discover a web of ancestral connections (African, East Indian, Amerindian, Scottish) that bear witness to Guyana's diverse racial heritage. ... in this memoir, Rickford invites us to sit with the unseen ancestors that inhabit his house of memory.

—From the *Foreword* by **John Agard**,
author of *Half-Caste*, numerous other books
of poetry and winner of the 2012 Queen's
Gold Medal for Poetry

Speaking my Soul

Speaking my Soul is the honest story of linguist John R. Rickford's life from his early years as the youngest of ten children in Guyana to his status as Emeritus Professor of Linguistics at Stanford, of the transformation of his identity from colored or mixed race in Guyana to black in the USA, and of his work championing Black Talk and its speakers.

This is an inspiring story of the personal and professional growth of a black scholar, from his life as an immigrant to the USA to a world-renowned expert who has made a leading contribution to the study of African American life, history, language and culture. In this engaging memoir, Rickford recalls landmark events for his racial identity like being elected president of the Black Student Association at the University of California, Santa Cruz; learning from black expeditions to the South Carolina Sea Islands, Jamaica, Belize and Ghana; and meeting or interviewing civil rights icons like Huey P. Newton, Rosa Parks and South African Dennis Brutus. He worked with Rachel Jeantel, Trayvon Martin's good friend, and key witness in the trial of George Zimmerman for his murder—Zimmerman's exoneration sparked the Black Lives Matter movement.

With a foreword by poet John Agard, this is the account of a former Director of African and African American Studies whose work has increased our understanding of the richness of African American language and our awareness of the education and criminal justice challenges facing African Americans. It is key reading for students and faculty in linguistics, mixed-race studies, African American studies and social justice.

John Russell Rickford is a former president of the Linguistics Society of America. He was elected to membership in the American Academy of Arts and Sciences and the National Academy of Sciences. Rickford is co-editor of *African-American English*, now available as a Routledge Linguistics Classic.

Speaking my Soul
Race, Life and Language

John Russell Rickford

Routledge
Taylor & Francis Group

LONDON AND NEW YORK

Cover image: © Linda Cicero, Stanford News Service

First published 2022
by Routledge
2 Park Square, Milton Park, Abingdon, Oxon OX14 4RN

and by Routledge
605 Third Avenue, New York, NY 10158

Routledge is an imprint of the Taylor & Francis Group, an informa business

© 2022 John Russell Rickford

British Library Cataloguing-in-Publication Data
A catalogue record for this book is available from the British Library

Library of Congress Cataloging-in-Publication Data
A catalog record has been requested for this book

ISBN: 978-1-032-06885-5 (hbk)
ISBN: 978-1-032-06883-1 (pbk)
ISBN: 978-1-003-20430-5 (ebk)

DOI: 10 4324/9781003204305

Typeset in Times New Roman
by Deanta Global Publishing Services, Chennai, India

Contents

Illustrations

Figures

Table

Foreword

By John Agard

In a special May 1966 Independence issue of the Queen's College newspaper, *QC Lictor* (Georgetown, Guyana) a sixteen-year-old editor wrote these words:

> While I would not deny the relevance of English and European historical studies, there is everything to say for West Indian, African or Asian studies being made a part of our A-level courses. Then, even if students fall short of academic perfection, they will at least have some idea of their common heritage.

The sixteen-year-old, who made that confidently adolescent yet prescient declaration (bearing in mind that the Caribbean Examinations Council (CXC) had not come into being until 1972) was John Rickford, who went on to pursue a much acclaimed career in sociolinguistics.

And I'm only too happy to say a few words by way of saluting Rickford's memoir. True, he's my friend from way back in teenage days, my peer, my fellow "limer" (as we called a chilling out buddy). And true, there are certain parallels in our evolution as two Guyanese boys.

But this moving and honest memoir is crucial to understanding the wider reaches of identity in a multiracial former British colony, and by extension, to the much-discussed question of identity in today's instantly connected global world.

Having himself in 2019 suffered an unexpected stroke (an illness that had killed his father), Rickford was motivated to further explore his family tree. When faced with our own mortality, exploring one's family tree (something we might have been putting off for ages) can suddenly take on a sense of urgency.

This leads Rickford to discover a web of ancestral connections (African, East Indian, Amerindian, Scottish) that bear witness to Guyana's diverse racial heritage. Guyana is in fact officially projected as a "land of six races"—the indigenous Amerindian, African, East Indian, Chinese, Portuguese, European/other. Here it's interesting to note that the Portuguese, having come as 19th century indentured laborers from Madeira, were differentiated from Europeans who were grouped with the other expatriates.

Of course, the different races would be conditioned by stereotyped notions about each other. Yet, out of that historically enforced co-existence, there emerged a Caribbean crucible brimming with racial and linguistic cross-fertilization.

And these two strands—ethnicity and language—turned out to be crucial to Rickford's personal development, influencing his decision to switch from literature to linguistics while an undergraduate at the University of California, Santa Cruz.

As Rickford recalls: "The switch from Literature to Linguistics was one of two transformations I underwent in my undergraduate years, the other being the change from conceiving myself as colored to defining myself as black. The two transitions were not unrelated. Learning to love Black Talk (my native Creolese— or Guyanese "patois"—and African American Vernacular English, or "AAVE") was of a piece with learning to love my black self, the African strands of my ancestry, my me."

However, the groundwork for such a transformation had already been laid in his sixth form days at Queen's College. Among the many teachers to whom Rickford pays homage is C.A. Yansen (or Yango, as he was fondly called). And it was in the previously mentioned 1966 Independence Issue of the *QC Lictor* (edited by head boy Rickford) that Yango had contributed an article entitled "Random Remarks On Creolese."

Here's what C.A. Yansen had to say about Guyanese Creolese, in his Foreword to the revised edition of *Random Remarks on Creolese*, 1993, ed by Sonja Jansen:

> Creolese is a living thing and clearly reflects the activities of all Guyanese in every walk of life: their hopes and fears, joys and sorrows, vices and virtues, achievements and failures; in fine, their reactions to all the vicissitudes of time and circumstance, and above all, their sense of humour, without which life indeed will not be worth much.

Subsequently, another Queen's College teacher, Richard Allsopp, would nurture Rickford's passion for linguistics. In his own words:

> I was even more influenced by the MA and PhD theses that Richard Allsopp, the first local head master of QC, had done in 1958 and 1962 on Guyanese Creole English, although I would not really read and appreciate them until I was doing my own PhD research in the 1970s. I was blown away by the fact that even before William Labov's 1966 emphasis on the value of eliciting casual speech and counting how often people used one feature rather than another, Allsopp had shown the value of recording informal, unmonitored speech and using quantitative measurements in his analysis of Guyanese speech.

At this point, let me take a moment to also pay tribute to the pivotal role of the teacher in Caribbean childhood (small days) as well as adolescence, for Rickford is of a generation who saw a teacher as a shining beacon with a blackboard for accomplice.

In my own case, at St Stanislaus College, an all-boys secondary school run by Jesuits in Georgetown, it was a Scottish priest, Father Stanley Maxwell ("Maxy" to us) who in my early teens would turn me on to words. Maxy made the dictionary an adventure. (Though I must also in passing mention the radio commentaries by the legendary commentator, John Arlott.)

Later in Sixth Form it was another inspiring teacher, Michael Gilkes, himself a poet and playwright who taught us Joyce's *A Portrait Of The Artist As A Young Man* and from whose lips I would first hear the words *epiphany* and *synasthesia*. (Sadly, Michael Gilkes died last year, one of the many who had fallen to the pandemic of our times.)

It is striking that in the course of his memoir Rickford pays homage to a veritable roll-call of teachers who have in some way contributed to his development, whether along the road of linguistics, history, or indeed poetry.

The switch to sociolinguistics would set him down the path of exploring an impressive range of dialects, including Gullah spoken by Sea Islanders, South Carolina; Garifuna of Belize; not to mention varieties of Caribbean Creole Englishes.

But this new linguistic path would also converge with a growing African consciousness fed by various sources—his role as President of the Black Students Alliance at the University of California, Santa Cruz; his reading of *The Autobiography of Malcolm X*; his introduction to Huey Newton, co-founder with Bobby Seale of the Black Panther Party; his hosting at Stanford University of an event for Civil Rights icon, Rosa Parks, who had refused to give up her seat on that Alabama bus one cold December night of 1955; his meeting with South African anti-apartheid activist and poet, Dennis Brutus; as well as the eye-opening experience of interacting with the Gullah-speaking Sea Islanders of South Carolina.

Away from the fluid **"shade-ism"** of the Caribbean and thrust into the harsher black/white polarization he was experiencing in the USA, Rickford embraces the Black Power ethos with a commitment that would make his mother back in Guyana express some concern over his new sprung goatee and dashiki attire, while his father concluded that his son had developed "a black complex."

In Rickford's own words,

> I *had* developed a "black" complex. Living in the US with its one-drop view of race. (I was 34% African, 14% South Asian, 48% European, and 3% Amerindian, as later DNA analyses revealed). The American system was very different from the highly gradated, shade-conscious Caribbean society in which we grew up, in which blacks were 100% African or nearly so, and people like me were colored, mulatto, brown, red, or mixed.

Meanwhile, staying with Guyana in the early 70's, my own dear Mom had been just as shellshocked as Rickford's dear Mom when she witnessed my neatly parted *Brylcreem*-gleaming hair (showing more of the Portuguese in me) suddenly sprout into an abundant Afro (showing more of the black on me). To bolster her argument, she was quick to point out that my hair looked like a bush fowl and that my fully black (that is to say, not mixed race) friends should be the ones turning Afro, yet they seemed to keep their woolly hair low and well groomed like Harry Belafonte or Sidney Poitier.

As regards this shifting of allegiances, it would be salutary to reflect a moment on Amin Maalouf, the Lebanese-French novelist's observation that "people often see themselves in terms of whichever one of their allegiances is most under attack."

And embracing the fact that identity cannot be compartmentalized, and that among his multiple tributaries, he is Arab, French, Maronite Christian, Maalouf radically suggests that people should be able to include in what they regard as their own identity a new ingredient, in "the sense of belonging to the human adventure" as well as their own.

As a poet, I find Maalouf's choice of the word "ingredient" both apt and appealing. And I'd like to sustain that culinary metaphor in relation to Rickford's memoir, for it was no less than young Rickford's own inspiring Queen's College teacher, C.A. Yansen (Yango) who chose to describe his *Random Remarks On Creolese* as a "cook-up with a bit of vocabulary, history, philology, grammar, glossary and semantics as the ingredients."

For those unfamiliar with that classic Guyanese dish—a cook-up is a mouth-watering medley of black-eyed peas and rice, with chicken or beef and okras, a Scotch Bonnet pepper among other spices, all boiling away in coconut milk, which gives it that distinctive flavor. Leftovers (or *lef-lef*) are often creatively added to the mix.

And I welcome Rickford's memoir as a cook-up of an honest and poignant personal recollection blended with a bit of ancestral detective work, seasoned with an exploration of identity, combined with a linguistic stir of varieties of Creolese, marinated in relevant references to poetry for which Rickford maintained a passion from his teenage days and beyond his switch from literature to linguistics.

For poetry, as Breyten Breytenbach, the outspoken Afrikaans writer reminds us, is about our multiplicity, our un-fixedness. About how we are modified by the ancestors and the ghosts, taken possession of by the invisible guests. Voices also need a house to sleep in.

This comment resonates not only with the fluidity of poetry but also with the multiplicity of identity. And in this memoir, Rickford invites us to sit with the unseen ancestors that inhabit his house of memory.

Prologue: the gift of stroke

John R. Rickford

It happened on September 10, 2019—exactly 50 years after I sent Dad a last let-ter from Santa Cruz, California that he would never receive, because he died four days later of a stroke at the age of 56. Two of my three brothers have since died of strokes, Peter in 1995 at 55, and Edward in 1998 at 63. Now, six days before my 70th birthday, was it to be my turn?

I was working seven days a week to clear out my office at Stanford University in Palo Alto, California, just north of Santa Cruz. I was retiring after almost 40 years in the Linguistics Department and was overdue to vacate my office. Suddenly it felt as though my words didn't sound right. Though I was only too familiar with the symptoms of stroke—weakness in arms or mouth, change in vision, change in speech, droopy mouth—I opted to send my doctor a non-urgent email. I said I seemed to be experiencing few symptoms besides slurred speech. My eyes hadn't been as sharp recently, but wasn't that just a function of age?

Within an hour my doctor had called my wife Angela and told her to get me to the Emergency Room right away!

> I reinforce the advice that you should be seen in the ER. This could be a rela-tively minor stroke on its way to becoming a major stroke.
>
> David Thom, MD, PhD

During the next several hours, I entered Stanford Hospital with Angela by my side, underwent two CT scans and an MRI, and was admitted to Intensive Care, where doctors worked assiduously to lower my blood pressure.

In the end I had four intravenous ports, two in each arm, including a very painful one in an artery. They *did* bring my blood pressure down to an acceptable level, and I fell asleep. But when I woke up, I had virtually no speech. I tried to talk to Angela, but only muffled noises came from my throat. I cried (something I rarely do), and I cried again the next day as my children came to visit me from Crestline, Hayward and Los Angeles in California, and Ithaca in New York.

That second day in the hospital, I had an angiogram, which involved the intro-duction of a radiopaque substance through an artery in my groin, transported to my brain through an artery. It showed significant narrowing of the arteries in my brain. But it was too risky to attempt widening them by balloon angioplasty, for as my stroke and vascular neurologist Dr. Neil Schwartz explained, one misstep and it would be "lights out!"

I also had to endure an MRI about eight in the evening. The ordeal triggered my claustrophobia, a condition that stemmed from having been confined by a nun to a school closet, at age four or five. The hospital gave me a sedative to calm me down, and the MRI operators told me I could squeeze a ball if I needed to come out. I squeezed it *three times* as the machine cranked out the most hideous radio frequencies (it sounded like a voodoo ceremony). They *did* pull me out each time, but they were increasingly impatient, and pushed me back in as soon as possible, complaining that I might ruin the entire MRI.

The MRI revealed that I had suffered five ischemic strokes on the left side of my brain—hence the difficulties with my speech.

Over the seven days I was in hospital, I received visits by numerous doctors and their teams of trailing interns, by three ministers who said a prayer with me (one from my church, one from the hospital chaplaincy, one from my brother's Mormon church who anointed me with oil), a few faculty colleagues, and dozens of nurses. Angela stayed with me night and day, sleeping uncomfortably in two chairs propped together. My children and grandchildren held a small celebration in my hospital room on September 16, my 70th birthday.

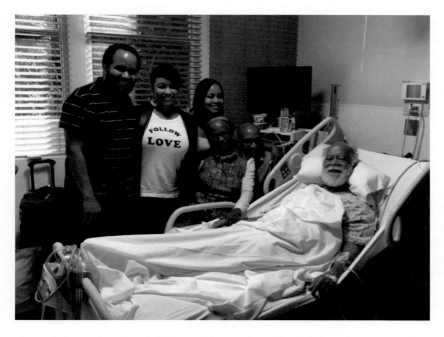

Figure 0.1 Angela and our children, Shiyama, Russell, Anakela, Luke, at my bedside in Stanford Hospital, on my 70th birthday, September 16, 2019, six days after my stroke.

One of the most helpful visits was from my emeritus faculty colleague David Abernethy on day three or four, when I was bemoaning my situation. He told me about another faculty member whom we both knew who had had a stroke and had been paralyzed on one half of his body for more than a year.

That prompted me to look around the unit and notice individuals who were much worse off than myself. Like the eight-year-old boy with his mother next door who cried "Ma-Maa" every few minutes. He appeared to have had a traumatic head injury. Or the guy whom I called my "stroke-mate" because he had had his stroke just two days after mine, but still couldn't speak. Or the many others like him whom I met at the Santa Clara County Rehabilitation Center where I spent another 12 days in therapy (speech, physical and occupational). Taking notice of these patients prompted me to count my blessings, and to see my stroke as a *gift* with some deeper, divine purpose.

It was not to write a book about strokes. That had been done in May 2019 by retired Stanford Professor, Debra E. Meyerson and her son Danny Zuckerman in a powerful book—*Identity Theft: Rediscovering Ourselves After Stroke*.

Nearly 50 *years* after my father's stroke, I realized how uncannily I had followed in his footsteps, and those of my deceased brothers and my maternal grandfather C.B. Wade. Except in this crucial respect: I had *survived*, spared by God and Fate and excellent doctors, and assisted by my wonderful wife Angela, to do something more.

The one big thing I wanted to do, before it was too late, was to write a memoir, to share with my family and perhaps more widely. I had already planned to take a Stanford Continuing Studies course, "Fast draft your way to a complete memoir," taught by the novelist and memoirist Rachel Herron.[1] And although I was still weak and recovering at the Santa Clara County Rehabilitation Center, I asked the administrators to let me go to the initial class meeting on September 23. Angela drove me and stayed with me throughout the three-hour class. That course, with about 20 students, was informative and inspiring, and is the reason I have this book to share with you today.

On Friday October 13, just a month after I had had my stroke, Angela and I flew to the 48th annual conference on New Ways of Analyzing Variation in Language (NWAV 48), held in 2019 at the University of Oregon in Eugene. I had been at almost every NWAV meeting since the first, but this was a challenge for me, both walking the several blocks to the conference site from the hotel, and speaking, since that was not back to normal yet. But I was encouraged by the warm greetings I received from colleagues and students, who had heard about my stroke and were surprised to see me out and about so soon.

My main reason for going, however, was because two of the three featured speakers at the conference were my former students, Renée Blake (New York University) and Devyani Sharma (Queen Mary University of London), whose dissertations I had supervised in 1997 and 2003 respectively. The significance of this and its relevance to my memoir did not strike me until later. Renée has Afro-Caribbean roots and Devyani is Indian, the two components of my genealogy and identity as a person of color that that I explore at depth in this memoir. They both gave excellent presentations, and I was able, in a tremulous voice, to request the microphone to ask questions of each of them afterward.

Figure 0.2 Renée Blake and Devyani Sharma, featured speakers at NWAV48, University of Oregon, October 2019.

Renée Blake and Isa Buchstaller were also co-editors of the surprise *festschrift* in my honor that had been presented to me in 2018, at NWAV-47 after my featured presentation at New York University. I'm still deeply moved when I recall their presenting me with the four preprint volumes of essays that would become *The Routledge Companion to the Work of John R. Rickford*, and my professors, colleagues, and former and current students streamed onto the stage, along with my wife, Angela, and our children and grandchildren.

I should add that this is not an exhaustive autobiography, but a memoir that focuses on aspects of my life and work in linguistics that relate to my race and identity. For readers interested in other roles I've played or other work I've done, see www.johnrickford.com, read Zion Mengesha's write-up in the *Journal of English Linguistics*,[2] or download the interviews conducted in 2019 by Michele Marincovich at https://historicalsociety.stanford.edu/publications/rickford-john.

Finally, note that the title of this memoir deliberately recalls the title of the book I co-authored with my son Russell in 2000: *Spoken Soul: The Story of Black English*.

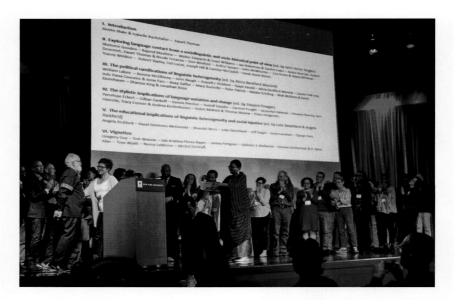

Figure 0.3 JRR being presented with draft volumes of the Routledge *Festschrift* by editors Isa Buchstaller and Renee Blake at NWAV47, Oct 2018, New York University.

For the marvelous memoir course that taught me how to write this book, and for their ever-positive feedback, I am grateful to Rachel Herron, and the students in that Fall 2019 Stanford Continuing Studies course. I'm thankful too to my good friends Ewart and Odette Thomas, who drove me to and from that course every week, since my driver's license had been revoked for about two months after my stroke. I am especially thankful to Maria Olujic, Lisa Trei and Mitra Solomon, the subgroup of students from that course who continued to meet regularly after the course ended, to discuss memoirs that we had read, and to provide feedback on our draft chapters. Their books will follow soon!

Super thanks to my wife Angela for feedback and encouragement throughout, from conception of this memoir, writing and revision. And to my son Russell, who read, critiqued and edited virtually every chapter of this memoir, even though I did not always follow his wise advice. I'm also grateful to Michael Mitchell for his detailed review of the manuscript, and his many helpful suggestions for improving it. My former student David Dabydeen, Emeritus Professor, University of Warwick, was especially helpful with Chapter 14. Thanks too to Shirin Yim Leos for helpful editorial feedback on several chapters. And to Rod Fletcher who helped me get a usable photo of the 1964–65 Queen's College staff!

I'm grateful too to the following family members who did interviews with me or otherwise helped with my genealogy and/or this memoir: my brother George Rickford and his daughter Caroline Kessel-Fell, my sisters June Fletcher, Dawn McTurk, and Nancy Rickford (especially helpful with old Rickford photos!), my nieces Debbie Camacho and Loraine Ayshah Jansen, and my cousins

Figure 0.4 The Routledge Companion to the Work of John R. Rickford.

Sheila Bender and Diane and Nadia El Amin, my children Shiyama Clunie, Anakela Washington and Luke Rickford. Thanks too to Rimskey Hastings, Lily Katchay and Keith Wilson, who also generously did interviews with me, and thanks especially to Roxana Kawall, my wonderful genealogical research assistant in Guyana, and Carol Tolman of Legacy Tree Genealogists. Joey Alberga, Diana Astwood, Elizabeth Phillips, Joel Samoff, Russell and Jo Ann Streeter also gave valuable feedback on the memoir draft. Thanks too to Kelly Batcher and Rebekah Quijas of the Stanford Linguistics Department for their administrative assistance and to Noah Lukeman for advice on agents and memoir publishing

Thanks too to Pamela Moreland of the Stanford News Service, to Shayna Kent and Kayla Judd of UCSC's Alumni Engagement, and to Peter Dunn of the University of Warwick Press and Media Relations office, for help with providing quality photos from their university archives.

Figure 0.5 L to R: John R. Rickford, Elizabeth C. Traugott, Olga Fischer, Rajend Mesthrie,
David Crystal, plenary speakers at the first meeting of the International Society
for the Linguistics of English (ISLE 1). U. Freiburg, Germany, 2008.

To John Agard for his perceptive foreword, and to all those who generously provided endorsements, I am deeply indebted.

To Louisa Semlyen and Eleni Steck of Routledge Press, who accepted my book proposal, and spent countless hours shepherding me through the intricacies of producing this book, I am enormously grateful, as I am to the copy-editor and to others who helped with its production or marketing.

Finally, a word of thanks to David Crystal, who notes in his excellent memoir *Just a Phrase I'm Going Through: My Life in Language* (Routledge 2009) that memoirs and autobiographies are rare in linguistics (p. 270), providing further inspiration for me to write mine. And to Elizabeth Closs Traugott, who as Chair of the Linguistics Department when I first came to Stanford in 1980, helped to invite and mentor me. Thanks too to Penny Eckert, Charles Ferguson, Ewart Thomas, Rob Podesva, Tom Wasow and Gina Wein who were important colleagues and supporters. I was the only underrepresented minority faculty member during my 39 years in Stanford's Linguistics Department. Hopefully, I will not be the last!

To anyone whom I have inadvertently forgotten to include in these acknowledgements, I apologize.

Notes

1 Herron, Rachel. 2018. *Fast-Draft Your Memoir: Write Your Life Story in 45 Hours.* HGA Publishing.
2 Mengesha, Zion. 2019. Interview with John Rickford. *Journal of English Linguistics* 47.4: 335–356.

1 Youngest of ten, and my monkey and rabbit

I was my mother's tenth and last child. My birth certificate says that I was born at "5, Princes St, Charlestown, Ward 7" in Georgetown, which was the address of Princeville Private Hospital, belonging to Dr. Randolph T. Bayley, who delivered all my siblings. The certificate also lists our residence as 118 Cowan Street, Kingston, which is where I lived for the first twelve years of my life.

Our home had two bedrooms: one for my mom and dad, and one for the children. My siblings and I were arrayed in bunk beds and a fold-down bed. I was always being asked (or told) to go outside so one of my five sisters could change "in private."

Later, my dad built a small third bedroom to accommodate two of the older brothers who remained after the eldest brother had gone to Edinburgh for college. Eventually he built a fourth bedroom downstairs which my brother George occupied, and I moved into bedroom number three.

Privacy was practically unimaginable. We had one bathroom, so for years, I was forced to sit on a potty outside the bathroom. There I endured the taunts of passing siblings while I did my business.

My earliest memory is of riding on my father's shoulders as we went to see Government House—all lit up in celebration of Queen Elizabeth's ascension to the throne, June 2, 1953. I was almost four. Significantly, my first memory is also my first *colonial* memory. So much of Guyanese culture and consciousness was oriented toward England, our "Mother Country," 4,600 miles away.

As a small child my fun days revolved around the forty-foot trench or canal in front of our house, beyond an unpaved road and a sloping grassy dam.

In that trench, I learned to fish, beginning with string and bent needles, before graduating to real hooks and nylon lines. The main fish—in fact the *only* fish—we caught was *kurass*, a member of the catfish family that would bite at worms, meat, flour-bait and almost anything else. The fishermen we envied were the ones who threw their circular cast nets into the canal and caught scale fish like *snook* and *cuffum*. We were only two blocks from the *koker* that opened the canal onto the sea at low tide and allowed sea fish like these to enter the canal.

I was constantly beside the canal, fishing, or catching *sheriga* crabs with string and salt fish. Many people refused to eat the lowly *kurass*, but I did so enthusiastically, cleaning and seasoning them myself. I remember a particularly good day in

DOI: 10.4324/9781003204305-1

which I caught maybe a dozen *kurass* of different sizes and put them to swim in the shower well. My parents were livid when they returned home and discovered my exploits. The slime, the smell—get them out!

The most ecstatic occasions were when the sugar estates upstream released their *bagasse* or sugar cane trash into the canal and the resulting oxygen-deprived *lease* water forced every fish—big and small, prized or despised—to the surface to breathe. In hindsight this was a clear act of pollution on the part of the sugar plantocracy, which historically had exploited both the people and ecologies of Guyana. But the surge of contaminated water also produced a bonanza.

I saw giant *kurass* and species of fish I didn't even know existed, all swimming sluggishly, gasping for air. People would wade into the water, wallop them over the head and pull them out. That happened twice in my young days, and I played hooky on both occasions to gaze in amazement at the scene. But I didn't try to catch any fish, fearing they might be tainted and unhealthy to eat.

Once a family of alligators moved in underneath the bridge about 200 yards from our home. There was at least a mother, about four feet long, and two babies. One guy tried to shoot them with a BB gun, but the bullets bounced off their hard hides. Until they moved out, we avoided swimming in the canal, although swimming was always forbidden as far as our parents were concerned.

And with good reason. We saw at least two boys who drowned, including one who dove in headfirst and never came up! My big brother Teddy, though, was an accomplished swimmer who would traverse the broad estuary of the Demerara river, about a mile wide.

One day a friend and I decided to build a "boat" consisting of a wooden box to conquer the mighty forty-foot. The holes between the slats had been filled in with melted tar from the hot road. We got two flat boards to use as paddles and marched down to the launching site like triumphant expeditioners, surrounded by excited young neighbors and passersby. We got off to a triumphant start. But halfway across, the boat began to take on water, and although we paddled faster, by the time we were about seven feet from the opposite shore, the vessel sank. We abandoned ship. Luckily, we could just barely touch the bottom, but unluckily for me, I cut my foot on an old glass bottle. Nevertheless, we were regaled as heroes by the cheering onlookers, and our "boat" was christened the "SS Sink-to-Bottom"!

I started school early, around the age of three, at Miss Gill's Little ABC. Later, I was transferred to the Stella Maris nursery school in Kingston, Georgetown, where I was taught by white nuns in long white habits. One of them locked me in a closet for some infraction. What could a four-year-old have done to deserve *that*? I was terrified. It was then, I believe, that my lifelong claustrophobia began. In any case I found a ball in that dark closet and began bouncing it against the wall. That annoyed the good nun even more and she flung open the door and let me out.

I spent the next five years at Sacred Heart Primary school, called "Main Street School" because of the street on which it stood. The school was divided into boys' and girls' sections, which were separated by the church. Nuns also taught the Big ABC class, and we used to torment them by putting our hands out for "licks" (lashes), then pulling them away at the last minute, so that the cane would get caught in their habit. They would have to disentangle themselves, grumbling and chiding us before resuming their task.

Beyond the preschool classes, the teachers were not nuns, but lay people. Most were rigid disciplinarians—savage *beat-men* and *beat-women* who devised increasingly sadistic punishments. Like Miss Philadelphia, who brought her husband's police baton to school and would roll it over our knuckles with the full force of her considerable weight. Or Mr. Hing, who kept his canes soaking in oil or water to increase their sting. The fact that the classes were overcrowded (60 and 70 students each) may have necessitated firm measures, but I think the whippings were simply part of tradition, our brutal inheritance from slavery and indenture.

Some teachers were unusually patient and kind, however, like my first-grade teacher Miss Ogle, who would stay after class and wait for hours, it seemed, while I figured out the answer to 2 + 2 or 3 × 6 as my mind drifted here and there. Then there was the third-grade teacher on whom I had a crush. She had only to look at me before I broke into a broad self-conscious smile.

I remember passionately the beautiful kites my father used to make for the youngest children at Easter. He was a skilled woodworker, who had made most

Figure 1.1a Smiley me, about eight, Cowan Street.

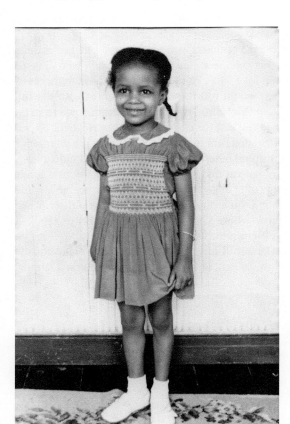

Figure 1.1b Smiley Angela, about same age, unknown to me then.

of our living room furniture from scratch. And he applied those skills each year to making five or six kites in stages, beginning about two months before Easter with the balsa wood frames, each one smaller than the next, tightly held together with string and suspended on nails on the wall. Then he would add the shiny, brightly colored Barbados paper (kite paper), glued section by section, and then the brown paper singing engine (the *bull*) on a string under the raised V *nose* at the top of the kite. Then the decorative frills or wings on each side, and lastly the *balla* of string and the tail interspersed with colored strips of cloth. We could feel the excitement of Easter approaching as the kites took shape, step by step.

On Easter Monday, a huge national holiday, we were off, walking briskly to the sea wall with our kites ruffling and eager to fly on our backs, tethered by the string of the *ballas* which we held in our hands. We would join thousands of people on the sea wall, where the wind from the ocean was strongest. (As far as I know, this extensive kite flying on Easter Monday is a distinctly Guyanese tradition.) There

Figure 1.2 A Guyanese kite, showing the raised V nose, and singing engine (*bull*). Kite by R. Bassoo, 2017.

Dad would help us to raise our kites in turn, adding more tail or less tail as needed, and trying to avoid the swinging tails of nearby kites, especially those that were armed with razors to cut your string. More than once, my kite was cut, and you would see it buckling back helplessly, meeting its demise in the sea, or in a tree, or on an electric wire. Even when those mishaps occurred, Easter kite flying was glorious magic, as thousands of kites sang and danced above us in the skies.

The space under our house was also the venue for countless games of cricket or bat-and-ball, police-and-thief or cowboys and Indians (played with cap guns). It was the arena, as well, for my high-jumping feats.

I first tried high jumping foot-first but didn't do well with that technique. I soon switched to my version of the Western roll, with the head and chest crossing the high jump bar first and the feet coming after. I mostly remember the bumps after I landed—cushioned somewhat by old mattresses behind the uprights—rather than the heights I reached! My delusions of grandeur might have been inspired by Walt Davis, the last jumper to hold the world record with the Western roll, soaring to a height of 6 ft. 11.5" in 1953. Interestingly enough, I only recently discovered that the Western roll technique had been invented at Stanford in 1912, first used by

George Horine (world record 6 ft., 7"). Maybe that was my future destiny calling me, although I would get to Stanford through books, not jumps.

I discovered early on that even I, the youngest, could escape obscurity and low status through academic excellence. By the time I was in sixth standard, at age ten, I was taking extra lessons with my classroom teacher, Mr. Arokium. When the Common Entrance Exam results came out, I had won a scholarship to the prestigious secondary school, Queen's College.

One more thing. While most children brought up in the Christian tradition get baptized in their first or second year, I didn't get baptized until I was nearly 12, on April 6, 1961! Why then? Well, I was planning to go on a QC scouting camp for about a week, and it involved biking up to the airport area, about 30 miles from Georgetown, along the narrow but crowded East Bank Road. My mom wouldn't give permission until I got baptized, presumably so that my place in heaven would be guaranteed if anything dire were to befall me. And why so late? Well, I don't know for sure, but it probably had to do with my "runt of the pack" status, and the fact that my parents were busy with their nine surviving children, having lost one just a few years before I was born. Mom asked two of my siblings and a brother-in-law (Edward, Dawn and Michael Norsworthy) to serve as godparents, and once the baptism was done, I was free to go!

Guyana in those years was not free from turmoil or violence. In the early 1960s, political divisions between Cheddi Jagan's People's Progressive Party (primarily East Indian) and Forbes Burnham's People's National Congress (primarily African) resulted in bloody racial clashes, euphemistically called "disturbances." The strife was fueled, in part, by the political interventions of the U.S. and the British, who favored the moderate Burnham over the left-wing Jagan.

I remember Dad putting on his St. John Ambulance Brigade uniform and heading into the night, amid the race-based rioting, to render first aid. We were terrified for him, and relieved when he returned unharmed.

One of Guyana's reigning ideals, especially since achieving independence in 1966, is the notion of unity despite (racial) diversity. The national motto, inscribed on the official Guyanese coat of arms is: "One people, one nation, one destiny."

However, that motto, with the idealism that the society has transcended race, was only necessary to counteract the years of racial disturbances that immediately preceded independence, and the decades of conflict and competition that preceded them. The reality is that despite the ideal of the fluidity or irrelevance of race, we remain obsessed with racial classification, between the so-called six primary races (Amerindians, Africans, East Indians, Portuguese, Chinese and Europeans) and the variety of mixtures between them.

The traditional conception of Guyana as a nation of "six races" actually belies the assertion that race is no longer a basis for division. The formulation of six "races," of course, is totally arbitrary. The fact that Guyanese traditionally distinguish "Portuguese" from "European" reflects in part the fact that the Portuguese in Guyana came primarily from the island of Madeira, about 1173 km away from Portugal, and held a lower status than that of English colonizers and planters and civil servants. The "six-race" characterization also reflects a particular schema of classification, and a pervasive one. The idea that there could be six "pure" categories and then various racial combinations is a total fiction. It has no biological basis. But it reflects a preoccupation with racial categorization as a primary way of understanding and ordering the world.

The point is that the construction and imparting/reproduction of racial meaning is a deeply entrenched way of ordering existence and understanding the world. It is *always* operating on multiple registers. It is *always* present, even when its presence is most vociferously denied. Racialization, the imparting of racial meaning—both in the Caribbean and in the U.S.—shaped my experience, identity and consciousness, even when (*especially* when) the prevailing ideal was racial harmony or the transcension of race altogether.

***

One of the most memorable events of my childhood was acquiring a black marmoset monkey and a white rabbit. I was seven or eight at the time.

Marmosets, native to South America, and about eight inches long, with an even longer tail, include several different species. Mine was a Goeldi's marmoset. The monkey-rabbit pair were a gift from a guy who lived around the corner, on Duke Street. He had noticed how much I admired the pair whenever I passed his yard, and he gave them to me along with a big cage. That cage helps me to date when I got it, since it was in the bottom-house space in which Dad built the downstairs room for my brother George a year or two later.

I was *ecstatic*. The monkey and the rabbit were inseparable. They had apparently been raised together from small and loved each other. They played all day long, she nervously chewing her cud and twitching her wet nose, he scratching his head and swinging athletically across the cage. At night, and several times a day, they snuggled together as they slept.

I used to take the monkey for bike rides. He would squat on my head, holding on to my hair tightly with his tiny hands, his tail trailing down my back. He gasped for air but loved the sensation as I rode faster and the wind grew stronger. The routine made us popular with friends and strangers alike.

The rabbit rarely went far from home, but sometimes, instead of just bringing back her favorite *zeb* grass, I would take her to where the grass grew wild and enjoy watching her luxuriate in the culinary variety—a self-serve all-you-can-eat grassery!

So it continued for a while. In the morning I rushed downstairs to feed and play with my two pets, and in the afternoon I could hardly wait to return from school to do the same.

But one day while the monkey was out of the cage, prancing around the yard, he attracted the attention of the family dog. I don't know if the dog was jealous of the attention being lavished on the monkey, or if he was simply roughhousing with him playfully the way dogs do, but for whatever reason he bit him. *Hard*! The monkey squealed in pain, and as I rushed over to rescue him, I shouted unhelpful admonishments to the dog, "Bad dog! Bad dog!"

Figure 1.3 Goeldi's marmoset monkey sitting on a vine, by DejaVuDesigns (Shutterstock 560550727).

I immediately took the monkey upstairs to tend to him, but he broke free and hid behind a closet. When I reached for him, he bit me for the first and only time. I knew then that he must have been in deep pain.

When I finally retrieved him, I plopped him on my head and pedaled off to the vet. We didn't have a car at the time. This time the monkey's grip was weak, and I had to steady him with one hand while I steered with the other. The ride to the vet seemed endless, devoid of the pleasure I usually derived from those monkey bike rides.

What happened after I reached the SPCA is a blur. I remember seeing all those ordinary animals—cats meowing and dogs barking in the waiting room—and I remember getting seen before people who had come before me because of the monkey's injury and pain. But when I left an hour later, my beloved marmoset monkey didn't accompany me. He had died, put to sleep by the vet to relieve him of his agony.

I rode home alone, tears streaming from my eyes, and went immediately to his cage to explain to his companion rabbit, who seemed lonelier and sadder than ever. And I gave him an extra-large feeding of *zeb* grass.

The next morning, I noticed that the grass had not been touched. I scoured the choicest spots for the richest, greenest *zeb* grass I could find, and replaced the uneaten grass from the night before with this juicy stuff. The rabbit just sat in her corner, chewing her cud despondently, refusing to eat. I stroked her. I told her how sorry I was that her mate had died. I pleaded with her to eat. All in vain.

Four or five days later, the rabbit also died, of suicide by starvation, or of heartbreak. It was almost impossible for me to comprehend. Both of my favorite pets gone in less than a week. It was a long time before I got over it. Perhaps I never did.

2 Forebears and cousins

My earliest lesson in genealogy, but also in race and power, came from my Aunt Tottie when I was less than eight. I would go to her for piano lessons, and before I entered her home on Duke Street, she told me something that she repeated often: "Your great grandfather on your mother's side was a Scotsman, with blond hair and blue eyes."

This was only a partial family history, ignoring African, East Indian and other elements in my genealogy, but it was supposed to impress on me "a common conception of colonial society: a conception in which things English and 'white' were valued highly, while things African and 'black' were valued lowly."[1] One recalls that Guyanese historian Walter Rodney, similarly noted that in French colonies like Guadeloupe, a class of black shining faces would learn that "the Gauls, our ancestors, had blue eyes."[2]

Moreover, Aunt Tottie's comment was not just an act of *omission*, but it was also about *construction*. She was staking a claim to "whiteness," and to beauty, virtue and power. At the time, I didn't believe it, any more than I heeded her admonition that I should brush my hair constantly and assiduously (demonstrated with the hairbrush she kept by the front door) as a way of taming the curls and knots—a legacy of my non-European ancestry.

Later, when I grew older and could formulate my own point of view, I would realize that while I loved Aunt Tottie and her sisters (including my mother), I completely rejected the colonial mentality that their family and society had instilled in them. In hindsight I can see the powerlessness that led them to absorb a colonial schema of racial prestige. One might even sympathize with the effort to construct a claim to a more valorized racial identity.

But such thinking is obviously based on the perverted logic of white supremacy. Rejecting such logic has been an important part of my attempt to forge an identity based on pride in my whole, true self, while developing a worldview that would enable me to positively and productively raise my family.

As has often been noted, race is a social construct. It is always relational. That is, "whiteness" is an identity and a sociological designation in contradistinction to non-whiteness. It is a position within a social hierarchy that imparts power and privilege. Whiteness is not a natural or empirical category.

DOI: 10.4324/9781003204305-2

By highlighting the "white" element, Aunt Tottie was reinforcing the lie of racial hierarchy, a lie that helped build the modern world while creating untold suffering, oppression and conflict. The claim to whiteness also implicitly referenced the 16-point distinction between "black" and "white" that had developed in the British West Indies in the 19th century, and she was locating us in the "white" half.

A West Indian history text that we first read in high school discussed the particular racial classification scheme that evolved in the British West Indies:

> There were distinctions of color among the general class of free black and colored people ranging from the Mustifino, who was "fifteen sixteenths white," through the Mustee, Quadroon and Mulatto to the Sambo, who was only "one fourth white." These distinctions led to a general striving after "whiteness" for social, political and economic reasons. . . .[3]

When the sixteen-point distinction collapsed later on, ethnically mixed people were simply known as *mulattoes* (the term previously reserved for "one-half white"), or *douglas*, if the mixture was between African and East Indian.[4] But one could claim by descent to be of higher status than a regular *mulatto* and one could, by successive marriages to "white" people aim to "elevate" the family status to that of a Quadroon, Mustee or Mustifino.

There was a similar system in New Orleans.[5] The colonial New Orleans distinctions included: *Passé blanc*, *Quinteroon* (15/16 White), *Octoroon* (7/8 White), *Quadroon* (3/4 White), *Mulatto* (1/2 White), *Griffe* (1/4 White), *Sacatra* (1/4 White), *Negro* (usually applied to one of full Negro blood).

With this in mind, let us review what we know of my *mother's* family. Mum's name was **Eula Sylvia Enid Wade** (November 10, 1905–March 8, 1984). Her mother was Rosina Wilson, the only child born on October 19, in either 1867 or 1866, to Henry Wilson, the white Scotsman Aunt Tottie (Marian Evelina Wilson) invoked frequently. Wilson, Rosina's dad, was Chief Engineer at Plantation Enmore, about two miles from Paradise, East Coast Demerara, shown on the map in Chapter 3 (Figure 3.1). But we don't know where he came from in Scotland, how long and when he lived in Guyana (British Guiana at the time), or in Barbados. Given that Wilson went out from Scotland to Guyana as an adult, and had a child in 1866 or 1867, he was probably born in 1846 or earlier. There are archival references in 1882 to him having built a steam cane mill in Golden Grove, East Coast Demerara.[6] There are other references to a Henry Wilson having gone into cattle farming, and to his owning property in Vreed-en-Hoop, west of the Demerara river in 1912,[7] but we're not certain this is the same Henry Wilson. All told, Wilson was probably in Guyana between 1860 and 1890, maybe as late as 1912. Whether he was buried in Guyana, Barbados or Scotland, remains unclear.

One interesting potential link to Henry Wilson is the fact that I share DNA with Norbert Errol Wilson (known as "T-Bone") and his daughter Zoe W. Wilson.[8] The link is clearly on my mother's side, because Marcia Bhagan, the

Figure 2.1 DNA third cousins, Norbert Wilson and his daughter Zoe, from Golden Grove, East Coast Demerara, where Henry Wilson built a steam mill in 1882.

great granddaughter of my mother's sister, Janet Wade, also shares a DNA connection to Norbert and Zoe Wilson. Moreover, Norbert Wilson's home village in Guyana is Golden Grove, East Coast Demerara, precisely where Henry Wilson constructed a steam mill in 1882. Golden Grove is about a mile east of Enmore, where Henry Wilson worked. Although the ethnic ancestry of Norbert Wilson is 96% African, and only 3% British, the 23andMe estimate of when the British ancestry came into his family is the 19th century, which would also coincide with when Henry Wilson was living and working nearby. 23andMe lists us as possible *third* cousins. We are continuing to explore this relationship.

About Henry Wilson's wife, my mother's grandmother, a mixed blood woman who came from Barbados, we know virtually nothing, not even her name or date of birth. My father, in a 1969 letter to me, says that they referred to her as a *mestee* [= *mustee*?], "of cream complexion." But this may have been wishful thinking, because my mother, several of her sisters and several of *my* sisters, regularly used hot combs to straighten their curly or kinky hair. And if my great-grandfather's Barbadian wife were "where the Negro element entered the family" (my father's words) she must have had more than a trace of this element, to have exerted such a strong influence on successive generations, despite her husband's white genealogy. We don't know whether she was actually Henry Wilson's wife, or a paramour, like Parvadi on my father's side. I have named this great grandmother of mine "Cleopatra" while the search for her identity continues.

The racism of Rosina Wilson's Scottish father was shown when her hand was sought in marriage by a wealthy brown-skinned man named Mascott. "I did not

Figure 2.2 My paternal grandparents Donald Howell Rickford and Millicent Beatrice (Davis) Rickford, with the first six of their ten children: Clockwise from left front: Una Marjorie Gwendolyn (seated, b. 1917). Beryl (b. 1919), Dorothy Elaine (b. 1914), Russell Howell (b. 1913), Neville Aubrey (b. 1915), Eric (b. 1920).

educate my daughter for a black man," stormed Rosina's father, according to my dad's letter of 1969. Eventually Rosina married Charles Benjamin Wade, the son of a "U.K. colonist" who was the owner of Plantation Woodlands on the Upper Demerara River. It was his third marriage, and he was older than her by almost thirty years.

My *father*, **Russell Howell Rickford** (March 1, 1913–September 14, 1969), was the eldest of ten children born to Donald and Millicent Rickford (see photo in Figure 2.4). Donald Howell, born either November 30, 1879 or September 21, 1884)[9] was one of two sons (the other was Geoffrey Howell) born to Walter Howell Rickford, a white sugar magnate at a plantation in the Corentyne and an East Indian indentured woman, whose name was "Parvadi."[10] (We have no birth certificate.)

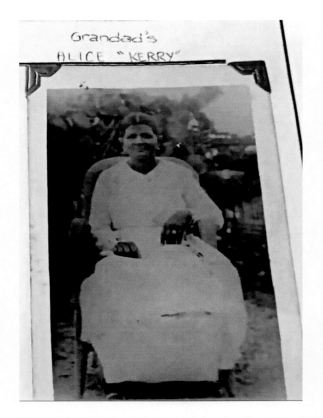

Figure 2.3 Alice Ann Mariaye Marimutha, Parvadi's daughter, and Donald Howell
Rickford's half-sister.

Although they both used the middle name of their father and he paid for their
education at Queen's College, Donald and Geoffrey were raised in the home
of Parvadi, where she lived with her indentured husband, with whom she had
a daughter, Alice Ann Mariaye Marimutha (or Maureemootha).[11] Alice Ann
Mariaye (Figure 2.3) married Robert Retnagheri Kerry and they had ten children, and adopted an eleventh.[12] In February 2020, in Toronto, Canada, my wife
Angela, my sister Nancy and I had a delightful visit and interview with the daughters of Dr. Joseph Kerry, Sheila (Kerry) Bender and Diane (Kerry) El Amin (see
Figure 3.4) and her daughter Nadia, who has constructed a detailed family tree on
ancestry.com.
    What of my paternal grandmother, Millicent? She was one of three children
born to Harriet Anne Jackman ("Aunt Annie"), and Harry Davis (who came from
St. Kitts to then British Guiana) in the 19th century. Millicent married my paternal grandfather Donald Rickford in 1912. From the one photo we have, George
Davis, Millicent's brother, was mixed, with some African ancestry. We know

Figure 2.4 My cousins Diane (Kerry) El Amin and Sheila (Kerry) Bender, holding photos of their parents, Joseph Chinden and Eileen Olga Kerry, Toronto, Canada, February 24, 2020.

little about Millicent and George's parents, beyond their names and the information that one of them came from St. Kitts. But Grandma Millicent is the only paternal grandparent I knew (and loved), and she and Donald had seven children. The youngest, Jean (known as "Aunt Bunny," shown in Figure 2.5) celebrated her 91st birthday in August 2020, in Florida.

Let us now look at the results of DNA testing using saliva samples. shown in Table 2.1.

While there is some question about the authoritativeness of DNA testing, it is striking how much the 23andme and Ancestry.com tests agree about the ethnic composition of my DNA. The first thing that's interesting is that my Aunt Bunny

Figure 2.5 Aunt Bunny (Jean Rickford) with Kitty first cousins, L to R: Richard, Brenda, John N. and Donald, April 2017.

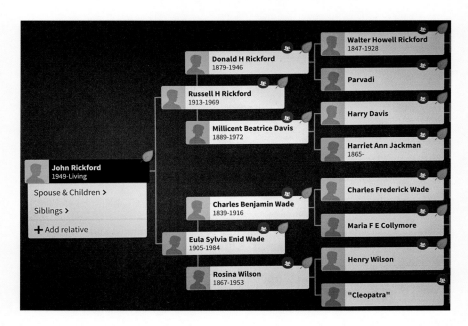

Figure 2.6 Partial family tree, showing my parents, grandparents and great grandparents.

Table 2.1 DNA results by ethnicity for my paternal Aunt Jean ("Bunny") and myself

DNA Company	23and Me	23andMe	Ancestry.com
Genetic Ancestry	Aunt Jean "Bunny" (my dad's sister)	John (me)	John (me)
African (sub-Saharan)	17%	34%	33%
East Indian (from India)	28%	13%	13%
Amerindian/Indigeneous	0%	3%	3%
European	54%	48%	50%
Unassigned	1%	2%	1%

has about twice as much (East-) Indian heritage as I do.[13] That is not surprising given that her father (Donald Rickford) clearly had East Indian roots from our great grandmother Parvadi.

What *is* surprising is that she had so much (17%) African heritage, while no one had explicitly mentioned black influence on their side of the family. It must have come both from Grandma Millicent herself, and maybe from Grandfather Donald Rickford, who does look a little like a *dougla*, a mixture of black and East Indian. Clearly the "black" elements in my ancestry came from both my mother's and my father's sides.

As for me, I am about 48% to 50% European, with twice as much African (34%) as East Indian/South Asian (13%) and Amerindian (3%) ancestry combined. Compare Harvard Professor Henry Louis Gates, of *Finding your Roots* fame, who is 50% sub-Saharan African and 50% European, and who notes that "The average African-American is 24 percent European."[14] Following the one-drop rule in the US (Blay 2014), I identify as black or African American and am proud to be known as a "person of color." Interestingly enough, four of my siblings and myself chose black spouses (Elizabeth, Nancy, Peter, me); four chose white spouses (Edward, Dawn, George, Pat) and one chose both (June). Although my Aunt Tottie emphasized the white element in our ethnic descent, we recognized that our forebears were more ethnically diverse, and made more diverse choices in our spouses.

Since my father and mother both came from big families, I naturally had many cousins. But my siblings and I were not close to all of them—sometimes I was the only one that was close to some of them—and therein lies a story or two.

My father's brother Neville (1915–1967) had eleven children (one died at age seven). They lived in a three-bedroom home in the village of Kitty, on the border of Georgetown. Uncle Neville was dark-skinned, and his wife Dorothy ("Dolly") Brady was primarily East Indian, but we would all have been considered "mixed" or "colored." I'm not sure how much my older brothers hung out with these Kitty cousins, but of the siblings in the younger half of my family, I hung out with them the most, by far. My dad and Uncle Neville used to exchange visits from time to time, and he would sometimes take me with him when he visited. The cousins would often meet at my Grandma's on Sunday afternoons, enjoying the usual fare of soft drinks, cake and ice cream.

Between these visits I became good friends with Donald, who was the same age as me, and we discovered our mutual love of fishing. The forty-foot (wide) canal that ran in front of my home was only a block or two from his home, and we spent a lot of time fishing in it for *kurass,* which would bite hooks baited with virtually anything edible. The more highly valued fish in that canal were the scale fish—*cuffum* and *snook* especially, which would only bite hooks baited with *silver bait* or *patwa,* which had to be caught in smaller drainage canals with tiny hooks and quite a different fishing technique. For *kurass* in the big canal, you used a bigger hook and a cork; when you got a bite, you had to wait until the entire cork went below the water and then wait for the line to get taut. Then you pulled hard on the string and pulled in the line, hook and hapless fish. For silver bait you would use a short line without a cork, and as soon as you got a reasonable bite, you would jerk the stick holding the line. Depending on how quick you were, the small fish would come flying out of the water and into the air, often falling wriggling behind you.

The Kitty Rickfords had a drainage canal teeming with *silver bait* and *patwa* near their home, and Donald helped me master the deft technique needed to catch them. In no time I was spending more of my time hanging out with Donald and his brothers, fishing for bait fish. Although we never succeeded in catching *snook* or *cuffum* with the live silver bait (these prized scale fish were picky biters), the dream of catching them inspired us to spend afternoons talking, laughing and hanging out by the side of the forty-foot canal.

I also began sleeping over at Donald's, enjoying the distinctive foods his mother made, like cook-up rice, with coconut milk and a compendium of vegetables and meats, or *metagee,* or split-pea soup on Sundays. My mom made some of these too, but everybody's recipe was slightly different, and the *chow chow* with *soury,* pepper and other vegetables pickling in a large jar was unique to Aunt Dolly. I also enjoyed our jaunts through an unfamiliar neighborhood with all the shortcuts Donald knew. Aunt Dolly was one of the sweetest, kindest and most generous people I knew. She would ask what I wanted to eat or do, and nothing was ever too much for her, even if she had to send one of her children off to the market to buy the ingredients.

Another "cousin" to whom I was especially close was cousin Archie Ramotar, the single out-of-wedlock son of Aunt Janet, my mother's sister, his wife Juliette Bacchus and their ten children (second cousins). Aunt Janet brought a breach-of-promise lawsuit against Archie's father, Archibald Noel Gainor Ramotar, after she became pregnant and he failed to marry her, but she lost the case. Having a baby out of wedlock must have been a huge scandal in the early 1900s, but she raised cousin Archie as a single mother, and his large family of ten children provided her with a bevy of grandchildren and a loving home for the rest of her life.

What I haven't mentioned so far is that Archie and Juliet lived in Better Hope, on the East Coast of Demerara, about seven or eight miles out of Georgetown. It was not that far, but it was considered "country," and the neighborhood contained many sugar workers (sugar cane cutters, weeders and so on). But for all of these reasons, I loved it. I would ride my bike there against the East Coast breeze, with the Atlantic

Figure 2.7 At our Ramotar cousins' home in Better Hope, Guyana, 1994. L to R, standing: Anthony, Noel (Dakiel), Joseph, Ignatius, Angela & John. L to R, seated: Archie & Juliette, Rolita (Noel's second daughter) & Samuel (Mary's eldest son).

waves crashing against the sea wall on my left, and cars, trucks, other bicyclists and carts pulled by donkeys and mules muscling in on the right. (Guyana drives on the left.) Sometimes it would take me as long as an hour, but I found it exhilarating.

Cousin Archie was an excellent pianist, with one of the rare pianos in the village in his home, but he also loved to drink. With my Aunt Janet often there, I was free to visit, and enjoyed walking through the open market, swimming in the nearby canal, sleeping over and eating Aunt Juliet's fine home cooking, particularly her specialty, *curry-and-roti.*

I became good friends with several of the children, including the eldest, the beautiful Mary whom I wanted to marry, and I confided this to one of my sisters. She sucked her teeth and sneered: "Don't be stupid, Johnny, cousins can't marry cousins," pouring cold water on my prepubescent fantasy.

Other siblings whom I came to know quite well included Ingrid, Mario (now a couturier in NYC), Margaret and Denise.[15] As far as I know, I was the only member of my family who ever slept in their home overnight, and certainly the only one who visited regularly.

When I returned home to work at the University of Guyana and begin field work for my PhD on language variation in Guyana from 1974 to1976, I chose the village of Better Hope as my research site. And the Ramotar home became the base from which I ventured out to record dozens of East Indian cane cutters and weeders and community members in or near their homes. This drew me even closer to my cousins. I was there several times a week.

Two sets of cousins that I didn't socialize much with were the Phillips and the Kerrys. My mother's sister Harriet Jane married Walter J.R. Phillips, a successful local businessman in the 1920s, and they had four children, Dorothy, Michael, Patrick ("Pat"), and Barbara Nancy. Walter Phillips and other siblings carried on the business started by C.A. Phillips in 1914, importing, wholesaling and selling foodstuffs, pharmaceuticals, cotton goods, paint, etc. to the tune of over two million Guyanese dollars annually in the late 1960s.[16] The mother of C.A. Phillips was apparently the aunt of Grandma Millicent, my dad's mom.

Aunt Harriet (born 1898) and her husband moved to England sometime after 1934, but Eric and one of the other siblings lived in a big compound with three houses, along with their mother, who had a separate cottage. They had children (second cousins to me) around my age. They lived just around the corner on Duke Street, the same two-block long street on which my aunts Tottie, Janet and Ivy lived, but in the more fancy block, upper (as against lower) Duke Street. I must have been there once or twice, but the memories of those visits are unclear and uncomfortable, almost as if I were tolerated instead of welcomed. I don't think the Phillips cousins were any lighter or more fair-skinned than we were, but they were probably considered higher class because of the wealth their family business generated.

The other "cousins" were the children of Dr. Frederick Kerry (born 1898), and his second wife, an English woman named Eleanor. They were Elizabeth, Patricia, Michael and Margaret. They didn't live that far from us in Georgetown, and we often went to Dr. Kerry for injections and minor injuries and illnesses, usually after hours. Frederick was one of the ten children of Alice Ann Mariaye Kerry, the sole daughter of "Parvadi." In short, my grandfather Donald and Uncle Fred Kerry shared in "Parvadi" a common East Indian mother.

Michael and Margaret were about the same age as me, and we certainly met at parties as teenagers (at least one held at their home). But we didn't hang out. One reason perhaps is that as the children of a medical doctor and an English woman, they would have been of a higher social class. They lived in a huge house at the corner of Camp and Church Streets that also doubled as Dr. Kerry's medical office. Also, I was never explicitly told they *were* my cousins—perhaps because to do so would have meant explaining the links to indenture and the fact that my grandfather and his brother were illegitimate, since their father, Walter Howell Rickford, never married their mother, Parvadi. Later I would learn that my dad regularly visited the Joseph Kerry family at Peter's Hall, on the East Bank, Demerara. But I didn't know that at the time.

Such are the mysteries of life, and relationships.

Notes

1 Anthropologist Raymond T Smith. 1960. *British Guiana*. London: Oxford University Press, p. 41.
2 Walter Rodney. 1972. *How Europe Underdeveloped Africa*. London Bogle L'Ouverture Publications,:p. 271.
3 The colonial system is described in F.R, Augier, S.C. Gordon, D.G. Hall, and M. Reckord. 1960. *The Making of the West Indies*, London: Longman's, p. 163.

4 See Richard Allsopp. 1996. *Dictionary of Caribbean English Usage*. Oxford: Oxford University Press.
5 Yada Ble. 2014. *(1)ne Drop: Shifting the Lens on Race*. Philadelphia, PA: BLACKprint, pp. 10–14.
6 Letter to the editor, *The Demerara Daily Chronicle,* September 5, 1882: 3. Georgetown. He also reportedly sold his portion of the steam mill (jointly owned with James William James) to Isaac Evelyn in 1884.
7 *British Guiana Official Gazette,* vol xxvi.
8 Wilson, Zoe. 2017. *Confessions of Love*, a book of poetry and photos, Las Vegas, NV.
9 The Rickford Family Dates calendar gives both the 13 and 30 November, 1879 as his birth. I take it one of these is a typo. *The BG Who's Who* says 21 September, 1884.
10 In an e-mail from Diane El Amin (Kerry) to Roxana Kawall, my research assistant, Diane says of her daughter: "Nadia visited me yesterday and told me that she got the information regarding Parvadi from my mom when she was researching our family history. She told her this because I was named after Parvadi, the mother of Mariaye."
11 *Marimutha* was how it was spelled in the note found in Diane's bible, and *Maureemootha* is how it is spelled for the person Roxana Kawall found in the archives b. 11 August, 1870 (same date as Alice Ann).
12 The Kerry children include Dr. George M. Kerry (1889–1967), Dr. Joseph C. Kerry (1894–1963), Dr. Frederick M. Kerry (1899–1978), Leopold P. "Paddy" Kerry (1901–1995), and Gladys Kerry Swamber (1909–1985) among others.
13 Neither my mother nor father was alive at the time I did my DNA tests, so I unfortunately have no DNA data on them.
14 See Gates' *Fresh Air* interview of January 21, 2019. https://www.npr.org/2019/01/21 /686531998/historian-henry-louis-gates-jr-on-dna-testing-and-finding-his-own-roots.
15 Marcia Bhagan, mentioned earlier in this chapter, is the daughter of Paul Ramotar and his wife Indira.
16 US Department of Commerce trade list, January 1968, p 16.

3 Baby Wade, my Mom

Everybody knew her as Baby Wade. My mother, Eula Sylvia Enid Wade (November 10, 1905–March 8,1984) was the thirteenth of fourteen children born to her parents, Charles Benjamin Wade and Rosina (Wilson) Wade. But the twelfth, Eulalie Helen, born in April 1904, died one and a half years later, just before mom was born. And the fourteenth, Edith Virginia, born in September 1908, lived for only ten days, ceding the status of "Baby" to Eula. As my mother joked later, "I told them that once I had come, everybody else had to go." Eula Sylvia was the youngest surviving child, not only of her mother's 14 children, but of her father's *24*, since he had one daughter with a woman he married in India at about 22, while in the British army. After his first wife died, he had nine other children (three died young) with a second wife in British Guiana.[1] After *she* died, at the age of 50, he married Rosina, only 20 or 21 at the time.

C.B. Wade, the father of my mother Baby Wade, was born in 1839 in British Guiana (renamed Guyana after independence in 1966), the son of an Englishman who had owned Plantation Woodlands on the Upper Demerara River. He himself had served as manager of Plantation Murrow or Dunoon, and as an overseer at La Bonne Intention (LBI) Plantation, before working as Town Overseer of Georgetown for 30 years before his death.

Grandfather Wade was also a Masonic Lodge man. One of the founders of the Union Lodge in Georgetown, he had often said that all he wanted to live for was to be Grandmaster of the Union Lodge. One evening in October 1916, he got his wish. But the excitement of the occasion was too much for him. As he was sitting in the chair, he had a stroke, and had to be taken home in a *gig*—"a light two-wheeled carriage pulled by one horse." He died at 77 on October 3, 1916. But not before getting a chance to say goodbye to all his children. As mom put it, when I recorded her in 1983, he "had a glorious death, all of us were round his bed, when he died. Half past five in the morning, too."

Of her father, Mom had only good things to say: "Nice man, man. Nice man. Blue, blue eyes like the sky … *oh*, he was sweet. He was nice … I miss him because he used to plant cane and fruit for me. Man believe in planting, man. Always. He believed in me, being the last child, you know. Oh, he was a nice person." It's interesting that she listed his blue eyes as among his key attributes—blue

DOI: 10.4324/9781003204305-3

eyes and blond hair were the features her sisters often invoked too as part of their claim to inherited "whiteness."

Mom was clearly a daddy favorite, and exploited it sometimes. Like the time "my mother gave me a sound whipping which I clearly deserved. And I didn't cry then." But three hours later, as her father was coming home from work, she "got behind the door and bawled ... When he opened the door, the first person he saw was Baby crying hard, behind the door. And he lifted me up, 'Why you crying?' 'Mother beat me for nothing.' And, stupid man, he lifted me up, and [said] 'Rose, why did you beat the child?'"

But despite the occasional advantages which being daddy's favorite bestowed, in many ways, Baby Wade was the "runt" of the pack, like I was. In such a large household, where she was and what she was doing were often ignored. As she said, "None of them worried with me. Too many were in the house." She was only ten when her dad died, and donning her school uniform as usual, she went to Mr. Sharples' school the next day, unnoticed by any of the family. They were making funeral wreaths and occupied with other funeral preparations. In mom's words, Mr. Sharples "sen' me back home. He was a friend of the family. He knew my father was dead. What de devil I doin' in school? I gone to school as usual. I knew he was dead. But I [was] due at school."

About Rosina Wade, my mom's mother, mom told me less, and was more critical when I interviewed her in July 1983. This grandmother died when I was four, so I can't really remember her, except for being pressured to kiss her dead body, which I resisted. She was a "colored" woman with an as-yet unidentified mixed race mother from Barbados.

With so many children, Grandma Rose never worked outside the home. But she earned a supplementary income by catering for various events, like the Union Lodge ceremony the night her husband became Grandmaster.

On one occasion she had made a dozen bottles of jelly (maybe guava jelly?) for someone in McKenzie, now Linden, a mining town 65 miles up the Demerara River. (See map, Figure 3.1) Mom, about 11 or 23 years old by then, saw these bottles of jelly, "eleven full" but "one was short." She said to herself, "I gon just take a teaspoon out of one and taste it." No sooner had she done this than she reasoned,

> Oh my, I must take out [some] of all eleven for them to look good. And I took a teaspoon ... I took out of all eleven. Naturally. So they would look equal, aint it? Hmmm, I said, it taste so nice, I must take another teaspoon. I took out of all eleven again. Ha! Ha! Well I was quite satisfied, and I went upstairs.
>
> Next morning, my mother came down early to send these goods up to McKenzie, found the bottles, you know, showing they'd been eaten out. Oh, she was sure my brother Percy [11 years older] had taken it. [Laughs uproariously.] ... Look, it took me until I was a grown woman before I could confess it was I who had taken out that jelly. I didn't dare! Percy said, "No, he hadn't." Course, they didn't believe him! I—my mother was so angry, I didn't DARE admit that I had taken that jelly!

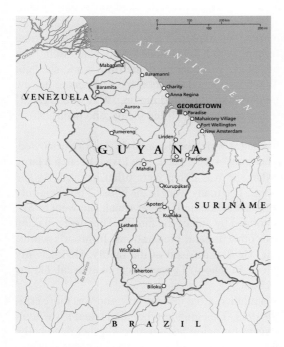

Figure 3.1 Map of Guyana, by Peter Hermes Furian. (Shutterstock.) 212368726.

I only knew three of Mom's siblings myself, Aunts Tottie (Marian, a music teacher), Janet (a seamstress) and Ivy (a ballet dancer and dance teacher). But some of the others I know from family lore.

Her sister Stella used to work at Government House, and went to England, where she became the second wife of Matthew Thomas Wilson in 1929, his first wife having died in 1923.[2] She probably passed for white in England, like my brother Edward later did in Oregon. Matthew Wilson was founder of the *Malvern Gazette*, and Stella wrote for it under the pen name "Suede." A famous family photo shows her hobnobbing in July 1936 with playwright George Bernard Shaw.

Another sister I never heard anything about is Amy Alethia Wade (b. November 2, 1900), who apparently married a colored or black jeweler, Charles Taylor. But I've recently learned that they had a daughter Pamela, and through her, a grandson Julian Halls (b. April 17, 1967) who played for the British National field hockey team in the 1996 and 2000 Summer Olympics. He won a bronze medal in the same sport in the 1998 Commonwealth Games.

Infamous and puzzling is the story of Mom's brother Cardigan Benjamin, or "Benjie," who went into the interior (the "bush") with two Americans seeking gold. The family never saw or heard from him again. According to my mom:

They come down and tell her that, they ran short of rations. And a boat was to go up the next week after they come down, and [they said] that he was on the bank, bidding them goodbye until they come back … Well, he staying to watch the shop. My mother say they must be eat him, cause they say they had to eat cockroach and all. Of course, that is what they tell Mother. And we've never seen or heard of him again.

Interestingly enough, when I first went to Angela's home, her mother told her after I had left this same story, about how my mother's brother had disappeared in the bush. *My* mother was critical of the way *her* mother had handled the incident. "And my mother ain' move to do a thing. You ever see woman like that?"

Part of Rosina's reluctance to do anything probably reflected a fear of the unequal power that a local Guyanese would have in a dispute with white expatriates—that one could not hope to successfully get justice, or even the truth, from two Americans. But maybe my mom's impatience with her mom also reflected something more general—Rosina's general unwillingness not to rock the boat for the nearly 40 years after her husband died and left her to raise a "string band of children." For instance, it is said that she only received three days' pay in pension after C.B. Wade died in 1916 but accepted it as "fate." And when her son Percy told her that he had sold her extensive property at Lodge for five dollars, she accepted this as well. As my brother George noted, "The idea of going to court for any right was anathema to her." And she never remarried.

Some of the family's color/class insecurities perhaps surfaced in other ways as well. For Tottie, the oldest daughter, had been well trained in the piano by Mr. O'John, and taught my mother, Aunt Stella and other relatives (including me) to play too. But she apparently wanted to become a nurse, and "Mother wouldn't have it. What?! Have a daughter there, inside of that place [the hospital, presumably having to tend to people of all colors and conditions]?" Interestingly enough, Dorothy Phillips, the daughter of her sister Harriet, who had been educated in England, *did* become a nurse. She fell in love with an English doctor, but although it was reciprocated, he told her that his family would never accept her, as she was "colored." As Dorothy told my niece Loraine Jansen, with whom she became good friends, it was just as well, if "he was that feeble." She never married. The same thing would happen, decades later, to another relative of mine. *After* they had been married and he realized the extent to which she had black relatives, he and his family became increasingly uncomfortable, and they eventually divorced.

All told, mom had, in her words, a "lovely childhood." She did well in school, was popular for her piano playing, played tennis and hockey, loved dancing and acting and reportedly had many suitors. In the photo below, taken on June 4, 1934, at the wedding of her sister to Diamond plantation manager Billy Campbell, Mom is standing behind her mother Rosina, whose veil had apparently dropped down to cover her mouth. Mom is sporting a stylish hat. Dorothy Phillips, the cousin who would be later spurned by the English doctor, is far left, and Aunt Harriet, Dorothy's mother, is far right, with her younger sister Barbara Nancy.

Figure 3.2 Dorothy Phillips, my first cousin. Her doctor friend didn't marry her, because she was "colored."

A month later, on July 14, 1934, Mom herself was married, to my father Russell, whom she had met some time earlier while they were acting in *The Adventures of Robin Hood*, staged by family friend Mildred Mansfield at the Girl Guides pavilion, top of Brickdam. He was Robin Hood, apparently, and she was Maid Marian. As my mom put it, "He was supposed to like me, Maid Marion, in the play. Well, the liking went on after. He was a nice lad, yuh know … a handsome lad … and ah can tell you, he's a persistent man. He don't give up."

Actually, my mom was almost eight years older than my dad, and partly because of this, his parents refused to give their consent to them getting married. They had to wait until he turned 21, on March 1, 1934. Mom never forgave Grandpa and Grandma Rickford for this delay, especially since they had my oldest sister, June, in 1933, almost a year before they were married! Dad fell from a coconut tree while he was picking coconuts for his beloved, six weeks before their wedding. He was confined to home, which explains why he is not present in the Aunt Ivy wedding photo. My mom and dad remained happily married for 34 years until he died of a stroke in September 1969. They had ten children in all, with me, the "Baby" Rickford, born in 1949.

The family nearly lost their lives in an accident at Garraway Stream in 1944. And neither me nor Nancy or Pat would have been born. Here is my

Figure 3.3 Aunt Ivy Wade and Billy Campbell's wedding, June 4, 1934: Front, L to R: Dorothy Phillips, Rosina Wade, Billy Campbell, Ivy (Wade) Campbell, Deryck Adamson, Harriet (Wade) Phillips, Barbara Nancy Phillips. Back, L to R: Mr. Wilson, Eula Wade, E.G. Forbes, Barbara Osborne, Walter Phillips (Harriet's husband), Johnny Adamson.

brother George's account, drawing on details from a recording I made with Mom in 1983:

> Tragedy nearly struck … in 1944 when the Rickfords lived at 108 miles Potaro and decided to have a family holiday in Tumatumari.[3] We travelled by a huge eight-wheeled "Thornycroft" lorry filled with passengers. My mother was seated in the front cab next to the driver with baby Elizabeth on her lap. The rest of the family were in the back with daddy. The driver attempted to turn the vehicle round at the Denham Suspension Bridge over Garraway Stream. The latter is a tributary of the Potaro River which eventually flows over the mighty Kaieteur Falls.
>
> The driver took his eyes off the road for a moment and was fumbling with the controls. The vehicle crashed through the railings alongside the bridge. Startled by the noise of the crash and my mother's scream the driver looked up, saw his predicament, and started shouting, "Oh me God, is where we going? Oh me God, is where we going?" Mummy had a grandstand view of the drama as it unfolded and recalls sending an urgent prayer heavenward.

Figure 3.4 My Mom, Eula Sylvia Enid Rickford, née Wade, on her wedding day, July
14, 1934.

Miraculously, the truck stopped with its two front wheels suspended in
midair over the fast-flowing river below! Having ascertained that the lorry
was going no further due to its wheels being firmly wedged against a lump of
granite, the driver and passengers proceeded to disembark through the back
of the vehicle. We were all shaken, but relieved."

Of the many memories I have of Mom, three stand out.

First, she was a *maestra* on the piano, primarily favoring classical master-
pieces. One of my favorites was her rendition of "Jesu, Joy of Man's Desiring" by
Johann Sebastian Bach (BWV Cantata 147). In July 1983, while she was visiting
us, I recorded her playing several of her favorite pieces and shared them with the
rest of the family on a cassette tape, the other side containing some of her many
personal narratives.

Second, she loved plants and flowers, and maintained a garden resplendent
with roses, orchids and bougainvilleas. Through divine good fortune, my wife
Angela has a similar love and a green thumb, as my annual Facebook postings of
her spring flowers will attest.

Third, she would often read to us in her youth, and I remember with great
fondness her reading, when I was already in high school, from Sam Selvon's
The Lonely Londoners. This was especially instructive and entertaining to me,
because it ran counter to my parents' usual advice to speak the Queen's English
(already complicated by the fact that in their informal usage, they used Creolese,
our English-based Creole, everyday, as did virtually every Guyanese). Here is a
sample of the dialogue in this marvelous book about West Indians from neighbor-
ing Trinidad who had emigrated to London:

Figure 3.5 My Mom and I, around 1959, when I was nine or ten.

"Who tell you my name and address?" Moses ask them.
"Oh, we get it from a fellar name Jackson who was up here last year."
"Jackson is a bitch," Moses say, "he know that I seeing hell myself."
"We have money," the fellars say, "we only want you to help we to get a place to stay and tell we how to get a work."
"That harder than money," Moses grunt. "I don't know why the hell you come to me."

Later I came to understand, write and teach about the systematic way in which Caribbean Creole English maintained grammatical distinctions while dispensing with some of the grammatical inflections of Standard English like past tense marking, present tense -*s*, copula *is/are* and the distinction between subject *we* and object *us*. But Mum's readings of Selvon were enough to introduce me to the ambiguous love/hate relationship that West Indians often have with what Kamau Brathwaite described as "nation language" vs the "Queen's English."[4] And they gave me my earliest love of language *and* linguistics.

Notes

1   C.B. Wade's second marriage was to Lydia Daly. One of their children was Virginia Wade, who married Benjamin Emmanuel Franker, the father of Colin Franker, our Bel Air Park neighbor. Colin (Kay) and Joy Franker Williams are the children of Colin and Muriel Franker. My mom, Baby Wade, was a half-sister of Virginia Wade.
2   See the biography and obituary of Matthew Thomas Stevens at https://tinyurl.com/ybfcjqve
3   These are places far from the coast where most Guyanese live, but in the hinterlands or "bush," where Dad used to work with BG Consolidated Goldfields. On the map in Figure 4.3, the closest named place is Mahdia.
4   Edward Kamau Brathwaite. 1984. *History of the Voice: The Development of Nation Language in Anglophone Caribbean Poetry*. London: New Beacon Books.

4   Siblings

Patricia(s), Peter

Mom and Dad had ten children, in this order:

> June Rosemary Rickford [1933–],
> Edward Noel (Teddy) Rickford [1934–1998],
> Dawn Elin Ann Rickford [1938–],
> Peter Howell Rickford [1940–1995],
> George Howell Rickford [1941–],
> Patricia Eula Rickford (died at one year old) [1943–1944],
> Elizabeth Ann Rickford [1944–],
> Stella Patricia (Pat) Rickford [1945–1999],
> Barbara Nancy Rickford [1948–], and
> John (Johnny) Russell Rickford [1949–].

Writing about every one of them would require a whole book! I've chosen to write about three siblings in this chapter, the two Patricias and my brother Peter, and my great-niece Paige Patricia.

Patricia Eula Rickford was the sixth child of Russell and Eula Rickford, and the only one who died in childhood. Born March 17, 1943, she died a year later, of dysentery. I would not be born until six years later, so of course I never knew her. But from all accounts she was a beautiful and greatly loved child, whose premature passing broke my parents' heart. My mother spoke of her often, although she gave birth to another child, Elizabeth Ann (named after Queen Elizabeth) on April 21, shortly after Patricia Eula Rickford died.

Early in March 1944, Mom began to have Braxton-Hicks (false contractions) as though she were about to go into labor with Elizabeth. So her doctor, the legendary Dr. Randolph T. Bayley, who delivered all ten of her children, admitted her to his nursing home as a precaution. Mom left baby Patricia with my Aunt Ivy for safekeeping. But Patricia developed dysentery there, and in a mistake common in a country where children often have gastroenteritis disorders, Ivy continued to feed her milk, instead of water or clear liquids.

When my mother heard about Patricia Eula's illness, she discharged herself from the nursing home and tried to find a doctor who could help her one-year-old child. But there was a big house fire in Kingston that occupied many of the

DOI: 10.4324/9781003204305-4

Figure 4.1 The Rickford family (Edward and Peter absent) at the wedding of my eldest sister June to Michael Norsworthy, December 2, 1961. L to R, standing: George, Patricia, my paternal Grandmother Millicent, Michael, June, Dad, Mom, Elizabeth. L to R, in front: Aunt Ivy, Nancy, Dawn, me (12).

firefighters and local doctors. Clutching her eight-month pregnant belly, she tried to get one doctor, then another, to help save her baby: "PLEASE. HELP ME. MY BABY IS DYING." But in vain. On March 19, 1944, Patricia Eula passed away. The first poignancy related to the name Patricia.

Just over a year after Elizabeth was born, on September 19, 1945, my mother gave birth to another girl, who was named Stella Patricia, in tribute to the lost Patricia Eula. Stella Patricia was always known as "Patricia" or "Patto" or "Pat" for short. Three of her qualities specially brought joy to her family members and friends:

1. Her laugh—difficult to describe, but it came easily and from deep within her body, and it was sustained and loud! I remember once when a few of us were sitting under an overhanging rock under Orinduik Falls, she kept laughing and shouting "Oh, we Oh we Oh"—like a female Tarzan!—while the words reverberated in the confined space and the rest of us cracked up. That was just like Pat. Her daughter Joanne described her laugh like this: "My mother had the most beautiful laugh. Unique—and loud—it was also very contagious and seemed to penetrate the souls of everyone surrounding her. Its strange first shriek, followed by a series of chuckles, was also the perfect detector: to find her, by a neighbor or on the other side of a vast supermarket, all we had to do was listen for her trademark. And it always came, like a wave

enveloping everyone, bringing us all into the sea of happiness that was my mother."

2. Her gift of gab. She was easy to talk to, able to converse on any topic, sensitive, interested, always with a good comeback to whatever you told her.
3. Her voracious love of reading. She would read novels anytime, anywhere. For instance, she would wash dishes with a book propped up behind the faucet, covered with plastic to prevent it getting wet from the splashing water.

But Pat started having epileptic seizures or fits in her late teenage years. Elizabeth, who was very close to Pat, recalled the first time she witnessed one. They were at the cinema, enjoying a movie, when Pat suddenly stood up straight, then collapsed on the ground in a seizure. Everyone was confused about what to do, but before too long she came out of it, and they just had to wait until Daddy came with the car to pick them up.

Dad himself had had an epileptic seizure or two, and we at least learned not to try to put a hand directly in his mouth. As mom said, "A person in a fit will bite down hard on it, unaware of how they're hurting you. Use a spoon or a cork to prevent them chewing up their own tongue."

Pat fell in love with a white divorcé from England named Ray Streeter, who was 17 years older than she was, and in 1970 they got married in Barbados, and made that small island their home. I was somewhat skeptical about the match, fearing that this might be yet another example of a British expatriate fascinated by a local girl of color (we already had several examples of that in our family history), and also apprehensive that she might end up having to care for him in his old age. Both fears were groundless. Whenever Angela and I visited their home, they seemed happy as clams, their lives enriched by a nearby beach, and two children who came in short order: Russell and Joanne. As far as I could tell, she had no seizures after they married, indicating that marrying Ray was a definite plus.

Pat was also a smoker, however, like her husband, and both of them enjoyed the occasional rum and Coke. Around 1997, she consulted her doctor about a persistent lump in her throat, which she feared might be cancerous. After a quick inspection, he dismissed it as "female hysteria" and prescribed Valium.

Although the lump continued to bother her, Pat postponed going back to her doctor about it, because he had been so dismissive the first time. When she finally returned to him, he quickly realized that she had cancer of the throat, and indeed that it had metastasized—spread to many other organs. A visit to England further confirmed this diagnosis. I helped to buy other putative remedies, like grasses from South America, which she requested, but they were futile against the Big C. On March 1, 1999, short of what would have been her 53rd birthday (September 19, 1999), she died.

I was there, at her home in Barbados, when she passed away. I had come a few days earlier and took turns singing Guyanese folksongs and campfire songs to her, along with my sister Nancy, and otherwise helping to take care of her in her unconscious state. But just before daybreak on September 3, I was awakened to join her husband Ray, her high school children Russell and Joanne, and my sister

Nancy by Pat's bedside. Her breathing had become slower and more labored. Eventually, she took in a last deep breath, and no outgoing breath followed. The second Patricia poignancy had occurred.

I turned to Ray and said, "Thank you for having taken such good care of my sister, and for having brought her so much happiness." The fact that he was older than her, and white, made no difference whatsoever. The only fact that mattered was that they had shared great happiness and love. His daughter Joanne Streeter confides:

> For the first time in my life, I see my father cry. Actually wail. He sits next to her bed, holding her hand, and bawls, the only way to describe it. I know he is devastated. This is the beautiful woman he adores, and he has had to sit helplessly at her side as her body is ravaged.

I didn't stay for the funeral. Communing with her for the last few days of her life was enough.

Figure 4.2 Ray and Pat Streeter (nee Rickford) on their wedding day, August 8, 1970, in Barbados.

The third Patricia in this multi-generation saga was born to Pat's son, Russell Streeter, and his wife Lisa Rampersad Streeter, on June 14, 2010. She was named Paige Patricia Streeter, her middle name commemorating her prematurely departed grandmother. In the birth announcement, Russell wrote: "Lisa is recovering, but is so thrilled at having a daughter that, when I left the hospital, she was feeling no pain!" Their first child had been a son, Samuel.

Angela and I first met Paige Patricia in June 2012. We were visiting my eldest sister June in Horley, near Gatwick airport in England, and Russell, Lisa, Samuel and Paige came over to join us. Paige was sick with leukemia and was trailing a six-foot long nasogastric tube from her left nostril. But it didn't stop her as she explored everything in my big sister's apartment, trailing the tube behind her. Her spirit was indomitable, and as this picture shows, her giggly laugh, reminiscent of her grandmother's, was sheer joy.

Shortly after this photo was taken, Paige won her first fight with leukemia. She was cancer-free! We saw and enjoyed her at subsequent family celebrations, like June's 80th birthday celebration in England in June 2013, and a big Rickford family reunion in Miami in April 2017.

But in August 2019, after a hiatus of six years, the leukemia returned, camouflaging itself at first as a liver problem, until its true and monstrous identity was laid bare. She was airlifted to King's College Hospital, London, and on August 14 we joined with others around the world to "offer up fervent prayers for her full recovery."

For the next eight months Paige went through a series of painful medical procedures while her parents took leave from work to be with her in Great Ormond

Figure 4.3 Paige Patricia Streeter giggling in the cocoon of her loving family: mom Lisa, brother Samuel, dad Russell, in my sister June's home, Horley, England, June 3, 2012.

Street Hospital and other hospitals in London, and her brother Samuel went to boarding school. I raised prayers repeatedly in First Presbyterian Church of Palo Alto—while others did likewise in private and in church communities far and wide. A WhatsApp group was started to share messages almost daily about her progress, and to support Russ and Lisa. My wife Angela represented us in that forum.

On January 2020, the most hopeful development of this entire period occurred. Eleven-year old Samuel, who was found to be a perfect match, donated bone marrow for a transplant. And miraculously, over the next month, the leukemia retreated, until Paige was cancer-free again.

But then she developed Idiopathic Pneumonia Syndrome, which happens in less than 20% of bone marrow transplants. She was treated with steroids for that, and then dialysis when she developed diabetes (her finger was pricked 23 times in one day!) and she needed a lung oscillator to breathe.

In the end it was too much for her nine-year-old body. The doctors said they had done everything for her and removed the cumbersome machines. On March 14, 2020, they brought in a musician to play the guitar and sing songs for her while her dad accompanied him on a tiny xylophone. And they left the family to enjoy her unencumbered for the last time. They hunkered down in a bed next to hers, hugging each other, and listened to Paige take her last breaths.

Five days short of the 76th anniversary of Patricia Eula's passing, Paige stopped breathing. The third and final poignancy.

Two parting notes, from her devastated parents. The first from dad Russell, Facebook, March 14:

> Today our beautiful, brave, strong little girl lost her fight and is now at peace. She fought for so long against this illness and her strength and positivity in the face of near constant pain and discomfort is truly inspirational. We are so thankful to have known her and been able to share so many happy times together. We will miss you so much.

The second from mom Lisa, who was too stunned to write anything to the WhatsApp support group on March 14, but sent this the following day:

> Woke up this morning feeling a sense of utter disbelief, despair and sadness. I am now truly broken. But we have to keep moving forward. Will pack up our things from Paige's room, including her craft. Then visit her one more time. Then head home afterwards.

A funeral was held Tuesday March 24, 2020. Due to the COVID-19 pandemic, less than two dozen people were allowed in the church in England. But it was live-streamed, reaching many more relatives and friends worldwide.

Of all my siblings, the one that leaps out as most different and distinctive is my brother Peter. He is commonly described as the most handsome of the lot, at least of the four boys, and the photo below shows how good-looking he was.

This fourth oldest child of my parents, born March 13, 1940, is also regarded as one of the kindest and most generous. He certainly knew more than anyone else in my family did about Nat King Cole, The Platters and other soul singers of the 1950s, and he had an enviable collection of 45s and long play records to boot. In this way he helped to introduce me to African American music, and the soul culture that my wife and I and our children would eventually adopt when we moved to the US.

Peter also had more black friends than any of my siblings did, and the beautiful teenaged bride that he married was also colored, with a black mother and father and siblings. For a while, they lived nearby. I hung out with them sometimes, even dreaming that I might sail away on a fishing trawler to the US with her dad, a trawler captain. Between his friends and in-laws, Peter helped to introduce me to the black side of Guyanese heritage.

As far as I know, Peter never rode a bicycle, and he certainly never drove a car. But he was a prodigious walker, and for many years he would cure meat at the Guyana Marketing Corporation. Everyone agrees that he made the sweetest, tenderest hams they have ever had! This skill he converted to the production of pickled fish, which he cured using a converted refrigerator and sold in bulk to the armed forces.

But this beautiful, generous, music-loving, ham-curing brother of mine also had less formal schooling than the rest of us. He probably had no more than an elementary education. He got into quarrels and even fights with my parents, especially Dad. I remember a row between him and my dad which became so heated that I crawled under a bed in the crowded bedroom that was home to so many of us and tried to close my ears.

And then there was the afternoon when he was trying to tune in foreign radio stations at home with the inevitable static this generated. My dad, probably concentrating on the accounting records for the company at which he worked, Panel Fitzpatrick, yelled at him over and over, "Turn that damned noise off! Keep it down!" But my brother, absorbed by the fine-tuning the process required, ignored him, until Dad did something I never saw him do before or since. He got up from his desk, tore the radio out of its socket, and tossed it through the living room window, where it splintered into innumerable pieces after falling 20 feet to the concrete pathway below. I remember staring at it from the window, aghast. I have blocked out of my mind what ensued, for that radio was the love and delight of my brother's teenage years.

Our family does not have many family portraits—just a few taken professionally at weddings or other special family gatherings. But Peter appears in none of those.

For the one thing I have not mentioned is that Peter had a physical disability, which my mother sometimes described as an astigmatism of the brain. "Astigmatism" is clearly not the right word, or perhaps I don't remember it accurately, since that describes an eye condition that causes blurred vision, something I don't recall Peter having. What is more likely is that Peter had a form of cerebral palsy, perhaps caused by damage to his brain before or during childbirth. It manifested itself in an uncoordinated gait, dysarthria and minor difficulties in speech.

Whatever the cause and precise diagnosis, Peter could not have succeeded and excelled in school as society and his family would have expected him to, and it was probably his frustration at his limitations that led to some of the outbursts and conflicts with Mom and Dad. This said, I am profoundly sorry that he is absent from the handful of family photos we have, for he was very much one of us, a beloved part of our family.

There is a happy loving photo of Peter just after his marriage to Hectorine in 1960 (she was 16 and he 20 at the time), celebrating with drinks at their little flat around the corner from our Cowan Street home (Figure 4.4). My mom, my dad and Peter are all smiling, and his new bride is sending him a shy, coquettish grin from across the room. I hope there were many more moments like this.

I got to know Peter better as an adult when Angela and I returned from graduate work at the University of Pennsylvania for six years from 1974 to 1980 to teach at the University of Guyana and do research for my PhD dissertation.

A few moments stand out, like the time he sent one of his children to get me early one morning to bring the tragic news that Hectorine had died. He had been showering to go to work early, and she had had an epileptic fit. Without anyone to

Figure 4.4 Peter, Dad, Mom and Hectorine, in Peter and Hectorine's apartment, Georgetown, September 1, 1960.

assist her, she had swallowed her tongue and died. I raced up to their Ruimveldt home to assist him, and Mom helped to get our Bel Air Park neighbor Judge Dan Jhappan to ensure that he would not be the object of suspicion.

Some years after that, we had him over to lunch, and a serving dish with half a dozen or more roti (flatbread, to be eaten with some curry chicken we had prepared) happened to be placed in front of him. "Eh eh," he said, "I thought all of this was for me to eat." He was probably speaking the truth, since he was a hearty eater, but I informed him, laughing, that it was intended to be sufficient for him *and* the five other people at the table—Angela, me, and the three kids we had at the time.

Similar too was his reaction to his doctor's recommendation in the late 1970s that he eliminate pork and other red meat from his diet and stick to white meat like fish and chicken. He told me, scornfully, that he had sucked his teeth at this suggestion: "I love me pork too much, Johnny!" Instead, he had started getting some bush tea from an herb woman in the market to help fight his high blood pressure and its common consequence, a stroke. These were the maladies of the Rickford family that had already claimed the lives of my dad, his brother Neville and his sister Cicely.

Figure 4.5 Peter Rickford, and his family, outside St. George's Cathedral, Georgetown, July 17, 1994.

I left Guyana in 1980 to take up a faculty appointment at Stanford University. By the time I returned to Guyana to organize the first big Rickford family reunion in summer 1994, Peter had already had a stroke that affected him and left him unable to stand and perform several basic functions, like going to the bathroom by himself. In the photo below, taken outside St George's Cathedral in Georgetown (our traditional worship site) where we gathered for a celebratory mass, he is seated on a folding chair. Surrounding him are three of his sons (Denbeigh, Peter Jr., Chris Ranveer), a daughter Diana, her husband Andrew, and three of Peter's grandchildren: Denbeigh Jr., Michelle and Melissa. About six months later, on January 27, 1995, he was dead, killed by a massive subsequent stroke. Interestingly enough, the funeral service revealed two other children most of us had not known about before but welcomed readily into the family: Donna and Eula Patricia, daughters of Christina, who had often feuded with his partner Brenda Desiree Charles, with whom Peter lived for many years following Hectorine's death.

It bears mentioning that Peter's seven children, and their children, have always been very friendly and helpful to Angela and myself and our children, and vice versa. I am a father figure to his son Peter Jr., and he (and Ranveer) helped install a commemorative plaque to my mom and dad in St George's Cathedral, and to replace it with a more durable one when it was broken in 2019.

Peter Jr. and I communicate frequently by phone and email, and he regularly either paints my parents' grave or arranges to have someone do it. Some of his children have also become close to my sister Dawn and her daughter Michelle. And we get together with them in big family gatherings whenever Angela and I are in Guyana. In this way I hope the love and inclusiveness of his nuclear family that Peter did not always enjoy from 10 to 20 is now realized, and lives on.

5   Queen's College (my high school)

At the age of ten, in September 1960, I set out for Queen's College (QC), one of the two most prestigious high schools for boys in British Guiana. It was only about four blocks away from my Cowan Street home, and two of my three older brothers had gone there. I rode to the sprawling yellow structure in my school uniform: short khaki pants, white shirt, cap and school tie indicating the "house" to which I had been assigned (*Austin House*, like my brothers).

I made my way to the front of the assembly hall, where the newbies were. Classes were seated by level, so as you rose higher in the hierarchy, you moved further back. As newbies, we were trying to follow all directions and do everything right.

The assembly was going according to plan until we came to the playing of "God save the Queen," the British National Anthem. The Queen of course was Queen Elizabeth II, as we were still a part of the British Empire at the time. The music teacher Miss Dolphin was cranking out the melody on the piano, when Mr. Jones strode to the front of the stage and urged us all to sing along. Like dutiful newbies we did. But in fact this was supposed to be a piano solo, and Mr. Jones, unbeknown to us, was having a nervous breakdown.

The headmaster, an Englishman named Mr. V.J. Sanger-Davies, who had served in Gambia before coming to Guyana, was getting quite agitated by this violation of protocol, and yelled at us to be quiet. But Mr. Jones, conducting by this time, and singing aloud himself, urged us to sing louder, making the headmaster more apoplectic. The situation was only saved by an older, wiser teacher named Mr. C. A. Yansen, who gently approached Mr. Jones, and putting his arms around him, persuaded him to exit stage left. It had been a memorable morning, and we buzzed about it all day and still remember it half a century later. In Guyana, psychological and psychiatric help, so widespread in North America and Europe, is limited for those who need it.

For the next seven years I would remain at QC, winning the 1965 prize for best results at the London University General Certificate of Education (GCE) Ordinary Level exams, and becoming president of the Junior Debating Society and the Literary and Debating Society. I was also editor of the school newspaper and the school magazine, and served as Head Boy, in charge of about two dozen seniors who were prefects. In the British system exemplified by Harry Potter's *Hogwarts*,

DOI: 10.4324/9781003204305-5

prefects are senior students with leadership roles and administrative authority—for instance they can put students into detention for infractions of various kinds.

In the University of London Advanced Level exams in 1967, I earned a distinction in English, a credit in History, and a C in French—sufficient with my high school leadership to win me a 1968 Fulbright Grant for undergraduate study in the US.

But my QC career was not the steady success that these highlights would suggest. For one thing, although I was captain of the table tennis team in my entering class, and played recreational cricket and soccer, I sucked at sports. I never even made a "Standard Point" in the inter-house sports competitions that led up to the annual Sports Day, although I came close to the required distance for the standard in the shot put.

I also had a tendency to be late, exacerbated when we moved in 1962–63 from Kingston, close to QC, to Bel Air Park at the edge of Georgetown, over a mile away by bike. Students who came late for morning assembly were corralled by the prefects, made to stand at the back of the hall, and forced to make the Walk of Shame to the front of the hall at the very end of assembly.

Latecomers were thus seen by the entire student body and by the staff. Derogatory comments by the headmaster were routine: "Hey, Rickford, you're late AGAIN! Are you going to use that bicycle flat-tire excuse again? I'll deal with you later." As I got older, I perfected the art of avoiding that ignominy by sneaking into the school in some other way than the main entrance. My most elaborate ruse was to lock my bike at the nearby Scouts ground, cross the canal on a precarious pipe that led to the QC sports field, enter the woodwork shop that had been deliberately left open to facilitate habitual miscreants like me, and then join the students going to their individual classrooms after general assembly!

I also had a few run-ins with the staff and or/principal. One of the first came in my entering year, when another student and I stayed after class, drew a bull's eye on the wall and used open compasses as darts trying to hit the bull's eye. The prefect who found us only gave us a detention, requiring us to stay after school and write lines or pick up leaves, rather than getting caned.

But during my second year at QC, the principal, V.J. Sanger-Davies called me into his office. There he had a graph of my rank in class every quarter and year: *third, fifth, seventh* by the end of year 1, and *seventh, eleventh* by the end of year 2.

"What's wrong with this graph?" he asked.

"Looks fine to me," or something similarly smart-alecky, I replied.

"It's going in the WRONG direction," he retorted, "And you are going to need something to TUNE you up."

That was my first inkling that I was to receive a caning. He made me bend over a chair, selected a cane from an array on his wall to match my posterior, then gave me six savage lashes, each of which left an oozing bruise on my behind and leg. (I was still in short pants and would remain so until I entered the sixth form, although when I was in Upper Fourth, I led a fruitless delegation to headmaster

Hetram to ask him to let fourth formers wear long pants.) When he was finished, Sanger-Davies tried to tickle me to make me laugh, but this was further proof that he was a sadist. I tried hard to hold in my tears, to maintain my dignity with him as with anyone who might be passing by the principal's office as I exited. Maybe his caning *did* motivate me to study harder, but I still think there were other ways he could have achieved the same result.

My second caning came when I left for the summer holidays without removing all my text-books from the lockers in the cloakroom adjacent to our classroom. The principal, who apparently had an annual habit of checking for this throughout the school, picked my lock and then called me to see him in his office.

"Ahh, Mr. Rickford, I see you 'forgot' these twelve books, you left them in your locked locker. Not only would this inconvenience the new students who are depending on those lockers for their classes next year, but they must have cost your parents great expense."

"I'm sorry, sir. I left in a hurry and planned to come back for them later."

"Ah, the best made plans of mice and men! What say I offer to sell them back to you, at a price?"

"What do you mean, sir?"

"Suppose I offered them to you at one lash per book?"

I must have gulped, for a caning with twelve lashes would be pretty much unbearable. And it was certainly unconventional.

"Cat got your tongue? OK, my best and final offer—I will give them back to you at the bargain rate of two books per lash."

It was not an offer with which I had any choice. In a minute he had selected the appropriate cane, made me bend over the chair in his office, and again inflicted six hard, painful lashes that left me oozing and bruised, as before.

Among the reasons these canings bothered me so much is because they were executed by a white expatriate, they involved attempts at humor, and they hearkened back to the days of slavery, to a plantation era in which they were instruments of subjugation and control.

This was most evident in an incident in my *elementary* school, Sacred Heart Roman Catholic, in which a student, only eight or nine years old at the time, had hit an annoying teacher and jumped out the window onto a zinc roof before making good his escape. He was a folk hero to fellow students for a while, but his mother came back to beg that he not be expelled, and the headmaster, assisted by his coterie of good nuns, made him an excruciating "deal." He would have to submit to a caning of "six of the best" before the entire assembled boys' half of the school.

On the fateful day we saw him paraded to the raised dais at the top of the school, held down by several older boys, while Mr. Smalls, the hardest hitting teacher on the staff, administered the punishment. He would raise the cane high up in the air, behind his back even, and slam it down on the boy's posterior with all the force he could muster, again and again. The boy howled in agony. I felt all of us, as unwilling onlookers, lost something in the process: a modicum of the freedom we had gained since slavery was abolished in 1838, about 120 years earlier.

At Queen's, our white expatriate headmaster was replaced by local scholars of color after 1962, ending 118 years of expatriate leadership. The first headmaster was an Afro-Guyanese and linguist, Dr. Richard Allsopp (1962–3), and the second an East Indian, Mr. Doodnauth Hetram (1963–69). The rest of the staff was overwhelmingly Afro- and Indo-Guyanese, with two Chinese teachers (Mr. Yhap and Ms. Akai). And it was overwhelmingly male. Some of the teachers who had gone to universities in England years earlier (like Mr. Trotz and Mr. Lowe) still retained the semi-British accents they had acquired then (they were considered at the time prestige markers) but most used Guyanese accents with English grammar in their formal register.

I had many excellent teachers at Queen's, but some stood out. Like the relatively short **Eddie London** (second from the left in front in Figure 5.1), who did not appreciate jokes or innuendos about his height. He told us that studying burns up phosphorus and lecithin in the brain, and encouraged us to replenish our supplies with "Wampole's Phospho-Lecithin," an elixir that I bought and consumed in copious quantities. Whether or not his theory was correct, he inculcated in us a respect for the process of studying (*bunnin* or "burning") that included physical

THE STAFF

Sitting: (l to r) Mr. N. K. Robinson, Miss Ivy Loncke, Mr. Moffat, Mr. E. London, Mr. N. A. Robinson, Mr. Barker (Deputy Headmaster), Mr. D. Locke, Mr. D. Hetram (Headmaster), Mr. C. Yansen, Mr. Yhap, Mr. Glasgow, Miss A. Akai, Mr. B. Chinapen.
Standing: (l to r) Mr. K. Brotherson, Mr. S. M. Insanally (partly hidden), Mr. T. Thompson, Mr. J. Gopaul, Mr. Mangal, Mr. I. Trotz, Mr. V. J. Ramraj, Mr. M. Barton, Mr. C. O. Perry, Mr. P. Jonas, Mr. King and Mr. C. Yearwood.

Figure 5.1 Queen's College, Guyana, staff members, 1964–65. The headmaster, Mr. D. Hetram (seated third from right), and the deputy headmaster, Mr. C.E. Barker are in academic robes.

exercise and replacing our regular incandescent bulbs with daylight bulbs. These strategies and this serious devotion to studying served us well as we went into our GCE O or Ordinary level and A or Advanced level exams, set and graded at British universities like the University of London.

I also remember **Sylvia Wynter**, the young (compared with Miss Akai), intellectually vibrant, beautiful and well-endowed Jamaican wife of Guyanese novelist and memoirist Jan Carew. She exposed us to many of the radical intellectual ideas and thinkers of the day. She only taught us for a year or so, but she got latecomers like me to come to school early. About 13 years after I graduated from QC, we became faculty colleagues at Stanford. And she was amused at my stories of how she set our hearts and minds on fire in those adolescent days.

Then there was the unflappable **C.A. [Clement Aloysius] Yansen** (seated third from the right, partly hidden, in the second row of the photo in Figure 5.1). I've already mentioned him as the teacher who helped to resolve the incident with Mr. Jones at assembly on my first day at QC. He had a straight-handled bicycle and starched white coat, and it was in his Third Form Latin class that I first discovered "Take Down." In this game, you would form a line around the walls of the classroom, and if you gave no answer or a wrong answer to a question, he would go to the person next to you and so on, until someone answered it correctly—at which point he would "take you down" or move up to your position, and you would keep moving down until you answered a question correctly. My initial experience with this exercise was so humiliating (I ended up near the bottom!) that I went home

Figure 5.2 Richard Allsopp, first Guyanese headmaster of Queen's College, pioneering student of sociolinguistic variation, author of the *Dictionary of Caribbean English Usage* (Oxford 1996).

and studied my Latin vocabulary and grammar assiduously. After that I could hold my own and remain in the top ten or so in "Take Down."

Yango was also a fount of jokes and "ole time" stories, many of them depending on dramatic contrasts between standard English and deep Creolese, the local name for the Creole English of Guyana. For instance, he told us of courting a woman, by moonlight, with a Shakespearean-like *soor* or "sweet-talk" that included the line, "Your eyes are like lodestars ['a star used to guide the course of a ship']" To this she was reported to have replied, "Ah know yuh lie, but say it again, man, say it again!"

Yango, at the invitation of *QC Lictor* supervisor Victor Ramraj, went on to write a column entitled "Random Remarks on Creolese" for the 1966 Independence Issue of the *QC Lictor* that I edited. He subsequently published it (in 1975) as a book with the same title. That work was influential in showing me that Creolese, although widely disparaged in comparison with Standard English, was an important local resource.

In 1979 Yango published a second volume, writing in the foreword that:

> Creolese is a living thing and clearly reflects the activities of all Guyanese in every walk of life: their hopes and fears, joys and sorrows, vices and virtues, achievements and failures; in fine, their reactions to all the vicissitudes of time and circumstance, and above all, their sense of humour, without which life indeed not be worth much.
>   *Boy, tings so bad wid me just now dat ah gat to tek me story (and) mek laff. Ay-yah-yah! Laugh, Pagliaccio!*
>   [JRR gloss: "Boy, things are so bad with me right now that I have to just laugh at my situation. Ay-yah-yah! Laugh, Italian clown!"]

In 1993 Sonja Jansen, his daughter, issued a new version of *Random Remarks on Creolese*, combining both of the earlier volumes.

I was even more influenced by the MA and PhD theses that **Richard Allsopp**, the first local headmaster of QC, had written in 1958 and 1962 on Guyanese Creole English,[1] although I would not really read and appreciate them until I was doing my own PhD research in the 1970s. I was amazed that even before William Labov's 1966 emphasis on the value of eliciting casual speech and counting *how often* people used one feature rather than another,[2] Allsopp had shown the value of recording informal, unmonitored speech and using quantitative measurements in his analysis of Guyanese speech. In fact, one key finding of my dissertation was that vowel laxing in Guyanese pronouns (whether a person said "yuh" instead of "you" for instance) followed pretty much the same pattern that Allsopp had revealed two decades earlier![3]

But all this is getting ahead of myself, for one of the teachers who played a pivotal role in my doing well at O levels, and going on to A levels, even before university, was a young teacher named **Roger Isaacs**. Roger taught me at QC in 1966, when I was in Upper Fourth. Like other adolescents, I had just discovered the opposite sex, and studying was not receiving the priority it deserved. Indeed,

I had begun to see some of the guys who had left school after O levels and joined the workforce, riding about town with shiny motorbikes and girls who hugged them tightly from behind. That seemed not a bad thing to aspire to.

Thus distracted, I did not do well in the first test Roger Isaacs gave us. Indeed, I did terribly, scoring less than 10 out of 100, and placed near the bottom of the class. Roger asked to see me in the corridor after class and told me bluntly that I could not be as stupid as my test score suggested because he had been at the University of the West Indies with my sister Elizabeth. And since *she* had been quite smart, *I* couldn't be that stupid. He insisted then than I come to his after-school lessons. If my parents couldn't afford it, he said, I could come for free. But come I would. And I did. In less than a term my score went up from 10 to 72, and I placed second in the class. I went on to do well in French at the O levels, and it became one of my three A level subjects.

What I learned in a deeper sense from Roger Isaacs (who also got me, Potter Henderson and Thrushie Griffith intoxicated one day by letting us polish off two bottles of rum at his home, chasing them with pine drink) was not to rush to judgment about students' abilities on the basis of their performance on a single exam. But to offer them extra attention, set them high expectations, increase their motivation and encourage them to work harder.

This is a lesson I have remembered and applied often in my university teaching, disagreeing with colleagues too quick to classify students as "bright" or "not bright" on the basis of limited evidence, and finding myself willing, even eager, to work with students whom others dismissed. I'm gratified to find some of these points extolled (and the inner genius argument challenged) in the 2008 book by Malcolm Gladwell entitled *Outliers: The Story of Success*. But in a sense Roger Isaacs knew and put into practice a lot of what was in the book, 40 plus years earlier.

Among the other great teachers I encountered in high school was **Mr. Bobby Moore**, who taught me History in Upper Fourth. Bobby often raised our consciousness in innovative ways. For instance, several pairs of students in our class were "sharing" one day (looking on together at a textbook because one or the other did not have their copies with them) when he suddenly interrupted the lesson and urged us to notice the "racial" character of the resulting pairs. To our surprise and embarrassment, the sharing was almost all along racial lines. Two Chinese boys were sharing over there, two black students over here, two mixed race students at the back, two East Indians by the window, and so on. I was sharing with Robinson, a colored or mixed race student. None of it was conscious, but it was nevertheless real.

Finally, I must pay respect to **Ms. Ivy Loncke** (seated extreme left in the front row in Figure 5.1), whom I was privileged to have as English teacher in my final, Upper Sixth year, at QC. The year before I had had **Victor Ramraj** (standing sixth from the right in the back row in Figure 5.1) also an excellent teacher, and the person who introduced me to my future wife, then Angela Marshall. Angela was being taught by Ruby, Victor's wife, at the Bishop's High School for Girls (BHS), about half a mile away, the sister school to QC.

Ivy Loncke shook me and others in our class out of our complacency. For one thing, she was the only teacher who, teaching both in a morning and an afternoon period, would give you homework to be done during the lunchbreak! Another way in which she stretched us was by giving us relatively low grades and requiring us to revise, sometimes more than once. "Fair. Could be better," she would write on our first submission, with the additional comment, "Rewrite." Your second attempt might come back with the comment, "Better. Rewrite." Your third rewrite might earn you her top accolade, "Good," and a suggestion that you compare that to the first version and note how significant an improvement it represented. I should add that Ms. Loncke never gave you a grade higher than 8 out of 10, inculcating in us the idea that there was a level of achievement beyond 8 that we could never quite reach, but for which we should always continue to strive.

Ms. Loncke also used to lend me books by Cambridge Professor F.R. Leavis and other critics that extended the scope of my preparation for the University of London GCE Advanced level exam and helped me secure a distinction in that subject. And when I had to deliver a speech as Head Boy to a crowded QC auditorium on Speech Day, she prepared me for this by having me stand behind a chair in her home and doing a rehearsal, urging me to avoid fidgeting and speak clearly.

Two years later, in October 1969, when I was just beginning my second year at the University of California, Santa Cruz, Ivy Loncke died, prematurely. The news hit me, five thousand miles away, hard. My favorite and most influential high school teacher was gone. But I went on trying to incorporate the lessons she had bequeathed to me.

Notes

1 Allsopp, Richard. 1958. *Pronominal Forms in the Dialect of English Used in Georgetown (British Guiana) and Its Environs by Persons Engaged in Non-Clerical Occupations.* M.A. thesis, London University, vols. 1 and 2.
    Allsopp, Richard. 1962. *Expressions of State and Action in the Dialect of English Used in the Georgetown Area of British Guiana.* Ph.D. thesis, London University.
2 William Labov. 1966. *The Social Stratification of English in New York City.* Washington, DC: Center for Applied Linguistics.
3 In my 1979 PhD. dissertation (*Variation in a Creole Continuum*, University of Pennsylvania), I found that how often the vowel was lax or reduced in Guyanese personal pronouns closely matched the ordering in Allsopp's MA study: Allsopp 1958: ju .80, de .67, shi .59, mi .56, wi .32, Rickford 1979: ju .84, de .68, shi .68, mi .48, wi .04.

6 Friends and girlfriends

One can learn a lot about who you are and where you live from the friends you keep. So let me run down what I can remember about the guy friends I had as a youngster, beginning with my primary school years, and then the girlfriends I had later (or imagined I had).

My earliest friends were products of my neighborhood, although one can still see in them influences of my parents and the race/class ideologies I grew up with. My closest friend until the age of ten was Geoffrey Jardim, the youngest child in the Jardim compound next door to us on Cowan Street, Kingston. That compound included three houses and a steel fabrication workshop that was always humming with activity. Most memorably, it included an old car frame with wheels, a steering wheel, and brakes, which we would push around the neighborhood and jump on once it had picked up enough speed.

Geoffrey had two older brothers, George and Alan, an older sister Elsie and a cousin Jean. They were all Portuguese. I enjoyed hanging out in their home and yard a lot, except for the time Geoffrey and someone else locked me in their dad's workshop, and I remember frantically looking for a place to escape, in vain. That undoubtedly contributed to my claustrophobia, together with the lock-up in a closet I received from the nuns at Stella Maris preschool. We spent the days capturing lizards, playing cowboys and Indians, and Police and Thief, admiring the cock-a-belly fish in the gutters, and fishing in the canal or trench beyond the road outside our homes.

One friend we had in common was Michael Trotman, an Afro-Guyanese whose mother Stella worked for the Jardims. His father used to close and open the gates to block off or facilitate traffic crossing the train lines on Parade Street when the trains were coming in or going out of the Georgetown train station, which was right across from where we lived. The Trotman family lived in a cottage right next to the gates. Michael was often with us, fishing, swimming, catching small insects and so on.

Another friend was Roger D'Ornellas, who lived around the corner on Barrack Street. I got to know him from Sacred Heart Roman Catholic school on Main Street (often referred to as Main Street School), which we both attended. To tell you the truth, I don't know precisely what his ethnicity was. His dad looked

DOI: 10.4324/9781003204305-6

Portuguese, and his mom and some of the other relatives in his home looked more "colored."

But in addition to many occasions playing cricket or bat-and-ball in the concrete driveway underneath his home, I remember his family inviting me on their picnics—once on the seawall facing the Atlantic Ocean, another time on a longer trip to Cheong's Creek up at the American base, about 30 miles away, near the airport. My family never went on picnics—we didn't have a car during my primary school days. I remember the fun of eating curry and roti, cheese straws and other culinary delights with the D'Ornellases, in addition to "swimming" in the creeks, playing games and otherwise enjoying those occasions. It was also a delight to go with them to Colgrain Pool (at the Georgetown Club), one of the benefits of Roger's dad being a Booker's executive. That went on for years until Roger's nephew "Bud-up" Edghill drowned, a tragic event that brought the pool trips to an end.

I had other friends at Main Street school. But the transition to high school at about ten or eleven represented a parting of the ways, so to speak. Portuguese or near-Portuguese boys, especially if they were Catholics, tended to go to St. Stanislaus College, not exclusively so, of course. Afro-Guyanese, mixed race or colored boys, and students who were not committed Catholics tended to go (if they did well enough on the Common Entrance exam) to Queen's College, again, not exclusively so. Geoffrey Jardim and Roger D'Ornellas went to Saint Stanislaus College and Karna and I went to Queen's. We were friendly enough when we bumped into each other after that, but gradually we developed and held fast to new friendships in our respective high schools.

At Queen's, my friendships tended to vary depending on my age/grade level and interests. But serious friendships, involving visits to each other's homes, were limited. Among my East Indian friends, Karna Singh, a friend from Main Street school, and the son of poet/writer Rajkumari Singh, was one of the closest, and it has continued up to today.

I had a number of Afro-Guyanese friends, including Colin Benjamin, who lived about three blocks from me in Bel Air, with whom I often biked to school, and we played ping pong frequently. Gordon Moore, in Kitty, was a friend I often visited at home, and I worked and talked constantly with Keith Gordon in the final year at QC when we served as Head and Deputy Head prefect respectively. I also spent a lot of time at Potter Henderson's home in Bent Street, where a group of us used to hang out regularly, scraping, repainting and modifying our bicycles, and getting our hair cut with a razor blade and comb, the common style at the time.

L.A.R. Grant was a black friend who I first got to know from when both of us were in Miss Akai's relatively small geography class. Like Roderick Fletcher and Charlie Cambridge and Keith Wilson, I became closer to him after we were in the U.S. I now communicate with them by email several times a week as part of a small QC Old Boy's group. Andrew McIntosh (mixed race: mother Portuguese, father mixed—African, Amerindian and white) is also part of that group, although we hung out in high school where he taught me to "feel" for *patwa* in the Light Street canal.

And yet, my three closest friends in high school, from about 1965 to 1967, were Brian Chan, Michael Dow and John(ny) Agard. Brian and Johnny were budding poets, like me, and we were contributors to several issues of the fledgling *Expression* magazine which were published in 1966, 1967 and beyond.[1] Brian's "If I could extract" was one of the very best poems in *Expression 1*, in my view (don't know if Brian would agree now).

Brian and Johnny both have book-length publications of their poetry now. Johnny lived around the corner from Brian, so even though he went to St. Stanislaus, we hung out regularly. Michael was not a poet, but he was an excellent raconteur, and on any given afternoon, we could be found at each other's homes, or drinking small lemonades and eating buns and tennis rolls at a nearby corner shop while *gyaafin* ("small talking") the time away. What was more, we had started going to teenage dance parties as a group, especially from 1966 on, and our girlfriends (Marilyn with Michael, Molly with Brian, Angela with me) knew and liked each other.

Oh, and I forgot to mention their ethnicities: Brian was half Chinese and half Portuguese. Michael's parents were both mixed race or colored; his mother was more Portuguese, and his father had more African influence. Johnny's mom was Portuguese and his father (whom I never met) was Afro-Guyanese, making him "mixed race," like me. He wrote a powerful poem about this in 2005, called "Half-caste." It is included in the General Certificate of Secondary Education exams in the UK, and has been the subject of many online analyses.[2] Agard employs sarcasm and feigns daftness to mock the derogatory term "half-caste" itself:

Half-caste by John Agard

Excuse me
standing on one leg
I'm half-caste

Explain yuself
wha yu mean
when yu say half-caste
yu mean when picasso
mix red an green
is a half-caste canvas/
explain yuself
wha u mean
when yu say half-caste
yu mean when light an shadow
mix in de sky
is a half-caste weather/
well in dat case
england weather
nearly always half-caste
in fact some o dem cloud

half-caste till dem overcast
so spiteful dem don't want de sun pass
ah rass/
explain yuself
wha yu mean
when yu say half-caste
yu mean tchaikovsky
sit down at dah
        piano
an mix a black key
wid a white key
is a half-caste symphony

Explain yuself
wha yu mean
Ah listening to yu wid de keen
half of mih ear
Ah looking at u wid de keen
half of mih eye
and when I'm introduced to yu
I'm sure you'll understand
why I offer yu half-a-hand
an when I sleep at night
I close half-a-eye
consequently when I dream
I dream half-a-dream
an when moon begin
        to glow
I half-caste human being
cast half-a-shadow
but yu come back tomorrow
wid de whole of yu eye
an de whole of yu ear
and de whole of yu mind

an I will tell yu
de other half
of my story

Towards the end of 1962, our family moved to Bel Air Park [BAP]. As my brother George remembers it, a number of the middle class people who lived there at the time had decided to emigrate to England or North America, in the wake of political "disturbances" which had begun to rock Guyana from 1961 to 1964, with killings, burning of homes and businesses and widespread political unrest.[3] This allowed us to buy a home in BAP more affordably than we might have in earlier years.

When we moved to BAP, I got a new set of friends, many of whom were from there or nearby Section "K" Campbellville. We used to hang out on a wooden structure at the top of Eping Avenue, where it branched into a roundabout. The new friends included Gerry Benjamin (primarily Portuguese) from Queen's College, William Eddie Campbell (primarily Chinese) and Gary Bannister, from Saint Stanislaus, Joey Alberga, who had already left school and was working in his father-in-law's business at the time, Sammy Warren (whose mom was a dance instructor) and Morris Jaundoo (East Indian). Of these, only Sammy would have been considered "Black" in Guyana. Joey, according to his mom's estimates, is about 50% Chinese, 45% Amerindian and 5% European.

Eddie says that we didn't see "race" at the time, mainly class. This could be so, partly confirmed by the fact that Dr. Nicholson (a bigwig at the Georgetown Hospital) and Shridath Ramphal (Attorney General of Guyana in 1965 and later Secretary General of the Commonwealth from 1975 to 1990), lived across from that wooden structure where we hung out. But it is also interesting that the ethnicities of the BAP/Section K guys included primarily Chinese, Portuguese, European and "mixed" ethnicities, with smaller contingents of Guyana's "six races" which included: East Indian, African (in Sammy) and Amerindian (primarily Joey).

One more friend must be mentioned, Paul Rimskey Hastings. I knew him through the Boy Scouts Troop at Queen's, where my brother George was the Scoutmaster. I ended up hanging out a lot at Rimskey's house and had some unique adventures with him because his family had a house in an Amerindian village named Aratack (near Santa Mission) on the Kamuni creek, a tribute of the Demerara River. Rimskey's dad was black, a descendant of a great grandfather who was a freed African enslaved person, and a great grandmother who was Arawak Indian. Through that connection, they had been able to buy land and build a home (which they went to for vacations) in the Aratack community. Rimskey's mom was mixed, but she was much lighter than his dad, and known for her expertise selling and fitting shoes at Bettencourt's store in Georgetown. I remember Rimskey taking me several times to Aratack, driving up the East Bank Road for about 25 miles, then crossing the turbulent Demerara in a speed boat, and boating up the Kamuni creek for another 14 miles or so. Swimming in the cool creek water was amazing!

But I also remember him, a colored or red man like me, having a hard time getting a dance at a party in Georgetown that included several fair-skinned and Portuguese girls. We had gone down the line of seated girls, one after the other, getting refusals when we extended our hands and asked, "Can I have this dance?" It was *very* embarrassing, because few girls would say "Yes" once the preceding girl(s) had said "No," and the boys would give you a hard time for being a loser. At one point, when he had had enough, Rimskey went to the kitchen, filled up a plate with food, and brought it to the last girl who had refused him. He said something like this, "People come to a party either to eat or to dance, and since you clearly don't want to dance, you should enjoy eating!" and left the tray of food in her lap. It might have been a bit harsh, but the brown and black boys felt vindicated, and Rimskey was the hero for the night.

I should add that several of my closest friends after I returned to Guyana to teach for six years in 1974–1980 were black, like Wordsworth McAndrew and Ian Robertson. But by that time my black identity had been firmly solidified from my six years studying and living in the U.S.

What of girlfriends? These were mainly fantasies, rarely if ever leading to more than a stolen kiss, if that. There was Ann Tucker, my next door Kingston neighbor whom I probably talked to once or twice, and Dorothy Ann Hubbard, my neighbor from round the corner whom I didn't have the courage to say I had liked until years later when she was visiting me with my wife and kids. Then there was Jane Wilson, the daughter of a British couple who became neighbors when I moved to BAP. I swapped Elvis Presley memorabilia with her for Hayley Mills memorabilia. (Embarrassed to admit now I was a Hayley Mills fan.) I remember visiting her a few times, but never the reverse, and dancing with her at a party in her bottom house. Then there was Pat Andersen, whose Norwegian father worked at Barclays Bank, and Maria Jagdeo, an East Indian girl in Bel Air Park for whom I wrote a poem entitled "To a Death" in 1966:

To A Death by John Rickford (Expression, June 1966)

Maria, we are dead
I place these black flowers at your head
Stare your placidity
And take my turgid place beside you;
Beside the long words that we read
Aloud into the lost years;
Beside the long years that we fondled
And found a love. Beside us tumbles
Blackness after that find
Flounders, after all the blunders choked
Our love, made it falter, splutter, go.

Maria, we are dead.

But "the lost years" in line 6 is probably an overstatement of our relationship. Apart from the odd house party, we met primarily at her front door. I don't think I was ever invited in. And while my poem proclaimed we were "dead," she probably didn't even know we were "alive."

My first serious girlfriend was Kateri Wendt, an Amerindian girl adopted by an American pilot and his wife who lived just across from the wooden structure where the BAP boys hung out. My earlier relationship with Rimskey, and our forays upriver to the Amerindian settlement at Aratack probably laid the groundwork for the liking I developed for Kateri. I had even had a brief fling with an Amerindian girl named Lucille, whom I towed to a downtown cinema on my bicycle from Peter's Hall, and took to a movie once, when she came to town.

Kateri's older sibling Theresa and her younger brother Michael had also been adopted by the Wendts. The parents banned Joey Alberga and me from visiting the home after we had been visiting for a year or so, when they caught him and Theresa snuggling up in the kitchen. At first, we were disappointed. But after that, the relationships became even more interesting, as the girls would flick the lights on and off when their parents went to sleep. We would then jump over their low back fence (with the conspirational OK of the watchman next door) and enter their home through the back door. Joey and Theresa were more adventurous than Kateri and me, even going out to a nightclub and pulling on a string attached to Kateri's toe to wake her up to open the door when they returned home after midnight.

Joey and I had a habit of going over to his cousin's house in Bel Air to listen to music, talk and eat after we left Kateri and Theresa. One night I lost track of time, and it was around 2 am when I got back home, opening the door gently so as not to wake anyone. Bam! My father's knuckles connected with my jaw. I was astounded, because I did not expect him to be awake, and because he had never hit me like that before. It was a long time since he had punished me physically any-how. But he was waiting up for me, and in response to his many questions about where I'd been so late and what I had been doing, I tried to come up with a story about my bike having broken down and having had to walk a long way home. I'm not sure he believed me, but his message was clear that these late nights wouldn't be tolerated, and that I would never succeed in high school if I kept them up.

Finally, there was Angela, my first black girlfriend, whom I started dating in 1966, and haven't stopped since. We have been dating for 55 years and have been married for 50. One might argue that the way had been prepared for me (and my parents) by the fact that two of my much older siblings (June and Peter) had married black spouses, but also by the fact that two sisters closer to me in age (Elizabeth, Nancy) had been dating black men (Bobby and Joe respectively). They eventually married them at separate churches but at a shared reception in July 1967. (The photo of Angela and me in Figure 6.1 was at their shared reception.)

How did our relationship begin? It was when I was trying to organize a big inter-high school organization in 1966, and invited students to come to QC from all over. The main event was a film I had borrowed from the U.S. Information Services, and I had even borrowed a movie projector. BUT when the time came to show the film, I realized that I had forgotten to get a take-up reel, without which the film could not be shown. (It was after hours at USIS, so no chance of getting one from there then.) I had to go on stage to say as much, making a mealy-mouthed apology and just hoping that the ground would open up and swallow me.

Afterwards, when I was about to leave, I noticed this cute student from Bishops' High School for girls (BHS, our sister school) waiting on her dad to come and pick her up. I began to repeat my abject apologies, but she stopped me, and told me not to get so upset. These things happen to everybody, she said. Those comforting words were soooo assuring to me, and I talked to her for a few more minutes until her dad arrived. The next day, I asked Mr. Victor Ramraj, my English teacher, if he could ask his wife Ruby, a teacher at BHS, to find out what Angela's name was. He did better than that, arranging a tea and sandwiches social event at their home for the small group of Sixth form students at each school who

Figure 6.1 John and Angela, July 1967, just after graduating from our respective high
    schools (QC, BHS).

were studying English Literature at the Advanced level for the GCE (General
Certificate of Education) exams. From that small get together, three relationships
were born: Angela and myself, Brian and Molly, and Michael and Marilyn. Brian
and Molly, like us, got married and stayed married.

On my first visit to Angela's home in Middle Street, her mom greeted me at
the door and asked me questions about my family for what seemed like an eter-
nity before she let me enter. Subsequent visits were, like the first, built around
studying together, sharing books and so on, usually with her mom watching from
across the room. But on August 27, 1966, I hosted a party at my home, and Angela
of course was invited. We danced and danced, and at some point I mustered up the
courage to ask if we could *go around* ("go steady"). She said yes, we had our first
kiss, and that was that. My diary notes read as follows:

> Tonight was a turning point in my relationship with Angela. I talked and said
> what I had to say. I held her, and we kissed. Not much of a kiss technically,

… but great. I realize how great an honor she gave me—first boy to kiss her. We sit in two chairs, hands together, and the tears of joy shone in my eyes. I promise to be around so long as she needs me. Mr. Marshall comes at 5 to 1, and some things are left undone. But I am happy. I am in love.

I was so excited, I stayed up talking with Brian and Johnny and Michael into the wee hours of the morning.

Three days later I wrote this poem for Angela:

From **No Rain Could Grow the Flowers** by John Rickford (August 30, 1966)
No rain could grow the flowers
That now entwine the bowers
Of my soul. Salt tears alone
Have made a soil out of my stone
Of heart. Your gentle touch does plough

Figure 6.2 John and Angela, at our wedding in San Mateo, CA., June 19, 1971.

This soil where steel was not enough
To even scratch the hardened soil
Which now watch how your touch does mock. …

I should add that Angela's mom and dad, whom I came to love and who even stayed with us for a while in our married homes, were strict, to the point that I wondered early on if my relationship with Angela could really develop. About a month after that memorable party at my house, for instance, I asked her dad if Angela and I could go for a walk around the block. Almost immediately, he asked, "Are you married?" I was dumbfounded at first, but muttered, "No." Not responding of course, would have been rude. "Well, there's your answer!" he said, and left the room.

I realized thereafter that I would have to win him over with patience and flattery. For instance, about a year after we had been going around, I got him to allow me to stay later than usual, and to not wait up to lock up the door and windows himself, by asking him to demonstrate how he could do push-ups with one hand. He graciously obliged, and even followed this with pull-ups on the metal bar suspended between the entrance to the dining room. By the time he had done all THAT, he was panting loudly and was clearly exhausted. I assured him I would help to lock up, and he could go upstairs to bed without worrying about us or the house. He glanced at our array of books on the dining table (actually, we were

Figure 6.3 The extended Rickford clan, June 16, 2016, just before our 45th wedding anniversary. Adults, L to R: Neale & Shiyama Clunie, Adrienne Clay & Russell Rickford, Angela & John Rickford, Marc & Anakela Washington, Luke Rickford. Grand-kids, L to R: Miles & Lance Clunie, Nyla Washington, Anaya Rickford, Kai & Bailey Washington.

usually playing footsie under the table), and went to bed with his nightly mixture of milk and raw eggs.

Almost two years after we had started going steady, in fall 1968, Angela and I both left Guyana for university studies, she to the University of the West Indies in Mona, Kingston, Jamaica, and me to the University of California at Santa Cruz. We wrote letters to each other constantly, and also exchanged tape recordings on small 3" x 3" reels (some of which we still have). Long distance phone calls were a rare and expensive luxury. But we did manage to meet in California in the summer of 1969 (see chapter 9), and in Guyana in the summer of 1970 (my surprise to her, after I took a Greyhound bus to Miami, and then flew home). On Juneteenth (June 19) 1971, she came to California just days after finishing her final exams, and we got married.

The photo of us celebrating our 45th wedding anniversary in 2016, with our four children, three spouses and six grandchildren shows how we have happily proliferated since then!

Notes

1 *Expression* 1 (June 1966) was edited by Brian Cotton and N.D. Williams. *Expression* 2 (March 1967) and *Expression* 3 and ½ (September 1967) were edited by N. D. Williams and M. Michael Drepaul. *Expression* 6 (March 1970) was edited by Jan Lowe, later Jan Lowe Shinebourne, who later became a published poet and novelist, as Williams did and several of the contributors.
2 For instance, https://poemanalysis.com/john-agard/half-caste/
3 See the "Real Political Event Chronology" in Aubrey McWatt and Donna Schweibert, 2019, *Red Man,* 360-365. Monee, IL: Self published.

7   Johnny and Johnny (Agard) and the police

I had one or two run ins with the cops in my preadolescent and teenage years.

When I was about ten, I was riding my bike at night without a bicycle light and was less than two blocks away from home when a policeman stepped out from behind a truck, held up his palm and yelled at me in a menacing tone.

"Stop! Weh yuh bicycle light?!"

I tried to come up with an explanation, but I was getting increasingly flustered as I spoke.

"De light was wukkin', but it just went out, an' I nearly reach house, ah mean, home, and please officer, gi' me a chance …"

But he interrupted me, threw my bicycle into the back of the truck, and ordered me to climb into the back too, with several similarly chastened "offenders" and their bikes. I was the youngest, I think, and I was shivering in fear that they would take us to the lock ups, and my parents wouldn't know how to find me. My life as I knew it was over …

Eventually, after the cops had caught a few other miscreants, they took us to the Brickdam police station, charged us formally (meaning they gave us an order to appear in court), impounded our bikes and left us to walk home.

Subsequently, I appeared in court, with my dad, and the judge gave me a fine of 25 dollars or a week in jail. My dad hesitated for a moment about which alternative he would accept (he was just trying to scare me), but in the end he paid the fine, gave me a long lecture about always riding with a light at night and otherwise steering clear of the law. And that was that.

That was nothing, however, compared to the experience my friend Johnny Agard and I had in our teenage years, when we were about 15 years old. We were both *red men*, mixtures of mainly African and European descent. We were considered mixed or colored, but not black in the shade-conscious Guyanese society when we were growing up. But we both embraced black identities in the racially polarized communities of the US and England when we immigrated years later, and we both married black women.

It was a rainy afternoon. We had been at Agard's home, snacking on small lemonades and buns and small talking about various things. The conversation

DOI: 10.4324/9781003204305-7

turned to a party we had been to the week before, and the dances we had had with these Matadial sisters, daughters of a local magistrate. None of us had ever dated an East Indian girl, so that was partly the source of our fascination. Suddenly we had the idea of going around to their home, not more than two blocks away, to see if we could attract their attention. And for some reason that escapes me now, we decided we would wear our raincoats, even though it was no longer raining.

Off we went. The home was a corner house, at the junction of two streets, and all the windows were shut because of the recent rain. But hanging out by the back fence, we thought we could hear the girls in the kitchen at the back of the house, which looked out on a spacious back yard with fruit trees. So we hunkered down against the fence and started making noises like a mewing cat, a barking dog and other animals, in the hope that this would attract them.

All to no avail, but we brave troubadours did not quit so easily. Fifteen minutes passed, half an hour. We started singing Beatles songs like "Yesterday" and "All my Loving." We were laughing and enjoying ourselves so much, the futility of the whole endeavor never hit us.

What we didn't know was that some youths had been jumping the fences of that home, and others, in recent weeks, and stealing fruit from neighborhood trees: mangoes, *genips*, *sapodillas* and so on. Shortly after we took up our position by the fence, a neighbor across the street had become suspicious, telephoning the Matadials to alert them. The police had also been called, and a vigilante group began to assemble in their yard to nab the would-be thieves (us!) if we tried to escape before the cops came. We were totally oblivious to the fact that these "vigilantes," armed with sticks, shovels and other implements, had quietly gathered in the neighbor's yard. And that the police were on their way.

After another ten minutes or so, when we had shifted from singing to calling out their names, "Ranee! Indira!" and got nothing but stony silence in return, we decided to call it quits. But as we crossed the gutter and returned to the road, a mob of men charged out of the neighbor's house across the street, intent on thwarting us from leaving. Shocked, we wondered whether if it was us they were after, or someone else. But before they could close the gap of 30 feet that separated us, a police car screeched to a halt between us, and two cops jumped out.

"You all stop right dere!" one bellowed. And I immediately froze.

But the other Johnny, scared out of his wits, took off running. One of the policemen immediately pulled his gun and said, "Tell yuh friend to stop or I gon shoot he dead!"

"Jahnny! Jahnny! Stop or dey gon kill yuh!" I shouted, and thankfully, Johnny halted.

The vigilante mob was only too eager to chase him down too, restrained only by the police.

By this time justice Matadial was on his front steps, surrounded by his wife and children, and fulminating about these damned fruit tree thieves, and what he would like to do with them. Johnny and I, in the grasp of the police, looked alternately confused and terrified.

Recognizing us, one of the Matadial girls cried out, "Oh God, i's Jahnny and Jahnny!" To which their indignant father replied that they couldn't possibly know these would-be thieves and ordered them inside.

The cops shoved us into the back of their car and drove us to the nearby Alberttown police station. A sizable crowd, a mixture of stick-brandishing vigilantes and curiosity seekers wanting to know what had happened, pressed against the car windows to look at us.

This was all a brand-new experience for us—to be in police custody, about to be charged with intent to steal and we kept protesting that we were only would-be paramours, intent on attracting the two girls who had recognized us on the steps.

But to no avail. They put us in a holding cell (more like a cage, with stiff chicken wire rather than steel bars) behind the intake counter and left us to stew for what seemed like hours before an interrogating detective could come to grill us.

We were completely petrified. One question Johnny A. asked was whether his mother, a Portuguese woman riding a duck belly bicycle, had come by to check on him. News travels fast in Georgetown, and she was a single parent, and he her only child. "Yes, she did come by," one of the officers said, "even before you all arrived." But she had gone on to the Brickdam police station after discovering we were not at Alberttown. Thinking about our angry parents made us even more anxious, as we worried about how best to explain and protest our innocence when the detective arrived.

The detective was a middle-aged man, Afro-Guyanese, with a serious and somewhat forbidding look. He began by telling us about reports they had received about fruit thieves in the area, and what a serious matter that was. In turn, we poured out our denials that we had gone to the Matadial house, not to steal anything, but like would be-Romeos, hoping to gain the favor of the two teenage Juliets that lived there, whom we knew and had danced with at a recent party.

The detective stared at us silently for a while. Then after looking at the names on the cops' intake report, he asked me, "Are you related to Russell Rickford, who used to work at B.G. Consolidated Goldfields in the interior?"

"Yes! Yes! He's my father!" I clamored.

"I used to work up dey, in de bush," he explained. And after a moment or two, he added, "Russell is a decent man, and I would never expect a son of his to be a thief!"

"Dat is true!" I exclaimed, briefly recounting the paramour story again, and noting that we were both students at the top schools for boys in Guyana—me at Queen's College, and Johnny A. at Saint Stanislaus College. "All right," he said, and left the room to consult with the cops who had arrested us.

After about 15 minutes, he returned to say that he believed our story. But that if we EVER came before them on similar charges, they would lock us up and throw away the key. "Now get out of here!" he said, trying to maintain a stern face.

We were out of there in no time.

For the record, I went on a few years later to win a US Scholarship to complete a BA in Sociolinguistics at UC Santa Cruz, a Danforth Fellowship to do my PhD in Linguistics at the University of Pennsylvania, and after teaching for six years at the University of Guyana, received a faculty position at Stanford University. I worked there for 39 years before being elected to the American Academy of Arts and Sciences in 2017, retiring from Stanford in 2019, and being elected to the National Academy of Sciences in 2021.

Johnny Agard went on to become famous as a poet, living in England with his Afro-Guyanese wife Grace Nichols (a poet and novelist). He has over 50 books and numerous performances to his credit. He writes primarily for children, but as Wikipedia notes, "His poems "Half-Caste" and "Checking Out Me History" have been featured in the English GCSE anthology since 2002, meaning that many students (aged 14–16) have studied his work for their GCSE English qualifications." Among his many awards, he was presented by Queen Elizabeth with the Queen's Gold Medal for Poetry in 2012, joining previous recipients like Derek Walcott, W.H. Auden and Philip Larkin.

In 2009, on my 60th birthday, John Agard wrote about our teenage experience with the Matadial sisters and the police, in the form of a "calypso" with a chorus, which he emailed me from England. It was sung at my 60th birthday

Figure 7.1   John Agard receiving the Queen's Gold Medal for Poetry from Queen Elizabeth II at Buckingham Palace, March 12, 2013 (SEAN DEMPSEY/AFP via Getty Images).

Figure 7.2 With Angela and actor John A. Lithgow at the American Academy of Arts and
  Sciences induction ceremony, Cambridge, MA, October 7, 2017.

celebration—and provides another version of the events which I've described in
this chapter. The "calypso" follows:

> *Calypso Ballad of Johnny and Johnny by John Agard*
>
> Johnny and Johnny were two teenage comrade
> One name Rickford and the other name Agard
> What got into dem, I don't know mih Lawd,
> But they start singing outside one Indian man yard
> Inside de house was de Indian man two gal pickney
> And they were friendly with Johnny and Johnny
> So the boys for a joke duck down by the paling
> To give two sisters a little serenading
> *One Johnny was a Saints boy and one from QC*
> *Two colleges known for respectability*
> *Yes, my friends, I know the inside story*
> *You see, I was one of dem romy Johnny*
> So Johnny and Johnny playing troubadour
> Singing to hell and go and giving encore
> The place was dark and the rain was pouring
> But their song was flirtatiously imploring
> *One Johnny was a Saints boy and one from QC*

Two colleges known for respectability
Yes, my friends, I know the inside story
You see, I was one of dem romy Johnny
Next ting you know police car on the scene
Mr Matadial warning his daughters, "Don't intervene,
Because dese boys who call themselves serenaders
Are nothing but no-good fruit tree raiders."
"Arrest dem, officer, arrest dem officer!"
One Johnny was a Saints boy and one from QC
Two colleges known for respectability
Yes, my friends, I know the inside story
You see, I was one of dem romy Johnny
Imagine Johnny and Johnny predicament
When they were accused of loitering with intent
These two boys from decent Georgetown location
Now they heading for Albertown Police Station.
Agard decide to keep he head well under cover
As de police drive past he mother veranda
And a police say "Young Rickford, you ain't shame?
Look how you letting down the Rickford name."
One Johnny was a Saints boy and one from QC
Two colleges known for respectability
Yes, my friends, I know the inside story
You see, I was one of dem romy Johnny
And so Johnny and Johnny busy pleading
Trying to impress police with books they reading
They say how they doing Shakespeare and Chaucer
And were serenading de Indian man two daughter
De police say, "Since you-all boys so literate
You better have a word with de Magistrate
But we will spare you, no need for bail
What you all need is a damn good cut-tail."
To cut a long story short, de police took pity
They play like they writing, and let the boys free
But, my friends, this ballad of Johnny and Johnny
Will live on in Agard and Rickford memory.
Happy 60 not out!
One Love
From Johnny A to Johnny R
(September 2009)

Note: Glossing a few of the Guyanese words for those not familiar with them, *pickney* = "children," *paling* = "fence, usually of wooden staves," and *romy* in 1960s slang, as a noun/adjective, meant something like "romantically inclined."

8   Going to America

In August 1968, I left Guyana, the only home, family and friends I had known for 18 years, for the United States of America, to a country, education and experiences that would utterly transform me. The only times I had even ventured to another country before were by sea for a one-week Boy Scout Camporee in Suriname, our South American neighbor to the East, and by canoe or *corial* to Brazil, our South-Western neighbor, on a one-day expedition from Lethem in the south (See map, Figure 3.1). Because my parents used to organize trips into the interior on a part-time basis (Guyana Travel Tours) I had flown to various waterfalls like Kaieteur and Orinduik and other attractions within Guyana in Dakota or Douglas DC-3 airplanes, often with side-facing seats. But I'd never flown on a Boeing 727 or bigger international aircraft. So this was a huge deal.

We made the 25-mile trek to Atkinson airport from our home in a Vauxhall station wagon that barely accommodated my luggage, my father, my mother and me. The airport was abuzz with excitement. Many travelers were accompanied by hordes of family members and friends, many of them boo-hooing loudly as the travelers said good-bye and disappeared from view as they entered the departure lounge or as they appeared striding towards the plane. I was determined to leave, by contrast, quietly and with a modicum of decorum. So when the time came to say good-bye, I hugged and kissed my mother and put out my hand to give my dad a parting handshake. But he said "What? You're too big to kiss your father?" Of course, I kissed him then.

I didn't fly directly to New York. I stopped in Trinidad and Tobago for two days to visit my Aunt Nora and Uncle Freddie, and their two children, Ruth Ann and Pauline, who had visited us in Guyana when I was younger. I enjoyed the sing-song lilt of their Trinidadian accents. A favorite way of eliciting the Trini accent was to ask them to say, "I going round de corner."

They would inevitably say it with the voice going up on the second syllable of *corner*, without pronouncing the r's, like this: *co'NUH*.

Then I flew to Curaçao in the Netherlands Antilles. My main purpose in going there was to buy a fancy camera, since Curaçao was a duty-free port, and it would be cheaper than elsewhere. I was really into photography at the time—still am. I can't remember if the camera I bought was a Nikon or Canon, but it was a more

DOI: 10.4324/9781003204305-8

sophisticated camera than I had, and once I got it, I was ready for my final stop: America, or more precisely, New York City.

My first several hours in the Big Apple (NYC) did not go well. I was supposed to take an Allegheny Airlines flight to State College, Pennsylvania, where my sister Elizabeth and her husband Bobby lived, but I couldn't find out what gate that was departing from. By the time I did, the flight—the last one heading to that destination for the day, had already left. I was really dejected, especially since I now neither knew nor recognized anyone. I was in a crowd of complete strangers, including more white people than I had ever been around in my life. I called my sister in desperation.

"Guess what, Elizabeth. You ain' gon' believe this, but I miss de flight to State College! An' i's de last flight fuh de night!"

"What?" she said, "How on earth yuh manage to do dat?"

"Man, dis place leff me *bassidy* ("confused"). It bigger dan anyplace I ever been, wid nuff nuff ("many") people, an nobody didn' know where Allegheny Airlines was."

"Yes, I know," she replied sympathetically. "Look, JFK is like a madhouse, people running all over like red ants. You gon have to take a Greyhound bus to come here. See if yuh can find yuh way to a Greyhound station."

I discovered I had to take a local bus to Grand Central, to the nearest Greyhound depot. But trying to leave John F. Kennedy airport—the busiest in the U.S.—and find the local bus to Grand Central was not an easy task. Dressed in a suit with a tie and a gold Guyana tie pin, and looking totally baffled, I was an obvious stranger and an easy mark. No sooner had I pulled my two suitcases onto the sidewalk outside the airport and stopped to get my bearings than a black guy asked me where I was heading. "To catch the bus to Grand Central" I blurted out. He immediately grabbed both suitcases and headed off at a brisk pace. I could barely keep up with him, protesting that I didn't need any help. After a block or so, he demanded "Two dollars!" Again, I protested that I did not ask him to help, but he repeated "TWO DOLLARS!!" in a way that was more command than request. I fumbled for my wallet and paid him, and he took off. Other immigrants have told me similar stories about their first day in America.

I still had another block or so to go, keeping my bags closer to me now, when, all of a sudden, the handle on the suitcase I had bought in Guyana from Gimpex, the low-cost Russian store, broke off! I remember it as the height of embarrassment, because I was in a pedestrian crossing at the time. The traffic light had changed against me, and cars were honking at me as I struggled to make my way to the other side, lugging that handle-less suitcase against me. But I did find my way to the bus stop without further ado, and boarded the local bus, again feeling lonely and desolate. For the first time in my life, I neither knew nor recognized anyone.

Two things stood out on that half hour trip to Grand Central. First, I was amazed to see a white man pushing a broom, sweeping the street outside the train station. It was something I had never witnessed in Guyana, where white people from North America or Europe invariably held positions of some prestige or importance. Secondly, there were streets on top of streets, sometimes two or three or four, as freeways curled above each other, something I had also never seen in Guyana, Suriname or rural Brazil. Streets, in my experience, were always on solid ground.

At the Greyhound bus station, I bought my tickets for the next trip to State College, which was leaving in about two hours, and looked for a seat in the packed waiting room. Luckily, I found one and grabbed it, pulling my suitcases close to me. I then removed the new camera that I had bought in Curaçao from my neck, placed it gently under my seat, then stood up to remove my suit jacket, folding it carefully before I sat down. But when I went to retrieve my camera from under the seat, I discovered to my shock and surprise that it was gone! I double checked my belongings to make sure I hadn't put it in a different place. But I realized in an instant that it had been stolen, and I also had a strong suspicion about who had stolen it. The seats were in pairs of long connected rows, back-to-back with seats facing in the opposite direction. And I remember that shortly after I sat down, a tall strapping black woman had taken the seat behind me. To my surprise, because seats were hard to come by, she had gotten up soon after she sat down, and by the time I looked to see where she had gone, she was expeditiously leaving through the exit. My camera, the focus of all my planning and saving and dreaming for months, was gone!

There was no question about my shouting "Stop! Thief!" I was in a novel and unfamiliar environment and could not be certain that *that* woman had stolen it, even though I was 90% sure. Even assuming I could catch up with her, which, with a handle-less suitcase, was almost impossible, I was terrified of what an accusation might bring me in terms of repercussions from her or one of her accomplices, with an hour and a half to go before my bus was to depart.

So instead, I meandered until I found a small police outpost in Grand Central and reported it to the cops there. The experience did not inspire confidence. They were joking about prostitutes and their main advice, when they chose to be distracted from their more absorbing conversation, was that if I saw the suspect again, I should let them know. I decided there and then that I would do nothing of the sort, and finding another seat, settled down to wait the remaining hour and a half in a cloud of gloom.

In retrospect, now that I've had more than 50 years of experience with public transportation in the U.S., I must have looked like a *doofus*, waiting for a Greyhound with my suit and tie and gold tie pin. So much so, that I would probably have robbed myself, were I looking for a victim. But at the time, I didn't see it that way. I was the hapless victim, and Americans—especially black Americans from my sample of two—were people I had to be cautious about.

The Greyhound trip to State College/Penn State was tedious but uneventful, and the three or four days I spent with my sister Elizabeth and her husband Bobby were a pleasant solace from the calamities at JFK and Grand Central. They sympathized with the theft of my camera, and even took me on a day trip to D.C. to see the Lincoln Memorial and other sights.

My ultimate destination was California and the University of California, Santa Cruz. But first I had to join other foreign students for a one-week orientation course held at MIT (the Massachusetts Institute of Technology) in the Cambridge. Most of it was fluff, advice about not calling people after 9 pm, and instructions to misspell English "honour" as American *honor*. There were also trips designed to impress us, for instance, to the Prudential Tower in Boston, which at 52 stories and 790 feet high, was the tallest building in North America outside of New York City when it was constructed in 1964.

But the trip that made the biggest impact on me was a subway ride to Roxbury that was not on the official schedule at all, organized for a few of us by a counselor who felt we were getting a one-sided introduction to the US of A. "I've had enough!" she screamed to a small group of us, after we came back from another touristy introduction to the land of milk and honey. "I'm gonna show you another side of America. Who wants to go with me to Roxbury?" I had no idea where Roxbury was, but I was game for anything new, and immediately said yes.

We had to take the subway to get there, however, descending deep into the bowels of the earth and venturing under the Charles River like moles. I am claustrophobic, and I had never seen or been on a subway before. I tried to compose myself as the subway wheezed and snarled through the underground, wrenching to the right or left as it went around corners. When we were traveling under the river, I wondered how they had managed to construct the tracks at that depth, and worried that the tunnel might suddenly spring a leak, allowing tons of water to engulf us. But everyone else acted as though it were the most normal thing in the world, so I kept assuring myself, "It's ok. It's ok. This too shall pass." Eventually we *did* get to our stop safely and ran up the staircase to fresh air and the world of people rather than moles.

Roxbury blew my mind. It was predominantly black—about 75% at that time.[1] Streets like Blue Hill Avenue that had been looted and set afire after the assassination of the Reverend Martin Luther King Jr. only four months earlier, in April 1968, stood in stark contrast to the Prudential Tower and the showy facades of Boston to which we had been treated. Moreover, people in Roxbury were poorer on average than those in Boston, and their neighborhoods showed it too. At the same time, Roxbury had been home to some of the leading African American big names in music (Donna Summer, R&B singer), sports (Jimmy Walker, NBA guard), education (Lucy Miller, early childhood) and politics. The last category includes Edmund Brooke, the first African American elected to the U.S. Senate in the 20th century, Louis Farrakhan,[2] leader of the Nation of Islam, and Malcolm X, whose activism, autobiography and assassination played such a central role in African American history.

Roxbury showed me that the U.S. *was* racially segregated and socio-economically stratified, something I would see in other cities and regions. But also, that in those segregated communities, black people could nevertheless survive and rise. I had not yet realized that, in America, I was not just mixed race or colored, but black. And that I could contribute to the understanding of problems of race, diversity, inequality and injustice that bedeviled this great country I had just begun to encounter as a stranger. That realization would come later, once I moved to the University of California, Santa Cruz (UCSC). There I would meet J. Herman Blake, who helped to write *Revolutionary Suicide* by Huey Newton, co-founder of the Black Panther Party, and through him Huey Newton himself. There I also joined and then led the Black Students' Association in agitating for a College of Malcom X with a diversity and justice focus.

Luckily, in 1971 I got a Danforth fellowship to do a PhD at the University of Pennsylvania. Once I realized that I was *not* returning to Guyana to teach high school, as originally planned, but would ultimately make America my home, my absorption with black and minority issues deepened. At first it was centered on Black English or Ebonics, its structure and relation to the creole varieties we spoke in Guyana and the Caribbean. But language is rooted in a larger social and political context, and my work kept bringing me into contact with key people and problems of being black in America and elsewhere.

Except for occasional visits, I was out of the U.S. for six years, from 1974 to 1980, while doing fieldwork in Better Hope/Cane Walk for my dissertation, recording canecutters, weeding gang workers (among others),[3] writing it up and teaching at the University of Guyana. (I even served as Assistant Dean of the

Figure 8.1 With Angela (pregnant with Anakela), Shiyama and Russell, Guyana National Park, 1977.

Faculty of Arts, under Dean Joycelyne Loncke, sister of my high school idol Ivy Loncke, during my last year.) During that period, our eldest child Shiyama survived a life-threatening attack of gastroenteritis, and we had two more children, Russell and Anakela.

After getting my PhD in 1979, I returned to the U.S., first as a one-year visiting professor at Stanford, then as a tenure track and tenured professor. Over the next 39 years, before retiring in 2019, I grew enormously as a linguist, and so did my family. Angela got her PhD at Stanford in Education in 1996 and started a 23-year career as Professor of Literacy at San Jose State University, the founding campus of California State University. Shiyama got her BA in Sociology at UC San Diego and her JD at UCLA; Russell got his BA at Howard University, a Historically Black College/University (HBCU) and his PhD in History at Columbia, and became a professor at Cornell; Anakela got her BA in Art and Psychology at Spelman (another HBCU) and her MA in Family and Family Therapy at Loyola Marymount; and Luke got his BA in English/Creative Writing at Stanford.

Figure 8.2 Angela and me with Russell in our PhD gowns, after he received his PhD, 2009.

Figure 8.3 Receiving the President's Award for Excellence through Diversity, Stanford, May 22, 2018. L to R: Neale Clunie, Angela Rickford, me, Lance and Miles Clunie, President Marc Tessier-Lavigne, my sister Elizabeth Phillips, my daughter Shiyama Clunie.

What most of my linguistics colleagues know little about is that I also grew over that period as a student of and contributor to black and diversity issues. I hosted a two-day visit by civil rights pioneer Rosa Parks, and directed the program in African and African American Studies for seven years. I learned a ton about South Africa when I interviewed Dennis Brutus in England in 1990. I worked closely with Rachel Jeantel, the close friend of Trayvon Martin, whose shooting by George Zimmerman and acquittal by a Florida jury, sparked the Black Lives Matter movement. (More on Brutus and Jeantel in later chapters.) I chaired Provost Etchemendy's Committee on Diversity among Stanford graduate students, and I received the 2018 President's Award for Excellence through Diversity from Stanford's president Marc Tessier-Lavigne (Figure 8.3). Every year, as part of my African American Vernacular English course, I took students over to St. John Missionary Baptist Church in East Palo Alto to experience black preaching at its best (from Pastor Ricky Williams), and to grow beyond the cocoon of Stanford and Palo Alto (Figure 8.4).

My son Russell would write a 633-page tome about Betty Shabazz, the wife of Malcom X, and he is currently writing about African Americans in Guyana, who made the opposite journey to the one I did. In all these ways and others, I think my

Figure 8.4 Outside St John Missionary Baptist Church in East Palo Alto with Pastor Ricky R. Williams and students in the final rendition of my AAVE course, April 7, 2019. As a way of showing our appreciation to Pastor Williams and St John for having welcomed us repeatedly over the years, we also asked Stanford's multi-ethnic Talisman a capella group to perform their amazing rendition of "Amazing Grace" during the service. Check out their incredible 2020 version, recorded individually because of COVID-19: https://www.youtube.com/watch?v=g8lilTTVsd8#action=share

family and I contributed to America, and especially to African America. But no doubt about it: when I first landed in 1968, I was a gawking tourist and a *doofus*.

Notes

1 See *Historical Trends in Boson Neighborhoods Since 1950*. BPDA Research Division. http://www.bostonplans.org/getattachment/89e8d5ee-e7a0-43a7-ab86-7f49a943eccb
2 Born in the Bronx, NYC, Farrakhan's parents were immigrants from St. Kitts and Jamaica.
3 See "Sociolinguistic fieldwork in a racial and political maelstrom," in Rickford, John R. 2019. *Variation, Versatility and Change in Sociolinguistics and Creole Studies*. Cambridge: Cambridge University Press, pp. 17–30.

9   University of California, Santa Cruz (UCSC), and the summer of 1969

UCSC was not on my university dream list. When I got a US scholarship in 1967, I was overjoyed, since it would give me the rare opportunity to go to college overseas. A fledgling University of Guyana had been started at my high school in 1963, using its classrooms at night, but it had *no* status at the time and few faculty or course offerings. *No way* could I afford to pay for college overseas, especially at one of the prestigious schools in the US, Canada or the UK. But given the US scholarship, I had my heart set on UC Berkeley, which had a rising reputation as an innovative, top-ranked school.

Unfortunately, Berkeley also had a reputation as a hotbed of student activism, and the agency administering my scholarship was determined to keep me away from that, though it never said so explicitly. They suggested instead that I try this new University of California (UC) campus at Santa Cruz, two hours South of Berkeley. UCSC had been started in 1965 with 650 students, which would be more similar in size (they said) to what I was accustomed to. I was enrolled in Stevenson College, which was started in 1966. They said if I didn't like it after a year, I could transfer to Berkeley. That sealed the deal.

And so in September 1968 I made my way to UCSC, via Trinidad, Curaçao, New York, Pennsylvania, a brief orientation course at MIT, a one week stay with Ann and Norton Benner and their children (my American host family in the San Francisco Bay Area), and a winding trip along the gorgeous Highway 1 coastline to the idyllic campus nestled among the pines and redwoods. As it turns out, I would not leave it until I graduated. On my one look-see visit to Berkeley, I couldn't even get in the room for the class I was interested in—it already had 400 students—and I watched it on closed-circuit TV. I contrasted this with the small classes and active discussions at UCSC and decided there was no way I would leave my campus for that one.

In tiny, new UCSC the youngest of the Russell Rickford and Baby Wade clan was transformed. My clean-shaven face was replaced within the first year by a goatee and mustache (which my mother didn't like), and subsequently by a full beard, which I've maintained for all but a few months of my adult life. My Literature major was replaced by a self-designed major in Sociolinguistics. And, most importantly, my identity was transformed from a mixed or colored person who was neither black nor white under the shade-conscious Caribbean system,

DOI: 10.4324/9781003204305-9

Figure 9.1 Professor Roger Keesing, Stevenson College, UC Santa Cruz, 1966–67 (Courtesy Special Collections, University Library, UCSC. Steve Rees photographs of the University of California, Santa Cruz)

into an African American under the American "one-drop" system. This may well have happened at Berkeley too. But it happened at UCSC, and some details of how it happened are worth mentioning.

First the switch from literature to sociolinguistics. Anthropology Professor Roger Keesing taught me in a Stevenson College freshman seminar, "Language in Society," that I took in my first quarter at UCSC. His work on Solomon Islands Pijin in the Pacific (East of Papua New Guinea) intrigued me, reminding me of my native Guyanese Creole [GC]. In fact, my final paper for that seminar, dated December 6, 1968, was entitled, "Creolese: A Search for Identity and Rebirth."

For instance, in Solomon Islands Pijin, you can say:[1]

> *mi luk-im pikipiki bulong iu astade*
> "I saw your pig yesterday."

In Guyanese Creole, this would be *mi sii yu pig yastade* or even more similarly *mi sii di pig wa bilong ta yu yastade*. Yes, there are differences, but the similarities in how the first person pronoun is expressed ("I," "me" and "my" are all *mi*) and the way the past tense is unmarked for action verbs (*luk, sii*, not *looked, saw*) is striking. I began to wonder whether the similarities between these geographically distant English-based contact varieties reflected parallel results due to parallel sociohistorical circumstances and processes or other factors.

Keesing also led me to readings in the nascent field of sociolinguistics (e.g. Labov 1966, Fishman 1970).[2] And after devouring Le Page's (1968) article on "Problems to be faced in the use of English as a medium of education in four West Indian territories"—one of which was Guyana—I was hooked, and designed my own major in Sociolinguistics.[3] As far as I know, I was the first person to graduate with a major in Sociolinguistics—a brand new field—anywhere.

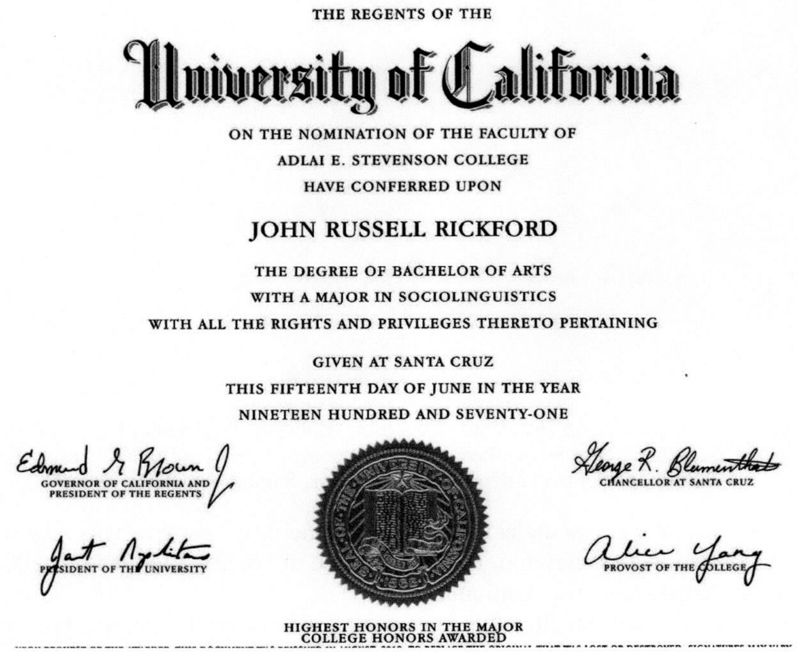

THE REGENTS OF THE

University of California

ON THE NOMINATION OF THE FACULTY OF
ADLAI E. STEVENSON COLLEGE
HAVE CONFERRED UPON

JOHN RUSSELL RICKFORD

THE DEGREE OF BACHELOR OF ARTS
WITH A MAJOR IN SOCIOLINGUISTICS
WITH ALL THE RIGHTS AND PRIVILEGES THERETO PERTAINING

GIVEN AT SANTA CRUZ
THIS FIFTEENTH DAY OF JUNE IN THE YEAR
NINETEEN HUNDRED AND SEVENTY-ONE

GOVERNOR OF CALIFORNIA AND
PRESIDENT OF THE REGENTS

PRESIDENT OF THE UNIVERSITY

CHANCELLOR AT SANTA CRUZ

PROVOST OF THE COLLEGE

HIGHEST HONORS IN THE MAJOR
COLLEGE HONORS AWARDED

Figure 9.2 My 1971 UCSC diploma of Bachelor of Arts with a self-designed major in "Sociolinguistics."

Le Page argued that in countries like Guyana, Belize, Jamaica, Trinidad and Barbados, one reason the English Language GCE pass rates were so low (10.7% to 23.1% in 1962) was that teachers did not recognize the systematic differences between the creole and the standard variety and could not help their students to bridge them successfully. He proposed that we have language specialists trained in "linguistics, psychological and sociological aspects of linguistic behavior… the processes of creolization, the principles of contrastive analysis, and the structure of the languages involved in their situation (e.g., Creole English, Creole French, English, Spanish, Maya) (p. 440)" to help teachers teach more effectively.

In summer 1970, I also took courses with Charles Ferguson, Joshua Fishman and other professors at the Stanford Sociolinguistics Institute, and I was so intrigued by everything they taught me that I resolved to do graduate work in linguistics if I were ever given the opportunity. I also wrote a senior honors thesis in 1971 entitled "De train dey ridin' on is full of dead man's bones: Language, Death and Damnation in the Two-Room Schoolhouse on Daufuskie."

Turning now to the *other* transformation that I had at UCSC, the transformation in my racial identity, let me begin with a story.

Shortly after arriving at UCSC in fall 1968, I saw two black students, Richard Townsend and Laura Luster giving out flyers advocating the creation of a "Malcolm X College." I took a flyer but was skeptical—I mean colleges were named after people like Adlai Stevenson II, the Democratic Party's nominee for US President in 1952 and 1953, and Ambassador to the UN from 1961 to 1965. The little I knew of Malcolm X—jailed from 1946 to 1952 for larceny—didn't seem to merit that distinction. But I *did* read *The Autobiography of Malcolm X*, published by co-author Alex Haley a few months after Malcolm's assassination, and it increased my understanding and respect for him enormously.

By my second year, I was speaking publicly in support of a "Malcolm X College," and I was doing so as President of the Black Student Alliance at UCSC! Moreover, the professor who later became a key mentor to me, J. Herman Blake, had done a televised interview with Malcolm X at Berkeley in 1963. My son Russell later published a 633-page biography of *Betty Shabazz*—the wife of Malcolm X, which contained a ton of information about Malcolm. And his mentor at Columbia, Manning Marable, wrote a Pulitzer Prize winning biography *Malcolm X: A Life of Reinvention* in 2011.

A repeated occurrence from the time I got on campus was that many of the black students began to call me "Brother" or "Bro," which surprised me at first because I had never thought of myself as black in the same way (US vs Caribbean systems, as noted above). But it also pleased me, at a time when I was isolated from my country, my girlfriend Angela and my regular friends, and feeling very lonely. In my first year, there were only about six or seven black students at Stevenson, and 25 in all at UCSC. The group was small, but tight.

The factor that shaped my identity most forcefully was a course on "Ethnic and Status Groups" taught by Professor J. Herman Blake during the second quarter of my first year. Some of us would refer to it as the "crying course"—since he would go through the trials and tribulations of each ethnic group in turn—Native Americans, Jews, African Americans, Latino Americans, Japanese and Chinese Americans and so on—and students in that group would be moved to tears. Blake was a powerful lecturer, his lectures bolstered by moving songs, sometimes sung by himself in a lugubrious bass.

In addition, he asked students to write our parents about our genealogy—this is how I came to write my dad about where our forebears came from. As I've noted in other chapters, his reply constitutes the single most important source of information about our family genealogy. Long before I had a DNA test, I already knew that our family had significant African and East Indian elements besides the "Scottish" element that my mother and her sisters emphasized.

Other events during my second and third year at UCSC helped to radicalize me (ironically, more than Berkeley might have!) and to reinforce my black identity. One was my work in drama, taking part in two plays, first as "Deacon George" who had witnessed the shooting of an innocent black man by a policeman in *Justifiable Homicide*, a play written and directed by UCSC Jewish professor Sheldon Feldner in December 1969.

Figure 9.3 UCSC Professor J. Herman Blake and me at my Palo Alto, California home, 2013.

The play, reportedly based on a true incident in Hunter's Point, San Francisco that occurred in 1967 was definitely *ahead* of its time, given the national and international outrage that followed the killing of George Floyd in Minneapolis in May 2020 by police officer Derek Chauvin. But it was also *behind* its time, since officer-involved shootings, especially of black men, had been happening long before. Deacon Willis George, whose part I played, had the opening testimony for the prosecution. He testified that Officer Allen David Shannon, who was not in police uniform and had not identified himself as a police officer, was waving his gun around when a crowd started to gather after he'd scraped George's car. He was also speaking abusively to Mrs. George ("Shut the fuck up, you black bitch"). Some of my lines as Deacon George catapulted me into the reality of racism, race relations and police injustice, especially in poor brown and black communities like Hunter's Point. I was definitely not the *doofus* about race in America who had landed at John F. Kennedy airport sixteenth months earlier:

> Deacon George: Officer Shannon waved the weapon around and said, "Get your heads back in niggers before I blow them off!" About this time Lee Washington came up with this stick. [A piece of scrap dowling.] …
>
> He hit Mister Shannon on the arm and Mister Shannon turned the gun on him …
>
> Mr. Shannon said, "Drop it! Drop that stick! God-dammit drop it!" Then he counted quickly, like this: "One, two, three!" …
>
> He shot Mister Washington down in cold blood. (Defense attorney's objection to this was sustained.) …

Mister Washington fell and moaned and kicked. Mister Shannon walked over and told him to shut up and then he kicked him in the side.

Interestingly enough, the court's judgment was "justifiable homicide." That was the norm in similar cases, even when the evidence against the police seemed overwhelming.

The second major role I played was as Caliban in Shakespeare's *The Tempest*. I wrote a *long* essay about portraying Caliban on different nights. Here is an excerpt:

> Another motif began to creep in—this was my blackness. It happened when I got to the part when I attack Prospero, grab his robe and yell defiantly at him … One night, rehearsing that part, I felt the bitterness and rage spewing out of me, and saw the scorn and anger expressed in Prospero's face. The moment reminded me of a similar one … in *Justifiable Homicide* … the racist representation of the white power elite fucking the defenseless but defiant black subject … I began to see Caliban as human, a black human with the shit falling all around him. I began to play him like a Panther—*mean*.

Another event, reckless now I think about it—was my leading a demonstration of UCSC students outside Soledad prison to protest the shooting deaths of three inmates on January 13, 1970, by tower guard Opie G. Miller. I could well have been shot dead by the tower guards who were glaring at us.

Finally, in my senior year (1970–71), when I served as a Teaching Assistant to Professor Blake while he was teaching "Ethnic and Status Groups" at Mills College, I drove with him weekly from Santa Cruz to Oakland, becoming quite close. One day he took me to the apartment of Huey P. Newton, co-founder of the Black Panther Party with Bobby Seale. Newton's autobiography *Revolutionary Suicide*, written with the assistance of Blake, was published in 1973.[4] The visit was a surreal experience. Huey struck me as extremely intelligent and discerning, and he completed a PhD in Social Philosophy at UCSC.

Other elements at UCSC shaped my black consciousness and identity—tutoring a low-income African American student (Wilbur Gowder), and spending a quarter on the South Carolina Sea Islands working in a Gullah speaking environment that reminded me of home. I should add that I had white and Asian friends as well as black, so I don't want to give the impression that consolidating my black identity meant neglecting people that weren't black.

One thing I should add is that up until my final year I believed that once I got my BA, and my US scholarship was over, I would have to return to Guyana to teach in high school, as I had been doing before I left. Any prospects of grad school seemed dim, because most graduate fellowships required US citizenship, which I would not get until 1992. The one fellowship that *was* open to everyone was the Danforth graduate fellowship, for which I applied.

My final Danforth interview was on the Stanford campus, at the home of Professor David Abernethy. To my delight, I *did* get one of the approximately 120

Danforths awarded in 1971. And although I went to the University of Pennsylvania for graduate study rather than Stanford, I returned to Stanford as a faculty member in 1980. Professor Abernethy and I became good friends, mounting a summer session at Stanford in Oxford in summer 1990. I'll describe that and what it meant to me and my identity in Chapter 14.

When the summer of 1969 began, I was bristling with anticipation.

My girlfriend Angela, from whom I'd been separated for *ten* months, was going to be joining me for the summer, actually living with me, day and night, for the first time in my life. A friend of mine in Los Angeles had written Angela's father in Guyana inviting her to stay at her place, and for some reason this strict man said yes!

Secondly, we would be driving to LA in a 1959 Volvo, staying with a friend Orel Knight. Granted I would not have university support over the summer, but Orel had assured me it would be easy to get a job, and with about 100 dollars in my wallet, I was excited about the prospect of this romantic adventure.

I greeted Angela at the airport, and after a couple days meeting friends, taking her to see San Francisco, and introducing her to UCSC, we embarked on the exciting drive to Los Angeles. Within a week of arriving in LA, two unfortunate things happened that we had not anticipated.

The first is that while driving the Volvo on the freeway, it threw a rod and died. The tow truck guy told us that not only could he give us *no* money for the car, but that I would have to pay him 20 dollars "to take this piece of junk off the road." I

Figure 9.4 With Angela at the beginning of the summer of 1969, in San Francisco, California.

felt terrible about having wrecked the car this friend had generously lent me, and I spent much of the summer worrying about how I would tell her and make it up to her. And we were of course car-less.

The second thing is that we realized without a so-called green card (a Permanent Residence or Alien Registration Card), we would not officially be allowed to work. Angela, who had banking experience from Guyana, breezed through her interview, and was offered a job with a bank in Los Angeles: "Just bring in your green card, and you can start tomorrow." But she only had a Visitor's or Tourist's Visa, and although I had a Student Visa, I was no more qualified to accept the offers I received than she was. With our initial 100 dollars rapidly evaporating, we had to call our prospective employers and say that we had changed our minds about their offers.

Orel had gotten us a room in the apartment building where he and another Guyanese friend William Roberts lived, and he kindly paid the rent and lent us money while we struggled. But without new income, we had to keep borrowing from Orel and Willie, which was humiliating.

In the end I got a succession of three jobs in which the employers either did not know nor care about their employees' immigration status.

The first was selling *Negro History Encylopedias*, a job I endured for seven weeks. As part of a group of neophyte black salesmen, I was subjugated to a daily routine of lectures about the product, accompanied by routinized affirmations:

> "What are we?
> Black salesmen!
> What do we sell?
> Black History!
> How do we sell it?
> Enthusiastically!
> I can't hear you!
> ENTHUSIASTICALLY!"

Then we would hit the streets for weeks of failure and despair, at the mercy of poor people in Watts who were interested but couldn't afford it, or rich people in Baldwin Hills who *could* afford it but weren't interested. I sold two encyclopedia sets in seven weeks, and one buyer had bad credit, so I made only 40 dollars. It didn't begin to cover the cost of the two bus trips and the meals I needed for this noon to night exercise in frustration I endured every day. In the end I realized the *biggest* sales job was on us, by salesmen who capitalized on our leads and never delivered the 500 dollars per month minimum pay they had promised.

The second gig I got that summer was through a Guyanese friend Keith Wilson, as a gas pump attendant at a Shell gas station. I told the manager that I had worked at various gas stations—Shell, Sunoco, Union 76 and so on—until he asked me to show him my uncalloused hands and he pronounced that I had never had a job requiring physical work in my life! But because I was a friend of Keith, and he only hired illegal aliens whom he paid less than minimum wage, he gave me a chance.

Figure 9.5 Keith Wilson (left), Jimmy and me at the Los Angeles gas station where we
worked, summer 1969.

Of course, I made mistakes. Like the time I put oil into the transmission fluid chamber and saw Keith's eyes open wide. We survived by pilfering Blue Chip Stamps
and through other means. I learned how to operate emergency trucks on the freeway and made some extra income from that. The boss was unsympathetic when I
told him about my father's death and the fact that I needed to leave without the cus-
tomary two weeks' notice. As I remember, he didn't give me my final paycheck.

My third job was working at Blue Cross, processing claims. I got this through
Orel, who was a medical student. He told the person in charge that I was also a
medical student and would bring in my paperwork subsequently. That job paid
decently, unlike the others, but I only had it for less than two weeks, at the end
of the summer. The main thing I remember was the admonition to deny any and
every claim we could!

Overall, I acutely remember the burning hunger Angela and I experienced, and
the longing with which we looked at people biting into hamburgers and licking
their lips and fingers. And I remember the empathy we developed for the have-
nots and the poor we encountered in public laundromats and elsewhere in East
LA, often exchanging smiles when we did not share a common language. And
the antipathy I developed for bosses who exploited workers for their profit, like
the black Negro History Encyclopedia bosses and the white boss of the Shell gas
station. Without the friendships of Orel, Willie and Keith, I don't know how we
would even have survived.

On September 14, 1969, my father died unexpectedly of a stroke, caused by a burst blood vessel in the brain. I was unable to buy an airline ticket to fly home. It was the final nightmare of the summer. I *was* able to buy an old Ford Falcon for 100 dollars, which I drove back to Santa Cruz and offered the student who had lent me the Volvo. She didn't accept it, saying the Volvo was old and half dead anyway. It was another lesson in the value of friendship. And Angela's sustenance throughout the summer was a solid lesson in love. We got married two years later.

Notes

1 Roger M. Keesing. 1988. *Melanesian Pidgin and the Oceanic Substrate*, p. 87. Stanford: Stanford University Press.
2 William Labov. 1966. *The Social Stratification of English in New York City*. Washington, DC: Center for Applied Linguistics.
   Joshua A. Fishman. 1970. *Sociolinguistics: A Brief Introduction*. New York: Newbury House.
3 Robert B., Le Page. 1968. Problems to be Faced in the Use of English as the Medium of Education in Four West Indian Territories. In Charles A. Ferguson, Joshua A. Fishman, and Jyotirindra Das Gupta, eds., *Language Problems of Developing Nations*. New York: Wiley and Sons, pp. 431–442.
4 Huey P. Newton, with J. Herman Blake. 1973. *Revolutionary Suicide*. New York: Harcourt, Brace, Jovanovich.

10 Forgive me, my son. Thank you, my parents

On May 18, 1969, Dad wrote me from our home in Guyana, South America. His letter began like this:

> My Dear Johnny,
> I got your letter of 13th May. It nearly tore my heart out. Forgive me. Forgive me, my son. I meant no such harm as you envisage.

The letter he was replying to was a four-page typewritten missive I had sent him. It accompanied a longer ten-page handwritten letter I'd written him on April 16, 1969, from the University of California, Santa Cruz, where I was in my first year. Somewhat uncomfortable with its contents, I had delayed mailing it. But on May 13, I put both letters in the mail.

And what was it that nearly tore his heart out? My letters were a response to a wonderful letter he had sent me on February 20, 1969, providing crucial information about our family that I needed for an assignment for Professor Herman Blake's class, "Ethnic and Status Groups."

The info he sent me has become the nucleus around which most efforts to trace our family genealogy in the half century since then have been built. And it earned me an excellent course evaluation in the class. So why did it trigger a response from me that "nearly tore his heart out"?

Because of the first two paragraphs at the beginning of Dad's February letter, together with reports from my siblings and neighbors that "Mom and Dad are upset about you."

In the first paragraph Dad provided further details, confessing that he was "alarmed" by my joining the Black Student Alliance and getting involved in the idea of a "Malcolm X" College. And he had asked, "Is it that America has given you a 'black' complex"?

Furthermore, he had cautioned that I was:

> not an American, merely a sojourner for a few brief years, gone there for the purpose of educating yourself. Self-expression may be a form of education. Maybe you think you can stop it from developing into radicalism. Good movements often start as non-violent ones, but can they be left so?

DOI: 10.4324/9781003204305-10

Secondly you are there on American govt. money. Don't bite the hand that feeds you.

In the second paragraph, he mentioned an incident in which a number of Caribbean students, including two from Guyana—one the son of former Prime Minister, Cheddi Jagan—had been jailed *that very month* for allegedly blowing up the computer center at Sir George Williams University in Montreal, causing millions of dollars in damage.[1] "It is said all thinking young men go through the communist stage," he warned. "Be careful."

In retrospect, and from the experience of being a father myself, that concern was fully understandable, since I wouldn't want to see a child of mine do something that drastic, with dire consequences for his/her life and career. Even in my April letter I had said that while recognizing how easily one can be swept up in the fervor and excitement of "movements," I trusted that he would credit me with the intelligence and good sense to review them critically and resist them.

But I *had* developed a "black" complex, living in the US with its one-drop view of race.[2] (I was 34% African, 14% East Indian, 48% European, and 3% Amerindian, as later DNA analyses revealed.) The American system was very different from the highly gradated, shade-conscious Caribbean society in which we grew up, in which people considered black were 100% African or nearly so, and people like me were colored, mulatto, brown, red or mixed.

I tried to explain this to Dad in my April 16 and May 14 letters. As I said, I had evolved a lot in the seven months since I had come to America, but the process was not complete:

> My father, my ideas have evolved since I left home and came here and thought about, and questioned intensely, certain things. I do not know myself well enough to pour forth me on this paper now, and I doubt that you shall understand something of what I am until I am back home again, and we can meet and talk and interact. But I still will try to communicate a sense of my evolving self as I see it.

I noted that I had come to be known by and accepted by all of the 25 black students on campus, who called me "Bro" or "Brother" whenever they passed me. (More than I had ever been by whites or near-whites in Guyana.) And that I was proud of my new black identity.

As I pointed out in one letter, I was driven to this identity because "in subtle, and sometimes not so subtle ways, America had made it clear that although I would be respected somewhat as a foreigner, my color made me different, and I would be viewed as such. There was a painful period of humiliation, inferiority and non-belonging after I made this discovery. I felt at times very lonely and small, a feeling of being lost, worse, being put aside, put down."

By contrast, I had found that I had a lot of things in common with the black students at UCSC, and more, "they had really beautiful ways and values amongst them that distinguished them from the type of America I was getting to know."

Moreover, "It was not long before I became one of them, and I am now. I identify far more with them, their culture, their values, than what America in general has to offer. They fill me with a sense of integrity and worth—the kinds of things one needs if one is to grow strong and do well in this society ... When I go on a bus and the eyes follow me, when I enter a crowded dining hall, there is no feeling of apprehension nor inadequacy. The symbols of blackness mean a lot too and reinforce my life. Black and Proud—and Beautiful."

Elaborating on this, I had noted in my April letter that "the most beautiful things I have found have come, quite frankly, from black people ... and it is these more than anything else I have the heart and soul to do. I believe it is a way to Truth, and I ask you to understand why I follow this way, and to accept and appreciate it."

Perhaps anticipating a point Dad would make in his reply, I had also added that "Nor do I want you to think I lead a separatist existence, not that I hold something against white people and do not 'get on' with them. I have some good white friends here, get on more or less well with lots of students, faculty, townspeople, etc. But a lot of the respect I now command derives precisely from the strength of my black identity."

In my May letter, however, I had said something more extreme. And this is probably the part that tore his heart out: *"Please know: I am not afraid to live my life alone, if you would have it so ... If for some strange reason you would rather not [maintain our links] then I will take my burdens and my hopes, my failures and my triumphs, my life, and go my way alone."*

Granted that I was only 18 at the time, but what a bunch of crap from the same guy who arriving nine months earlier, was so overwhelmed by being a stranger in a strange land, he used to pull back the curtains in his dorm to survey the scene before heading out! The same guy whom Resident Assistant, Glenn Omatsu had to accompany to the dining hall to allay his apprehensions about the unfamiliarity and novelty of everything and everyone there?

I did concede in my letter that "You are my father and my family. There is nothing closer, more fully a part of me ... And I feel a deep bond with, a need for you."

It was this element that Dad used to assuage me. He told me that he'd been busy with his accounting work, and his trips into the interior with "Guyana Travel Tours." And that when he was not busy with these things, he'd been lazy and apathetic, or spending "hours with Mummy just sitting and chatting" (thank goodness!) and occupied with the other kids and grandkids.

But he gave me the most humbling apology a parent could offer: "I did not imagine that you could put such a bad interpretation on my 'silence', but I understand it and ask your pardon; there is no real excuse."

Moreover, "It would be a great loss if I could not share with you your hopes and aspirations, and if you could not turn to me for assistance, material or otherwise, in times of need ... don't cut yourself off."

He noted that it was an "enlightenment" to read my letters and understand the way I felt about so many things. In fact, he noted, chiding me for this, that I should have written to share my ideas and experiences before, because as it turns out, my thinking was not so much different from his. He had voted People's National Congress (PNC, the party run by Afro-Guyanese LFS Burnham) not The United Force (TUF, the party run by Portuguese Guyanese Peter D'Aiguar), in the Guyana elections of 1964. In this respect he had disagreed with Mummy and the rest of the household.

And in the 1968 election, not only was he a stronger PNC supporter than he'd been before, but so was Mummy. The black PNC had, in his opinion, shaped up well. "It was the fair-skinned D'Aiguar, backed by fair-skinned people, who made the trouble."

He also confessed that he had reacted against the European staff at his office and their insecurity about a black government by not inviting them to his home for two years. "I have had so much experience of their insincerity that I have, probably stupidly, cut myself off from the normal intercourse that should happen between people working together." But he felt this was not right and he tried to remind me of the larger perspective: "Some of my children have married white people; some have married black. The important thing is to evaluate people as men and women, without any prejudice."

This, in turn, would become a guiding tenet of my life.

I was so elated about this rapprochement between us, that I wrote Dad at least two letters (which I unfortunately don't have a copy of), as evidenced by his reference to "your recent letters and other material" in a letter to me of June 4. He also wrote a short letter, that began, "I am taking advantage of a new stamp issue [enclosed] to send you a note to show *I am still alive*" [emphasis added].

I myself had written Mom and Dad a long letter on Sep 10 detailing the tough experiences of the summer, events which demonstrated that I could not make it alone, despite my bluster. Without university support for the summer and without the required green card, my girlfriend Angela and I could get no legal work, and often starved once our meager resources ran out. I pumped gas at a station that hired mainly illegals and paid us below minimum wage.

But Dad never got that letter, because, on September 14, two days before my 20th birthday, I got a phone call from my oldest brother Teddy:

Operator: "Long distance calling … I have a call for Mr. John Rickford, from a party in Oregon. Go ahead, sir."
Teddy: "Hello."
John: "Oh hi, Teddy. Thanks for that $50 for the car. Man, I was to write to thank you, but I was so busy, you know, and ahm—"
Teddy: "Your father is dead, boy."

Dad was 56. I was shocked, and utterly heartbroken. As recounted in my letter to my mother on Oct 5, I reacted like this:

> Why does the world seem so strange, so sudden, and why these thick sad voices in my ears? "He had breakfast with mummy and went upstairs and fell off the bed and died of a stroke, an aneurysm."
>
> Oh my father, my father, my father. No.

I only broke down real bad twice that day, Mom. Only twice I couldn't stop the huge gasping breathless heaving of tears and crawled to the window and felt sick inside and couldn't stop, and felt so small and lost and so far away from all of you so many thousands of miles, and most of all from my father. Daddy.

Oh mom, oh mom, we had come so close, Dad and I, and were to come so much closer. Oh mom, oh mom, I wanted to do so many things for him, for you, for both of you. Oh mom, I wanted him to see me graduate, and graduate real well, and make him so proud. I wanted both of you to have an anniversary holiday. I wanted you to spend your days in peace and love and quiet and together alone. Oh mom, the world is fragile and delicate: the thin white porcelain is cracked, and the pieces are confusion. …

And Mom, Mom, when you told me how his hands were turning blue, I remembered his hands, his hands and me. I remember them holding a chisel on the workbench making glorious things. I remember them pasting the paper on the kites for us to fly [on] so many Easter Mondays. I remember them showing me how to build *Meccano* sets and how to drive a car and change tires. I remember them carving beef on Sundays and gripping the handle on the leather briefcase that he owned. I remember them firmly holding mine as we bade goodbye (and farewell!) at the airport one year ago. I don't remember them blue. Don't let them take him away.

I had only one regret, remembering our saying goodbye at the airport a year ago for what would be the last time. I think I tried to shake his hand goodbye, embarrassed to do anything more with so many people around. But he said "What?

Figure 10.1 My dad, Russell Howell Rickford, Kingston, Georgetown, September 1, 1960.

You're too big to kiss your father?" And of course, I kissed him then. I would smother him with kisses now.

But I was also tremendously grateful that this giant of a father excused my sophomoric grandstanding and begged *my* pardon, allowing us to make up. I can hardly imagine how tortured my life would have been without this.

I remember trying to raise the 550 dollars needed for the airfare to fly home for the funeral. I had raised 275 dollars. But it was not enough fast enough. And I could not go home to see Dad one last time.

Monday was my day of mourning, the day of the funeral. At two o'clock I dressed for church in my black tie with a "J" in the middle (Dad had one just like it with an "R") and went into a chapel, "Our Lady of Solitude." I lit candles for him and cried and prayed for his soul in afterlife, for Mom, and the rest of the family and for myself, for strength and guidance.

This poem by e.e. cummings which I quoted in full in the letter to my mom, captures my feelings. I will reproduce only its first and last verses:

From my father moved through dooms of love*, by e.e. cummings*

my father moved through dooms of love
through sames of am through haves of give,
singing each morning out of each night
my father moved through depths of height
…
and nothing quite so least as truth
—I say though hate were why men breathe—
because my Father lived his soul
love is the whole and more than all

Cummings (1940)

Angela, who was with me in Los Angeles when my father died, was incredibly supportive. Neither of us had lost a parent before. And she allowed me to cry on her shoulder, and go over my many regrets about not getting to see him again, and to repeat what a great dad he had been.

Within a week of Dad's dying, though, Angela had to fly back to Jamaica to resume her university studies.

As I drove home from the airport, "Leaving on a jet plane" was playing on the radio. And I was left lonelier, but also wiser, more chastened.

In December 1983, 14 years after my dad's death, Mom fell in the bathroom in Guyana. At first, she didn't pay too much attention to it, but the pain got steadily worse, and in the end, she was admitted to St Joseph's Mercy hospital. The doctor who was assigned to her case was Sister Ligouri Cantlin, who, after becoming "the first Roman Catholic nun to be certified as a surgeon by the American Board of Surgery,"[3] had worked for 16 years in India before coming to Mercy Hospital in 1978.

Dr. Ligouri performed surgery on Mom in February 1984, but Mom wasn't getting better, remaining bloated and suffering diarrhea and vomiting. The doctor said she would have to operate again, which alarmed me, because she had done the same "two operation" routine on my Aunt Dorothy, who had been suffering from diverticulitis in 1978. And *she* had not survived. I remember Aunt Dorothy telling me, with foreboding, "I don't want that woman to cut me again." The next day she had the operation and died.

I was scheduled to teach my last class of the spring quarter in March 1984. I was only in my fourth year at Stanford, had a pregnant wife and three children and had not returned to Guyana since immigrating to the US in 1980. I asked my good friend Ewart Thomas, a senior faculty member, if he thought I should go. "Yes," he said immediately, "for if she dies, you will always regret it."

On Tuesday March 7, 1984, I wrote this entry in my appointment book:

> An incredible thing: I have tonight, after a day of agonized uncertainty, decided to go to New York to meet Nancy and Teddy and Fiona (my brother, sister and niece) to go to Guyana to see Mom, help her survive [her] operation, recover, live … or as God wills.

And I was *off,* taking three or four flights, and arriving at the hospital about an hour before the scheduled second surgery. My appointment book for Thursday March 8, 1984 records these details:

> I saw Mom and talked with her about 7:30 am, showed her our children's art work they'd sent for her. She smiled, talked, joked, then they wheeled her away for her second intestinal operation. And she never "woke up," not that we could see, at least. Maybe in heaven. R.I.P.

My first indication that something might be wrong came when I dropped in to see our former family doctor, Dr. Balwant Singh, near the hospital. When I told him Dr. Ligouri had operated on Mom two weeks before and was now opening her up again, he said that at her age, and in her condition, "Morbidity is very high." I wasn't clear what *morbidity* meant, but it was clearly negative, and I hurried back to the hospital.

Sometime after 1 pm they brought Mom, still anesthetized, back to her room. The surgery had been very long (and additionally stressful for her) because they had apparently cut her on the wrong side, and after realizing that the problem was on the other side, had to suture her up and open her up on the other side, which required another dose of anesthesia.

Then other problems arose. Our niece Fiona, a nurse in Oregon, had pleaded with Dr. Ligouri to let her assist with the surgery, but the doctor said no. Fiona soon realized that there was a problem with the main IV supplying medication to Mom. It was not in properly, so that a big pool of liquid was forming under her and at her side. When we alerted them to this, a nurse came in and removed the IV altogether, which struck us as odd, because it must have had some purpose to begin with. The next thing Fiona noticed was that her color was pallid—she again complained about that.

Around 7 pm, with Mom still unconscious, Drs. Ligouri and Searwar came to her room, booted us all out, and said to us after a few minutes that we should say our farewells, since she didn't have much longer to live. They were right. Within five or ten minutes she breathed her last breath and died. 7:35 pm. In keeping with Guyanese tradition, we placed two coins over her eyes so they would remain closed.

Some of my siblings were strong and silent. But I cried, feeling for the first time the hard reality of Odetta's soulful rendition of the spiritual that dates back to slavery, "Sometimes I feel like a Motherless child, … a long way from home."

I wrote this poem about the day's events. Never shared it with anyone.

Baby Wade's Last Reverie by John Rickford

I knew when I saw them (almost all) around my bed
—Calgary and Oregon and California added now to
St Philip and Prashad Nagar and Bel Air—that time was short.
I greeted them with warmth, and mustered up the strength
To smile at the drawings they showed me and
Answer the questions they asked, and
Joke about the doctor pushing 90. (Actually 70.)
Actually, I was happy just to look
at their faces and listen to their chatter
And close my eyes and think of the
Rest of the brood and Russell …
But when I snuggled up for a better dream
The tubes twisted and complained me back to reality,
To that white room in St Joseph's Mercy Hospital,
In Kingston, Georgetown, Guyana, with the sun rising
And a breeze blowing and the children standing around.
They came too soon for me, those men in white
With the gurney. I hadn't exhausted the preciousness
of the last moments. I wasn't ready again to face
the bright lights and the gleaming silver or the sharp pain.
I protested their rough handling, but took the children's kisses
and good wishes and glanced once more at their faces and went along.
Watching these strangers' eyes—slits above masks in
bright light, I felt tired and drifted back to my reverie
about Russell and Garraway Stream and my father the Grandmaster
and Mother Rosina and my lost brother Benjie and all …
I was breathing heavily when they brought me back.
"Russell, i's me. Baby."

Mom's funeral service was held on Monday March 12, 1984, after her death announcement was printed in the local newspapers and broadcast, accompanied by melancholy music, on the local radio stations:

RICKFORD—The death is announced of **EULA RICKFORD**, of Bel Air Park, which took place on March 8, 1984. She was the wife of the late Russell Rickford, mother of June Fletcher, Edward Rickford, Dawn McTurk, Peter

Rickford, George Rickford, Elizabeth Phillips, Patricia Streeter, Nancy Nunes-de-Souza, and John R. Rickford; sister of Ivy Campbell and Harriet Phillips, grandmother of Deborah Badley, Lorraine Compton, Judy Phillips and thirty others, great grandmother of Nicole and eight others. The funeral of the late **EULA RICKFORD** will take place on Monday, 12th March 1984 at 4:30 p.m. at St. George's Cathedral.

I helped to plan the funeral service with the help of the Right Reverend Randolph George, Bishop of Guyana and a family friend. He also conducted the service. Apart from standards like "There is a Green Hill Far Away," and "The Lord's My Shepherd" there was one hymn I included, "O Love that wilt not let me go" because I'd heard it was one of Mummy's favorites. It has since become one of my favorites, which I would like to have sung at my funeral. I will quote here only the first verse:

> O love that will not let me go,
> I rest my weary soul in Thee:
> I give Thee back the life I owe,
> That in Thine oceans depths its flow
> May richer, fuller be.

Beautiful and moving though these words were, it was the last verse of "Amazing Grace"—a verse that is not often sung—that reduced me to body-shaking tears:

> When we've been there ten thousand years,
> Bright shining as the sun,
> We've no less days to sing God's praise,
> Than when we'd first begun.

I left Guyana two days later, returning to the solace of Angela and our children.
    Thank you, my parents.

Notes

1 Sir George Williams University was merged with Loyola College in 1974, to become Concordia University.
2 Yaba Blay. 2014. *(1)ne Drop. Shifting the Lens on Race*. Philadelphia, PA: BLACKprint.
3 Obituary in *The Philadelphia Inquirer*, June 4, 1990. https://tinyurl.com/y7ytfb4t

11 How I fell in love with linguistics and Black Talk

Even before I left high school, I had fallen in love with language and literature. From my mother's reading out loud from Samuel Selvon's *The Lonely Londoners*, my curling up with the adventures of *Ali Baba and the Forty Thieves* from our home library and borrowing incessantly the *Hardy Boys* and other books from the Carnegie Public Free Library (now the National Library of Guyana) in Georgetown, I knew from a young age the delight that could be derived from fiction. Hanging out with John Agard and Brian Chan, publishing poems with them in *Expression* and closely reading Shakespeare and Chaucer and Wordsworth and Eliot under the tutelage of high school teachers like Ivy Loncke and Victor Ramraj deepened my love of poetry.

In fact, on the inside back cover of Louis Untermeyer's *A Concise Treasury of Great Poems, English and American*, which I bought in August 1966, I had penned this juvenile but earnest epilogue:

> Five hundred and fifty-eight pages,
> Read at various times in different stages
> Have yielded this overwhelming thought:
> This is the greatest book I ever bought. –J.R.R.

Thanks to Ivy Loncke's excellent teaching, I earned a distinction in English Literature at the London University GCE Advanced level exams in 1967. And I planned to major in literature when I began my undergraduate study at the University of California, Santa Cruz in 1968.

Then I discovered linguistics, the scientific study of language. As I have noted in an earlier chapter, the switch from literature to linguistics was one of two transformations I underwent in my undergraduate years, the other being the change from conceiving myself as colored to defining myself as black. The two transitions were not unrelated. Learning to love Black Talk (my native Creolese and African American Vernacular English, or "AAVE") was of a piece with learning to love my black self, the African strands of my ancestry, my *me*.

Black Talk is the title of Geneva Smitherman's invaluable 1994 glossary of AAVE words and phrases.[1] But it is also the title of J. Graham Cruickshank's earlier 1917 book on Guyanese Creole,[2] so I will use it to refer simultaneously to both. Note,

DOI: 10.4324/9781003204305-11

however that while Black Talk in Guyana was first created and used by enslaved Africans, it was adopted and adapted by East Indian indentured servants, and peoples of other ethnicities thereafter. I will also use the term to include the creole Englishes of the Caribbean, in Jamaica, Trinidad, Barbados and elsewhere.

The late poet and essayist Edward Kamau Brathwaite coined the term *nation language* for the creole English of the Caribbean, "the language of slaves and laborers":[3]

> Nation language is the language which is influenced very strongly by the African model, the African aspect of our New World/Caribbean heritage. English it may be in terms of some of its lexical features. But in its contours, its rhythm and its timbre, its sound explosions, it is not English, even though the words as you hear them, might be English to a greater or lesser degree.
>
> (p. 13)

Brathwaite illustrates the point with several examples, including this poem by the late Jamaican dub poet Michael Smith, which, like the sound poems of Jamaican Linton Kwesi Johnson and other nation language poets, "comes out of the same experience as the music of contemporary popular song: using the same riddims, the same voice-spreads, syllable clusters, blue notes, ostinado ["a short melody or pattern that is constantly repeated"], syncopation and pauses":[4]

"Mi cyaan believe it" by Michael Smith (excerpt)

Mi sey mi cyaan believe it
Mi sey mi cyaan believe it
room dem a rent
mi apply widin
but as mi go in
cockroach an scarpian also come in
an mi cyaan believe it
one likkle bwoy come blow im horn
an mi look pan im wid scorn
an mi realize ow mi fine bwoy pickney
was a victim a de trix
dem kall partisan pally-trix
an mi ban mi belly an mi baal
an mi ban mi belly an mi baal
Lawwwwwwwd
Mi cyaan believe it …
[*English gloss*, JRR]
I say, I can't believe it
I say, I can't believe it
rooms for rent
I apply within

but as I go in
cockroaches and scorpions also come in
a little boy comes and blows his horn
and I look on him with scorn
and I realize that my fine boy child
was a victim of the tricks
they call partisan poli-trics
and I bind my belly and I bawl
and I bind my belly and I bawl
Loooooord
I can't believe it …

Although I first learned to love linguistics at UC Santa Cruz, it was while studying for my PhD at the University of Pennsylvania that I learned how to really love Black Talk and to reveal the complexities and richness of its system. It was easy to love Chaucer, Shakespeare, Wordsworth and the celebrated poets and playwrights of English, for almost everyone loved them, and thousands of books had been written extolling them. Loving Black Talk, showing why it should be analyzed and cherished, and defending it and its speakers against its many detractors was more challenging. As a linguist I would write about many subjects, but none more frequently than Black Talk (creoles and AAVE).

After discovering linguistics in college, I enrolled at Penn for graduate school to study under Bill Labov. Labov had helped create the academic subfield studying sociolinguistic variation and change. He had led a major study of AAVE in Harlem in the late 1960s, resulting in two influential books published in 1972.[5] This white scholar was *de* man when it came to my two key interests: the study of language in society and Black Talk.

Labov taught me about fieldwork, how to go into the community and record speakers using their language in as natural and informal a setting as possible, which we did in 1972 in his "Study of the Speech Community" course. Group 4, that year, consisting primarily of black students, including John Baugh and myself, but also a white student, Martha Pennington, studied *be* in AAVE, and produced a 38-page report. Our scope included habitual *be* as in "I can't get no sleep in the afternoon, 'cause these kids *be* making so much noise" and the future perfect *be* done as in "Before you know it, he *be done* rolled off the couch!" Labov responded with two pages of typewritten comments and questions, something I came to appreciate even more when I sent him dissertation chapter drafts from Guyana analyzing the data from my field work. He would send me by return mail, pages and pages of feedback. He also accommodated me in his home when I flew to Philadelphia from Guyana to consult about my dissertation, and eventually defend it, giving generously of his time and advice. True, he stretched my 1979 dissertation to more than 600 pages, but he improved it considerably in the process. Gracias, professor.

Labov taught me by instruction and example how to combine theoretical and descriptive linguistics with applied concerns of social opportunity and equality. He helped inspire much of the work I later did on the educational and legal

Figure 11.1 With my mentor Professor William Labov, at his home in Philadelphia, PA, March 22, 2012.

challenges facing speakers of Black Talk in the Caribbean and the U.S. Love is not love if it does nothing to enhance the lives of those we love.

What do I love about Black Talk? Let me offer some examples of the allure of this language.

The first is from a recording I made on Daufuskie Island, South Carolina, in 1970.[6] The speaker was Deacon Walter "Plummy" Simmons, normally a subsistence farmer, dredge worker and the driver of the island's only tractor, delivering a prayer in a praise house one Sunday morning. The full prayer is much longer, and it is accompanied by the humming and singing of the deacon's wife, Agnes. But even in this short excerpt we can appreciate its poetry:

> An den, den, den, our Father
> we—we got some boys
> an we got some girls
> walkin up an down wid a
> stiff neck an a rebellious heart …
> Tell dem, our Father, dat
> de train dey ridin on
> is full of dead man's bones.
> Make dem know, our Father
> dat de house is on fire,

an de roof is what burnin down …
Make dem know, our Father,
Dat when you thunder in de Eas'
No man can thunder in de Wes'
after you.

Note the parallelism of the deacon's repeated phrases, sometimes for inclusion ("we got some boys, an we got some girls"), other times for contrast (God's thundering in the East is followed by man's thundering in the West, in a feeble attempt to equal Him). And feel the drama in the central metaphor of the train ridden by rebellious youth being "full of dead man's bones." Or the urgency with which the roof is described as not just aflame but "burning down." This from a farmer as well as a poet and wordsmith.

My next example is from Guyana. The speaker is Anna, a 36-year-old Afro-Guyanese huckster of fruits and vegetables from Buxton, famous as one of the first villages to be bought by former enslaved persons after emancipation in 1838.[7] Here she is complaining, in front of customers and hucksters, about the pace of business in Bourda market, Georgetown:

Ting baad. Nutten ain' sellin at dis market! Every maanin you gat fu wake up t'ree o'clak. Longtime, ting useta sell. Now, it worse. People ain' wan' buy nutten. Aaz yuh tell dem how de price goin', dey say, 'Ting dear. ee dear. Shop ting dear. Market ting dear. All ting dear.' Nutten na ah sell, right? Me come out from Buxton, right? Me ah taak de truth. Nutten na ah sell, right?

English Gloss:
    "Things are bad. Nothing is selling at this market. Every morning you have to wake up at three o'clock. Long ago, things used to sell. Now, it's worse. People don't want to buy anything. As soon as you tell them how the price is going, they say, 'Tings are dear.
    It is dear. Shop things are dear. Market things are dear. All things are dear.' Nothing is selling, right? I come out from Buxton, right? I'm talking the truth. Nothing is selling, right?"

Stylistically, we see again, as in Michael Smith's dub poem and Walter Simmons' prayer, the pervasiveness of repetition for dramatic effect (*Nutten na ah sell*; *ting dear, e dear*). But notice too the variation in grammatical form, from the more urban *ain Verb+in* (*Nutten ain sellin'*) to the more rural *na ah Verb* (*nutten na ah sell*). Note, as well, the deep creole use of *me* as pronoun subject, which occurs throughout Anna's discourse on sluggish market sales, in contrast with the more urban, English-like use of "I" or "Ah" as first person pronoun, which occurs elsewhere in the interview, for instance when Anna is talking about bicycle thefts:

Dis las' bicycle I lass deh, *ah* tek it out bout t'ree month.
    "This last bicycle I lost there, I took it out about three months [earlier]."

Finally, note that plurals are unmarked most of the time in Anna's speech (***ting baad, t'ree mont'***), but when needed, they can be marked with English *-s* (*tings*) or Creole *dem* (*de **ting** dem* or ***dem ting***). In short, Anna has a vast arsenal—a wide array of grammatical resources—with which to express herself.

My third example is from a 49-year-old East Indian cattle farmer named Lohtan, talking about the death of his baby daughter. To introduce the framework for the analysis of his narrative, I need to mention Dell Hymes, my second major influence at Penn. Hymes had edited an important 1971 book which was my reference source for decades, *Pidginization and Creolization of Languages*. It grew out of a 1968 conference held at the University of the West Indies, Jamaica. An anthropologist and poet, he was also co-creator of *ethnopoetics*, which argues that narratives are organized into lines and groups of lines based on stress, tone group and other factors, and tend to constitute sets in terms of a few pattern numbers, commonly two and four.[8] Dell's wife Virginia had been one of the early exemplars of ethnopoetics, and helped to organize Lohtan's narrative into the line structure shown below.

In Lohtan's narrative, the significant pattern number is two. The story has two major scenes: the *hospital*, where Lohtan goes to visit his sick daughter (apparently suffering from gastroenteritis), and his *home*, where his friend Baka comes to tell him in the night that his child has died. I will focus only on the second half of the narrative, where two households are contrasted, one belonging to Lohtan and his grief-stricken wife, and the home next door, where there is dancing, music and feasting in preparation for a wedding the next morning.[9]

Well, she tell me say ee see one light come. See one light
    come until when ee turn back. Ee say ee see de
    light. Say, "Pickney dead fi true." Ee jump right
    away, say, "Pickney dead fi true." Well, ee start to holler,
    shout an ting. Well, ee start to shout, an well, aal de peo-   5
well de music stap right away. Dem say, "Wuh happen?"
Well, all, me tel am say, "Pickney dead." Well, de music
    stop. Well de boy na gat fuh married mornin time?
Go an hurry bring de pickney come. Order coffin an
    ting fas, yuh know, an we bury am jus' nine o' clock,   10
because de people get weddin, you understand? You know, as de
    pickney dead, we cyaan humbug de weddin, yuh
    understan? An aal awee live neighbour, yuh understan? So
    me say, "De pickney dead already. Let we carry bury
    am." But de people dem, no music dey na play no mo. Dem   15
    stop, yuh know?
Gloss:
Well–well, she told me that she'd seen a light coming.
Seen the light come and seen it turn back. She said that she'd seen the
    light. She said, "The child is dead for real!" She took off right away,
    shouting, "The child is dead for real!" Well she started to holler,

shout and carry on. Well, she started to shout, and well, all the   5
pe(ople), well the music stopped right away. They said, "What happened?"
Well, all, I told them, "The child is dead." Well the music
stopped. Well, the boy still had to get married in the morning.
We hurried and brought the child home. Ordered a coffin and
so on fast, you know. And we buried her at nine o'clock,   10
because the people had a wedding, you understand? You know, as the
child was (already) dead, we shouldn't humbug ("spoil") the wedding, you
understand? I mean, we all lived as neighbors, you understand? So w-
I said, "The child is dead already. Let's carry her and bury
her." But the people, no music did they play any more. They   15
stopped, you know?

Note the repetition of propositions in pairs throughout the narrative:[10] ee *see one light come. See one light come. Pickney dead fi true. Pickney dead fi true.* The effect is to slow the narrative, letting the individual events and details sink in, as they do when tragedy unfolds. This is in contrast to lines 9–10, in which the repetition of clauses and the use of introductory *well*s stop, and contrary devices—like the piling up of predicates in the serial verb construction (*hurry bring de pickney come*), and the omission of subject pronouns (*order coffin*)—are deployed to convey the speed with which arrangements for the burial were executed.

Now people grant that writers have the ability to transform actual or imagined experience into art, but we are less prepared to recognize such strategies by ordinary people in oral narratives, particularly those dealing with personal experience. Note that while the events of the death of Lohtan's daughter are drawn from raw experience, that experience is filtered through Lohtan's sensibilites, and becomes, for him as for other oral narrators, a matter of art. Lohtan's verbal craftsmanship is evident not only in the structure of his speech, but in his selection of just the right points of detail for elaboration or omission, as when the neighbors are told simply, *pickney dead*, and their reaction is conveyed in one brief sentence: *Well, de music stop.*

The theme of the story is mutual consideration among neighbors and the importance of interpersonal cooperation. The neighbors halt their music as soon as they receive news of the girl's death.[11] Lohtan, in return, hurries to bury his daughter to avoid interrupting the wedding. The proliferation of *you know*s and *you understan*s in the last seven lines of the narrative represent insistent appeals to the listener to comprehend why the narrator acted as he did (burying the child so quickly), and to grasp the larger thematic significance of the narrative.

People also contend that vernacular or creole varieties are sufficient for discussing concrete or everyday matters, but not for engaging philosophical topics like life and death and cooperation among neighbors. This extract clearly shows this to be untrue, as does Granny's lament (see Chapter 14) that the work of a sugar cane weeder is so hard, that you "throw down youself a de bank and yuh say, "Lord, a when dis cutlass a go come out a me han? E betta me dead, before me a live."

Figure 11.2 Interviewing playwright August Wilson in Ujamaa Lounge, Stanford, January 14, 1999, about his realization that he had to put the voices of black people in his plays to make them come alive.

My final example is from AAVE or Spoken Soul, and from the literary master of this genre, the playwright August Wilson.[12] When I interviewed Wilson at Stanford in 1999, he explained that when he first started writing plays, he thought he had to put high-flown language into the mouths of his characters to make "art" out of it.[13] That didn't work, and it was only when he began listening to the voices of black people in his native Pittsburgh, and putting that language in his plays that, that the dialogue soared. *Fences* and *The Piano Lesson*, from his ten play "Pittsburgh Cycle," each documenting a decade of the 20th century, won Pulitzer Prizes.

The following exchange, from *Fences*, is between Troy, a 53-year-old former Negro League baseball player, his wife Rose and his friend Bono:[14]

ROSE: You gonna drink yourself to death. You don't need to be drinking like that.

TROY: Death ain't nothing. I done seen him. Done wrassled with him. You can't tell me nothing about death. Death ain't nothing but a fastball on the outside corner. And you know what I'll do to that! Lookee here, Bono ... am I lying? You get one of them fastballs, about waist high, over the outside corner of the plate where you can get the meat of the bat on it ... and good god! You can kiss it goodbye. Now, am I lying?

BONO: Naw, you telling the truth there. I seen you do it.

TROY: If I'm lying ... that 450 feet worth of lying! (*Pause.*) That's all death is to me. A fastball on the outside corner.

ROSE: I don't know why you want to get on talking about death.
TROY: Ain't nothing wrong with talking about death. That's part of life.
Everybody gonna die. You gonna die. I'm gonna die. Bono's gonna die. Hell,
we all gonna die.

Whenever I needed a text in my AAVE course for students to identify and discuss
AAVE features, an extract from one of Wilson's plays invariably filled the bill.
In this text, for instance, there are several cases in which, in keeping with AAVE
grammar, the present tense *is/are* copula is absent (*Everybody Ø gonna die, You Ø
gonna die*), but by AAVE rules too, first person *am* or *'m* is obligatorily preserved
(*I'm gonna die*). Note too his use of preverbal *done* to mark completion (*done
seen him. Done wrassled with him.*) Wilson's wonderful dialogue stamps his
characters as black people informally using Black Talk, enjoying the vernacular.
Again, these speakers deploy the dialect to engage expansive, existential issues,
like the inevitability of death.

Wilson is an aficionado of the vernacular,[15] in company with James Baldwin,
Claude Brown, June Jordan, Toni Morrison and other African American writers.
Baldwin described AAVE as "this passion, this skill, … this incredible music,"[16]
and Jordan identified "three qualities of Black English—the presence of life, voice
and clarity—that testify to a distinctive Black value system."[17]

For me, as a student of language in society, loving languages or dialects is not
enough. We need to also find ways to use linguistics to make a positive difference in the world. Labov first showed how linguistics could help ensure justice
in criminal cases, when he succeeded in showing that Paul Prinzivalli, a cargo
handler, "did not and could not have made" recorded bomb threats against Pan
American airlines in Los Angeles in 1987.[18] The crucial evidence was that the
bomb threat caller was clearly from Boston (with long *oh* as in *bomb* and short *oh*
as in *off* merged), while Prinzivalli was from New York (with long *oh* and short
oh separate).

In the case of speakers of Black Talk, the need for positive interventions is
especially great, because black people face discrimination in almost every area
of life—when encountering police and courts, applying for jobs and apartments,
seeking health care or education, and more.[19] In almost every case, the discrimination is worse when those black people speak Black Talk. As I will show in Chapter
16, the vital testimony of Rachel Jeantel, Trayvon Martin's good friend, was dis-
regarded in the 2013 trial of George Zimmerman for Martin's murder because her
speech was either not understood by jurors or interpreted as less credible.

Over the years I have contributed to several court cases in which I had to correct the official transcripts of AAVE speakers; it is striking how inaccurate the
police or court transcriptions can be, apparently done by people with no acquaint-
ance with Black Talk.[20]

On one occasion I assisted in the legal defense of a black woman (let's
call her Tamika) who was using a common American expression that a Drug
Enforcement Agency officer agent misunderstood or, more likely, pretended
not to understand. The officer, searching for drugs, boarded a bus and asked

an African American woman if he could do a body pat-down. She replied "I'm good," meaning "No," and remained seated to reinforce that she was not consenting to this intrusion. The officer proceeded with the search, without her permission, and found an incriminating substance under her bra. She was arrested and taken to jail. Her case is yet another example of a grotesque system that relies on racial and class profiling (drug sweeps on buses!) and criminalization of low-level offenses to feed mass incarceration's insatiable desire to cage black and brown bodies.

Her defense lawyer contacted me and asked whether I could provide linguistic evidence that "I'm good" meant "No," since the prosecution lawyers were asserted that it meant the opposite. At issue was the legality of the search if conducted without Tamika's permission.

I submitted several pieces of evidence in a formal deposition.[21]

The first kind of evidence I provided was from crossword puzzles, like one from a 2007 edition of *The New York Times*, in which the clue was "Nothing for me, thanks," and the solution was "I'm good." In another crossword, from 2018, the clue was "I'm good, thanks" and the solution was "Nah."

Then I turned to the unabridged *Oxford English Dictionary* [OED], more authoritative than the *Urban Dictionary* which the prosecution usually invoked. The OED defined *I'm good* as originally from the U.S., "used in response to a question or request," and meaning "no thank you." The dictionary's first example was from 1966, suggesting that this usage was relatively new:

> 1966 J. Ball *Cool Cottontail* x. 113 "More beer?" "*I'm still good*, thanks."

To get a better sense of its development over time, I did a computer search of the billion-word *Corpus of Contemporary English* (COCA), where I found 80 examples of *I'm good*, meaning "No, thanks" in response to a question or offer, as in this example:

> 2011 The waitress turned to Charlotte again. "Are you sure I can't get you anything? Maybe an appetizer or salad?" # *No, I'm good*. Really." From *Love, Honor and Betray*.

The COCA data showed that the use of *I'm good* = "No" has been steadily increasing since the 1990s, particularly in the 2012–2017 period in which Tamika's usage occurred.

The COCA data also refuted two contentions of the prosecuting attorney in this case. First, contrary to his allegation that *I'm good* only meant "No, thanks" when used in response to offers of food and drink (therefore NOT including Tamika's usage), only a third of the COCA examples were like this. Secondly, the prosecutor also alleged that for *I'm good* to mean "No, thanks," it has to be preceded by, "No," "Naw" or another negative. But while this was true in just over a half of the COCA examples, in the other half, no explicit negative was included, as in Tamika's case.

I also looked at 75 *I'm good* examples from Twitter, most of them from African Americans. These all meant "No, Thanks," but they often signal disagreement with or rejection of a hypothetical or actual situation, as in:

> if a dude i fw is giving someone else the same energy he's giving me, they can have em. *I'm good*, lol.
>
> (Tylar Phillips, October 28, 2018)

And among black users, there was also this extra element: *I'm good, luv, enjoy*:

> "Projecting your own insecurities unto me. *I'm good luv, enjoy*! (harms)"

As in the COCA corpora, about half the time *I'm good* was not preceded by "No" or "Nah."

The result of this and some experimental evidence I included in my deposition was that Tamika's final sentence after a plea bargain (less than 4% of cases go to trial) was two years instead of ten, a significant reduction of the time that would otherwise have been the case. She is now free.

Love is not love if it does nothing to enhance the lives of those we love, or the community members who speak the languages we love.

Notes

1 Geneva Smitherman. 1994, 2000. *Black Talk: Words and Phrases from the Hood to the Amen Corner*. Boston, MA: Houghton Mifflin.

2 J. Graham Cruickshank. 1917. *Black Talk, being Notes on Negro Dialect in British Guiana*. Demerara: Argosy.

3 Edward Kamau Brathwaite. 1984. *History of the Voice: The Development of Nation Language in Anglophone Caribbean Poetry*. London, Port of Spain: New Beacon, p. 5. Interestingly enough, on the same page he also refers to the "very excellent" presentation that had preceded his by "Dennis Brutus, the South African poet-and-activist-in-exile." See chapter 16 of this memoir for my 1990 interview with Dennis Brutus.

4 The words, from Brathwaite. 1984. *History of the Voice*, p. 46–47, differ slightly from those in the reading by Michael Smith at https://www.youtube.com/watch?v=-RF v7WqpcQQ.

5 William Labov. 1972a. *Sociolinguistic Patterns.* Philadelphia, PA: University of Pennsylvania Press; and 1972b. *Language in the Inner City: Studies in the Black English Vernacular*. Philadelphia, PA: University of Pennsylvania Press.

6 For a longer version of this prayer, and more analysis, see John R. Rickford and Russell J. Rickford. 2000. *Spoken Soul: The Story of Black English.* New York: Wiley, pp. 41–45.

7 For more of Anna's texts, and further analysis, see John R. Rickford. 1987. *Dimensions of a Creole Continuum: History, Texts and Linguistic Analysis of Guyanese Creole.* Stanford: Stanford University Press, pp. 231–237.

8 Dell Hymes. 1987. A Note on Ethnopoetics and Sociolinguistics. *Working Papers in Educational Linguistics* 3.2.
     https://repository.upenn.edu/wpel/vol3/iss2/1/

9 For the full narrative, and analysis, see John R. Rickford. 1986. "Me Tarzan, You Jane" Adequacy, Expressiveness, and the Creole Speaker." *Journal of Linguistics*

12: 281–310. Note too that *ee* is the deep creole non-object pronoun, which corresponds to subject "*he, she* or *it*" or possessive "*his, her* or *its*" in Standard English The deep creole object pronoun is *am*, corresponding to "*him, her* or *it*" as in lines 10 and 15 of Lohtan's narrative.

10 I am grateful to Elizabeth Closs Traugott for first drawing my attention to the existence of these paired structures.

11 Note how the cessation of the music is emphasized in 1106 by the fronting or topicalization of the object and the triple negative: *noo myuuzik dee na plee no moo*.

12 On March 17, 2021, the U.S. Post Office unveiled a new stamp honoring August Wilson, #44 in its Black Heritage series: https://youtu.be/P6wjB7s7I9g

13 See John Russell Rickford and Russell John Rickford. 2000. *Spoken Soul*. New York: Wiley, pp. 29–30.

14 *Fences*, set in the 1950s, is part of Wilson's ten-play Pittsburgh cycle, and in 1987 won a Pulitzer Prize for Drama and a Tony Award for Best Play. It is also a full length 2014 movie, produced and directed by Denzel Washington.

15 See now the December 2020 Netflix movie release of Wilson's *Ma Rainey's Black Bottom*: https://www.theatlantic.com/culture/archive/2020/12/ma-raineys-black-bottom-netflix/617445/

16 James Baldwin. July 29, 1979. "If Black English isn't a Language, Then Tell me What is," *The New York Times*.

17 June Jordan. 1985. "Nobody Mean More to me Than You and the Future Life of Willie Jordan." In her book, *On Call: Political Essays*. Boston, MA: South End Press, pp. 123–139.

18 William Labov. 1987. "How I Got Into Linguistics, and What I Got Out of It." www.ling.upenn.edu/~wlabov/HowIgot.html

19 See John Baugh. 2018. *Linguistics in Pursuit of Justice*. Cambridge: Cambridge University Press.

20 See Taylor Jones, Jessica Rose Kalbfeld, Ryan Hancock, and Robin Clark. 2019. "Testifying While Black: An Experimental Study of Court Reporter Accuracy in Transcription of African American English." *Language* 95.2: e216–e252.

21 I was assisted in this research by Stanford students Mea Anderson, Susan Chang, Julia Gong, and Zion Mengesha.

12 The Sea Islands

Dashiki in Suitcase if Required

In Spring 1970 I spent ten weeks in the blackest region of the United States, one in which African roots still show and Caribbean similarities are most visible. I was on Daufuskie Island, South Carolina, a 9 × 2.5-mile sliver of an island near Hilton Head, its bigger and better-known neighbor. Both are part of a chain of more than 100 Sea Islands stretching from South Carolina to Georgia and northern Florida. On most of these islands, as in the corresponding coastal Low Country, black people constituted 90% or more of the population for much of the last two centuries. On Daufuskie in 1970, there were over 120 black residents and only 8 or 10 white people. There were hundreds more black people in earlier decades, before pollution from chemical plants along the Savannah River contaminated the island's famed oyster banks. Shucking oysters had been the primary occupation on the island.

According to one scholar, the high proportion of black people to white people in this former rice and cotton farming region is one of the factors that made the Sea Islands "The most direct repository of living African culture to be found anywhere in North America."[1] Another factor is that enslaved people from Africa were brought here much later than elsewhere in the U.S. The slave ship *Wanderer* illegally unloaded a "cargo" of 400 enslaved people on Jekyll Island, Georgia, in 1858, although the slave trade to the U.S. had ended officially in 1808. Moreover, the remoteness of some of the islands—Daufuskie, for example, may only be reached by boat—limited acculturation to the norms of mainstream, white culture.

For these and other reasons, Daufuskie's connnections with Africa and the Caribbean were striking. When I first visited the Sea Islands, the linguistic and cultural similarities to my native Guyanese and Caribbean background were everywhere. The distinctive Gullah or Sea Island Creole dialect was very similar, in some ways, to Guyanese and other Caribbean Creole Englishes. Sea Islanders use words like *juk* (from the African Fulani *jukka* "to poke"), *deh* ("to be," or where a person or thing is), *(d)a* (for an action that one is doing, or usually does) and *bina* (for an action that one used to do, or was doing in the past), as in these examples, which resemble Caribbean Creole English:

"Dem chii'ren tek an *juk* [poke] dey foot through de screen." (Blossom Robinson)

DOI: 10.4324/9781003204305-12

Figure 12.1 The Sea Islands of S. Carolina (copyright Molly Joseph Fine Art).

"My aunt useta live in Washington, wa buil' da house … wa Rufus *deh* [is] in." (Sarah Grant)

"You ain' see how de grass *da* die ["is dying"], Hamp?" (Edna Bryan)

"How bout da ting wa Buddy *bina tell* [was telling] you bout da tree?" (Johnny Hamilton)

Lorenzo Dow Turner, an African American linguist, documented African and Caribbean similarities like these in his 1949 classic, *Africanisms in the Gullah Dialect*. The word "Gullah" may be a shortened form of "Angola," from where some of the residents of this area came. Or it may be a form of *gula*, the name of a group in Liberia, according to Turner.

Gullah people pound cassava and plantain with pestles in huge mortars, as some people in Africa and the Caribbean traditionally do. They use similar nets and ways of fishing. In style and function their baskets resemble those found in Senegal, Nigeria, Togo, Benin and Ghana, and their wood carvings look like those created by the Djuka people in Suriname, next door to Guyana.[2]

How did I get to this mecca of Africa in America? Through an exchange program that J. Herman Blake had started at the University of California, Santa Cruz, in 1968, to expand the learning of students outside the classroom while doing community service. Professor Blake began sending pairs of students to Daufuskie each quarter. Then he extended the program to other organizations in South Carolina (Beaufort and the Hilton Head Fishing Co-op), and to various counties

Figure 12.2 JRR and Frank Smith (right) with other UCSC students in Beaufort County, S. Carolina, Spring 1970. Prof. J Herman Blake is in the center, with his nephew, Jerome.

in California. Students had to sign up for at least 15 units of credit and independent work in sociology, linguistics or other subjects, while committing to serve the needs of the local community.

Frank Smith, a white student from Atascadero, California, and I were the "California boys" destined for Daufuskie that Spring. I was the first black student to go there. Frank and I didn't know each other, but we got acquainted during a four-day Greyhound bus trip that wound through Arizona, New Mexico, Texas, Mississippi, Alabama and Georgia before reaching South Carolina. For me it was an amazing introduction to parts of America I had never seen. As we got deeper into the South, I encountered racist looks and cold shoulders in some of the places we stopped to eat. This made me feel uncomfortable, terrified even, and I hurried back to the safety of the Greyhound bus as quickly as possible. I also fantasized about being Dick Gregory, the black comedian, and voicing his putative words in a similarly threatening establishment:

> A white waitress told me: "We don't serve colored people here." I told her: "That's all right, I don't eat colored people. Bring me a whole fried chicken." Three white boys—Klu, Kluck and Klan—said, "Boy, we're giving you fair warning. Anything you do to that chicken, we're gonna do to you." So I picked up that chicken and I kissed it.

Our Greyhound bus pulled into Savannah, Georgia, at 10:15 p.m. By the time we got to bed in our cabin on Hilton Head island, it was 1:30 a.m. Tom Barnwell from the Hilton Head Fishing Co-op was coming to pick us up for the short ride to Daufuskie at 8 a.m. Exhausted, we missed our 7 a.m. alarm and were only awakened by Barnwell banging on the door at 8:30.

"Shit! We ready to go an you people still sleepin?! Wha' is dis, man?"

Embarrassed, we hurried about getting our things together to leave.

Down at the dock, we boarded the co-op boat, the *Captain Dave*. I stood in the cabin for most of the trip with members of the co-op, which had been launched in 1966. They included Captain Dave himself, a delightful old man who spoke Gullah so rapidly it was sometimes difficult for me to understand, and for Frank, it seemed, impossible. Also joining us was Mrs. Dossier, a Barbadian woman representing the Episcopalian Church. Barnwell and I got on extremely well, the more so since he had been to Guyana (whose full name is The Cooperative Republic of Guyana) to learn more about the co-op movement, and I was familiar with many of the people and places he recalled. Throughout the trip, we talked and laughed in our respective but mutually intelligible creole dialects while feasting on crab and shrimp.

Everyone seemed to accept me very well and I got on with them easily. This moment of cultural recognition was immensely satisfying to me, quieting my fears about venturing into unfamiliar territory, and replacing them with a sense that my Guyanese creole and culture would mesh well with Gullah language and culture. At several points during the ten-week stay, Frank would ask me to translate the Gullah that older Sea Islanders spoke. I would joke, "These are YOUR people, man—Americans like you!" while recognizing that the similarities between their dialect and mine made it easier for me to understand. Later, I gave talks and wrote about the local Gullah language and culture often, emphasizing that in this locale, the African roots still show.

As we approached the island, I got nervous. This was the place we had heard so much about. It was real! I scrutinized every tree and bush and boat. This would be home for the next ten weeks. Once we got to the landing, Cap'n Dave and Tom assured me that the home in which we would stay, belonging to retired schoolteacher Frances Jones, was "jus' around the corner." It took several such corners before we got there. It felt like walking a mile in the soft sand, with huge oak trees bedecked in Spanish moss standing like sentries on either side of the unpaved road. Eventually we got there, with Barnwell hollering out, "Frances, I bring some people fuh you."

Miss Frances cut a striking figure—standing on one leg with a crutch, the other one paralyzed by polio—but there was no question as to who was in charge. Cap'n Dave asked her to settle the argument between him and Barnwell about which was the shortest way to her house, a single-level, two-bedroom building in white with blue trim near the school. She simply said, "He's right, and you're wrong." And that was that. We also met several of the local adults who were visiting her home, including the legendary Fastman or Weatherman, who would give you lengthy forecasts about the weather at a breakneck pace:

We expectin Nort-eas wind 10 to 20 mph, an we have showers, a CHANCE of showers or thundershowers, dis kind of ting, today an tonight, thru Wednesday, but we don' expectin too much o' heavy showers, not so quick.

There were several animals in Miss Frances's yard—an old horse named "Freedom," several hens and a crowing rooster, a big sow named Bebe and two puppies. The trees were full of squirrels, which Miss Frances would pick off with a rifle and cook for breakfast.

Before they left, Barnwell, Mrs. Dossier and I had a chat about how they thought the local black folk related to the contemporary politics of black pride and black power. They gave me the black power handshake and told me to feel free to introduce and use black literature and history in the grade 1–8 school if we were allowed to work there. Previous California boys had been forbidden by head teacher Ms. Johnson to work in the schools on the pretext that they lacked credentials. Barnwell cautioned me to use black educational materials mainly with the kids, for older people might misinterpret my intentions and squeal on me to Mr. Burns, the white authority figure on the island. Burns, perhaps alarmed by student activists of the 1960s who had traveled to the South to register black voters and fight segregation, had confided to the author Pat Conroy his unfounded fear that Mr. Blake and his students "are communists trained in Havana. If they keep comin' to the island, there is bound to be trouble."[3] At Professor Blake's suggestion, I had shaved off my beard (associated at the time with Fidel Castro), and kept it off, to allay such suspicions.

After the Hilton Head Co-op people left, Miss Frances sat down with Frank and me to find out what we liked to eat. I told her I didn't dislike anything, and she

Figure 12.3 Miss Frances Jones, in whose home Frank and I stayed on Daufuskie Island, Spring 1970.

smiled and said "Well, you is the same as me, anyway." After lunch, she talked about previous California boys and what we might do most effectively during our stay. But she interrupted the conversation to suggest we go down to the landing to meet the island boat, returning from Savannah at 4 p.m. There were no groceries or stores on the island, so everyone had to take a one-hour trip by boat either to Savannah, Georgia or to Bluffton, South Carolina, to shop.

That was an amazing experience! Frank and I were on the landing platform, nervous and self-conscious, but trying to hide this by rapidly talking and laughing with each other. When the island boat was about 40 feet out, we could make out about 25 people on it, with their groceries, chicken fencing, and other purchases piled high around them. They were laughing and talking and shifting around all at once, trying to get a view of the new California boys.

After the boat had docked, the islanders proceeded to climb up to the landing, sometimes saying hi, shaking our hands, or otherwise introducing themselves. We heard the youngsters, especially, exchanging their first impressions of us: "Who's de paleface one?" "He ain't got no nose!" and so on. But we had no time to dwell on any of this, for we joined the men in lugging bags, boxes and 100-pound bags of grain and flour up the sloping gangplank. The women and children looked on carefully, running up to us as we brought things off the boat to check whether it was theirs or not, and directing us to put it here or there with their other stuff. Less than an hour later, with this frenzy over, the boat unloaded, and the goods in cars, donkey carts or wagons, the islanders trailed off along the path to their homes. Our muscles were *sore*.

Figure 12.4 Frank and I lugging boxes of groceries up the gangplank after the island boat docked, Spring 1970.

The remaining ten weeks were busy. We were soon helping to plant crops in long rows—okra, corn, peas, beans—(something we didn't know diddly about before!), fixing fences and repairing roofs in the hot sun. We also began driving the island truck, meeting people at the dock and carrying them and their belongings home. We used the truck to take the kids to youth meetings and to explore the island. We were amazed to learn we would be allowed to teach—the first of the California boys to be granted this honor. We worked every day in Pat Conroy's classroom (grades 5–8) and in Mrs. Johnson's class (grades 1–4). Mrs. Johnson had confided to Pat Conroy that the real reason she had been opposed to Blake's California boys is that all of them had been white, and she feared interracial romance:[4]

> We can't let white boys and colored girls rub elbows too much. Them boys are young bulls with no cows on this island 'cept them colored cows. We can't afford to have no half-breed cows on this island.

Since I was "colored" myself, the concern about interracial rendezvous didn't apply to me. But I had also visited her home a day or two after I arrived to make small talk, and that seemed to assuage her fears.

We took the kids to their first movie in a cinema in Savannah—*A Man Called Horse*, a western show about a white Englishman who is captured by the Sioux people. I remember them squirming and screaming as actor Richard Harris was suspended by pins in his chest in the painful Sioux initiation ceremony. Only later did I realize that the movie was essentially based on a racist premise, that a white man who is enslaved by the Sioux could seamlessly adopt their culture and become their leader.

Even more ambitiously, we went as drivers and assistant tour leaders on an eight-day road trip to Washington, DC that Pat Conroy organized for the kids in grades 5–8. It was absolutely eye-opening for them, and a learning experience for me too, as I had never been to North Carolina or Virginia. Conroy wrote about the trip, its significance for the kids and our involvement in it, in *The Water is Wide*.[5]

While on Daufuskie, I recorded songs, stories and life accounts from some of the most memorable characters on the island. Frances Jones, our 59-year-old host, taught us so much during our stay. One of the most fascinating things was the story she told me about her enslaved great grandparents, who, she said, had levitated and flown back to Africa after receiving a whipping.

Years later, in Guyana, I heard a similar story from an old man named Damon. He told me that his great-grandfather, a former enslaved person from the Popo tribe, told him that slaves who were brought on deck for fresh air during the Middle Passage would chant and sing African songs, and as the rhythm grew stronger, they would just take off and *fly*, back to Africa. After a while the crew kept them below deck for fear of losing all their enslaved people.

From further research, I discovered that stories of enslaved people who could fly occur in Jamaica, Suriname and Cuba, all over South Carolina and Georgia, and in African American literature and folklore, (e.g. Toni Morrison's *Song of Solomon* and Virginia Hamilton's *The People Could Fly*). These stories are or course not just fantasies but reflect a black culture of resistance and self-preservation. It is also possible to interpret them as a metaphor for the many enslaved Africans who may have thrown themselves overboard during the Middle Passage, committing suicide rather than accepting enslavement. However, Esteban Montejo, a Cuban enslaved person, said explicitly that Africans didn't escape by committing suicide, "They flew through the sky and returned to their own lands."[6]

What is the significance of this widespread African American motif? I have argued that:

> this is one of those originally African elements that has been remodeled or reinterpreted by the experience of the Middle Passage and slavery, maybe providing a symbolic release from experiences that one could transcend in no other way … the existence of this possibility of flight—like the related belief that slaves who were being beaten could have the hurt telepathically transferred to the slave master's wife … —was one of the few aces that slaves had up their sleeves. It's significant in the stories that they often pulled these aces when the harshness of their New World experiences became most pronounced--for instance, after a whipping—from which it provided symbolic relief.[7]

The fact that I was from the Caribbean helped me to see how widespread these folk stories were across the black diaspora. As Melville Herskovits argued 80 years ago in *The Myth of the Negro Past*, many elements of African American culture cannot be fully appreciated or understood without the larger perspective of Africa and the Caribbean.

Another person who schooled me in the riches of the Sea Island was Walter Simmons, a 72-year-old farmer known as "Plummy" who worked on the dredges for a while. He was a deacon in the church or praise house on the Cooper River side of the island, where he played a key role because ordained ministers rarely came to Daufuskie. The key element in the service was the prayer, and his prayers were always rich in metaphor and poetry, phrasal parallelism and contrast, as discussed, with an example, in Chapter 11.

But Plummy, like his friend Johnny Hamilton, was also a master "liar," a maestro in the telling of tall tales—a vibrant folk tradition in the African American South and the Caribbean:[8]

> I see a man raise a watermelon once. Dis watermelon was on de side of a hill, you know, … An dat watermelon grow so large, until dey, he roll it up on de side there in a low place, an' been usin' it for a BRIDGE! People used to come by from everywhere to look at dat watermelon. … An dey had to— every two or three days dey had to put another wedge on the side of um to keep um from rolling down, you know?
>
> An dey been about five thousan' people been there been lookin at dat melon that Friday afternoon. An one of dem wedge slip out, an dat melon start down de hill. An when it strike itself in front o' dem rock, it break in half, an de water come out of um drowned over five hundred head of people![9]

Beautiful as the island was, it also had its discomforts, which explains in part why many white people avoided living on the Sea Islands. Alligators and snakes of all varieties—including rattlesnakes—abounded. Ticks would cling to your clothes as you walked and would swell up with your blood behind your knee or in your armpits if they escaped your nightly body inspections. Then you'd have to light a match, blow it out, and place it while still hot on the tick to persuade it to back out. Frank and I shared a double bed and at night used a chamber pot to avoid making the trek to the outhouse fifty or more feet away in the dark. There was no running water or toilets in any of the black homes.

I spent much of my time on Daufuskie worrying how I would be viewed and accepted in the larger world, especially in the blackest region of the U.S. Sure, America followed the "one-drop" rule—by law and by custom, anyone with a trace of black ancestry was considered black—but half of my ancestry was white, and there weren't many racially mixed people on the Sea Islands. I wrote a poem about this early on that began like this:

> Excuse me.
> I am from
> a distant family.
> Credentials:
> Dark skin, a
> nose bent in,
> thick lips and
> curly hair.
> Dashiki
> in suitcase
> if required.

So when I heard the children asking on day one, "Who's the paleface one?" and "He ain't got no nose," I was alternately worried that they thought I wasn't black enough and comforted that they were recognizing the African elements of my ancestry. Every previous California boy had been white. It was what they'd come to expect from the visitors from UC Santa Cruz. But I was also encouraged by the readiness of Barnwell and other Hilton Head Co-op members to accept me, and by Lyn Dozier and Miss Jones ("Well you is the same as me, anyway").

Other experiences on the island were alienating. In the first week, I was talking to Mr. and Mrs. Varney, an older white couple, when Mrs. Varney remarked casually that South Carolina was nothing but "Niggers and jackasses." Now South Carolina had always had a higher proportion of African Americans than any other US colony, leading one observer to comment in 1737 that it "looks more like a negro country than like a country settled by white people."[10] But it was the casual way she dropped the N-word into the conversation, pairing it with *jackass*, that unnerved me. Did she perhaps think I was white, and was accustomed to talking like this? Or did she realize I was black and was essentially saying "I don't give

Figure 12.5 "Dashiki in suitcase if required." JRR with Charlie Channel in 1971, the second black "California boy" to go to Daufuskie Island under Prof. Blake's Cowell Extra-Mural Program.

a shit." I wasn't sure, but I beat a hasty retreat before saying something equally obnoxious that might imperil the program.

Two other incidents of racial explication involved black people. The first was when I met Agnes Washington, the 76-year-old mother of Susie Smith, 40, with whom I would stay on a subsequent trip. She asked me, "Tell me, are you white or black?"

Me: "Black."
Suzie: "Aww, Mom, you mean you didn' know?"
Mrs Washington: "I thought you was a Chinaman."

The second incident occurred when I was introduced to the black woman with whom two California girls were living while working in Bluffton, South Carolina. The woman said to me, "My, you've got a wonderful *tan*." I corrected her, identifying myself as black ("Dashiki in suitcase if required") but as I wrote in my diary that night:

> I felt so bad, so embarrassed, so disappointed, betrayed, insulted, invisible—everything all at once. Am I so yellow my black is unrecognizable? Was it the white company I was in, the fact I was introduced as a U.C. student, and she hadn't met a black one before? Or was it something in her? I don't know, but I felt depressed and uncomfortable in her house all that evening. Talked to Herman [Blake] for about 15–20 minutes later in the night [mainly about the work we were doing, and plans for the future] and felt better afterwards … He really encouraged me. Said, "Call anytime. Collect." And left saying "Right on, brother."

Less than two weeks after we arrived on the island, Pat Conroy invited Frank and me to his home in Bluffton. It was a pleasant diversion, allowing us to get to know him better and plan for the forthcoming trip to DC with the Daufuskie children. But there were several awkward moments between us, most having to do with my black identity. Coming into Bluffton, for instance, he joked about how racist the people there were: "They would hang you from a tree, my son!" And in showing us historic Beaufort, he pointed out a big house with quarters for former enslaved persons in the back. He claimed to be worried about the reaction some of his neighbors would have to his associating with me, and my staying in his home.

Some of this might just have been Pat's continuous humor, but he'd already told us about how he used to go "nigger-knocking" (throwing rocks, clay pots and so on at black folk) with teenage friends before he reformed. When we went out with his white friend Brian, to buy bootleg whiskey, he made me duck down to avoid being seen, since the bootleggers, he said, would shoot us if they found out he had brought a black person to see that illegal activity. I was terrified.

The next day, Pat brought me the book *Dark Symphony*, open to a poem by Langston Hughes entitled *Mulatto*. He never explained why he was showing me this or entered into a literary discussion of the poem. But it left me uncomfortable:

"Mulatto" by Langston Hughes (excerpts)
I am your son, white man! …
You are my son!
Like hell! …
The Southern night is full of stars,
Great big yellow stars.
O, sweet as earth,
Dusk dark bodies
Give sweet birth
To little yellow bastard boys.
Git on back there in the night,
You ain't white …

What I might have said to him if he did open himself up to discussion, is that by this stage in the evolution of my identity, I was *not* asking any white man to recognize and claim me. I did *not* see myself as "a little yellow Bastard boy." If anything, I was fully embracing my blackness and East Indian-ness, my status as a "person of color."

I met two other people off Daufuskie—both black, and both leading community organizers—who reinforced and inspired my black identity. The first was Frieda Mitchell, a black woman whom Herman Blake insisted we meet. Co-director of a community development project at Penn Center on St Helena Island, she had done significant work in child care and civil rights.[11] Frieda came to meet me at Conroy's home. The first thing she said when she saw me was, "If I'd known you were a brother [black man], I'd have tried to contact you long before." I enjoyed driving around with her and her sister, talking about the problems of black communities on Daufuskie and the Sea Islands, while doing household chores, picking up garden supplies and groceries.

Mitchell made me feel at home from the start. She encouraged me to move ahead with a Black History and Literature program, which the kids needed, because they were not getting it in the school, and not sufficiently, at home. However, like Tom Barnwell, she warned me to be careful with Ms. Johnson as a potential saboteur. It was also great to be with Melinda Barnett, a black student from UC Santa Cruz who used to help me cut my hair back in California. She was also working in Herman's program in the Beaufort area. We enjoyed hours and hours of "black talk." Frank, Kitty and Cathy came over later.

I also was fortunate to meet Septima Poinsette Clark, whom Martin Luther King, Jr., sometimes described as "The Mother of the Civil Rights Movement."[12] She is known for her work with the NAACP [National Association for the Advancement of Colored People] and for spearheading literacy education and anti-segregation workshops at the Highlander Folk School in Tennessee, which she wrote about in her autobiography, *Echo in My Soul*. Rosa Parks had attended a workshop at Highlander before participating in the Montgomery Bus Boycott.

The occasion on which I met Septima Clark was a celebration of her 72nd birthday at the United Methodist Church in Charleston. I presented her with a statement I had written, at Herman Blake's request, on behalf of The University of California at Santa Cruz. My statement, a single-spaced page typed on a manual typewriter, was long, but ended with this paragraph:

> Septima, we are proud today to call you sister. Through all the tumult and the strife, you have kept your music ringing. Thousands of people have heard your "echo," and following, have steadily advanced. We are proud to join with them today in thanking you for teaching them your tunes and showing us their way.

Septima Clark didn't directly say anything to me about identity. Being in the presence of "this daughter of a laundrywoman and a former slave"[13] who had become a giant in grassroots education and an icon of the Civil Rights Movement was inspiring enough. I felt privileged to have been able to write and deliver a statement in her honor. The glow lasted for days.

One of the greatest boosts to my identity came from one of the eighth-grade students on Daufuskie, Ervin Simmons, who was especially interested in the Black History and Literature topics I discussed that quarter. Ten days after I left for California, he wrote me a letter signed "Your soul friend, Ervin Simmons," which included a drawing from a photo of me the previous year, with my bigger Afro and beard ("last year picture") and this touching note: "To one of my best Soul Friends. Who will always be steering for the right thing in life: John R. Rickford." In 1982, Ervin completed a bachelor's degree in Sociology at Oakes College, UCSC, where Herman Blake was the founding provost. They co-authored a remarkable paper in 2008 about his experience.[14] He was among the first Daufuskie students to complete an undergraduate degree, and three of his four children now have college degrees, too.

Two days before we left Daufuskie, I staged a "People Get Ready" program of poetry, song and dance at the Cooper River Church. It was designed to bridge the gap between the old and young (about 10 adults and 26 children participated), to combine the sacred and the secular, darkness and light, tears and laughter, and to showcase some of the black poetry and song I had been introducing them to both in the classroom and at weekly youth meetings.

The program included prayers and scripture readings by deacons Joseph Grant, Isaiah Graves, and Walter Simmons, songs by Edna Bryan, Frances Jones and Agnes Simmons and various poems, all by black poets, and all but one read by children. The poems included W.E.B. DuBois' "Song of the Smoke," read by Alfred Smith, which begins:

I am the Smoke King
I am black! …

And Countee Cullen's "Epitaph for my Grandmother," read by Sallie Ann Robinson:[15]

This lovely flower fell to seed;
Work gently, sun and rain;
She held it as her dying creed
That she would grow again.

And Langston Hughes' "Dream Boogie," read by Ervin Simmons:

Good morning, daddy!
Ain't you heard
The boogie-woogie rumble
Of a dream deferred? …

During part 3 of the program, the "Finale," Frank and I showed slides of the trip to Washington D.C., which everyone was eager to see, and after some responses and remarks, Sarah Grant, the oldest resident of the island, and the woman who as a midwife, had helped to deliver many of them, sang, "Thank you, Jesus!"

The next day, Frank and I went around the island saying goodbye to everyone, for we were flying back to California the next day. But we also went to our last praise meeting, where, moved by the deacon's prayer and songs like "Pass me Not O Gentle Savior," I fell on my knees to pray out loud, weeping profusely and shaking all over as if possessed by the Holy Spirit. My brothers and sisters, who at first seemed so far away, were now so near and strong behind me: "That's allright." "Have mercy." Purged and weary, I sat with my head in my hands and Miss Jones started to sing "Why not Now?" Everybody said it was a wonderful prayer meeting, and there was much crying and laughing as we sang and hugged and shook each other's hands. Daufuskie had been a cathartic and unforgettable experience.

Goodbyes that day and the next morning were tough. The ones my diary helps me recall include seven-year-old Eleanor, who asked for my address so she could write me, although she could barely write the alphabet. Frank assures her there'll be more students in September, and she asks, "Will they be white or colored?" And Richmond Wiley, so distinctive in so many ways, who says, "You guys put 'fuskie in de light" and wipes his eyes and hurries inside. Flossie Robinson says, "We sure will hate to see you go. You is de best two yet. I swear we sure will hate to see you go." Goodbye to Donkey and Estella Hamilton, perhaps the poorest couple, financially, but richest, culturally, that we met. We are overwhelmed by their offer of $1.35 to split between us. And Miss Jones, after talking with us about the program, just sits and broods as we pack that night. Goodbye is the loneliest word I know.

At the landing in the morning, more goodbyes, including Mr. and Mrs. Varney, who wished me the very best—incredibly, she, of the "niggers and jackasses" comment, has tears in her eyes. It reminds me of Frieda Mitchell telling *The New York Times* in 2008 that she asked Martin Luther King Jr. on one of his visits, "How can you tell me to love people who treat me as if I were not human?" King told her to love the image of God in every person, regardless of their outward actions. Mitchell remembered that for the rest of her life.[16]

Finally, I should say that in this blackest part of America, I learned that loving blackness and black people absolutely did not mean that I could not like and even love white people. Over the ten weeks I was on the Sea Islands, my fellow California boy, Frank Smith, and I got on each other's nerves from time to time, as people living that closely together inevitably do. But half a century later, this white guy is one of the closest friends from my college days. As Ervin Simmons told me in an email on August 12, 2020, "You and Frank are still profound in my life." Hell, we're still profound in *each other's* lives. And we'll always be.

Notes

1 John Szwed, Yale.
2 See Juanita Jackson, Sabra Slaughter and J. Herman Blake. 1974. The Sea Islands as a Cultural Resource, *The Black Scholar* 5.6: 32–39, and Patricia Jones-Jackson.

1987. *When Roots Die: Endangered Traditions on the Sea Islands.* Athens, Georgia and London: U of Georgia Press.
3 Conroy, Pat. 1972. *The Water is Wide.* Boston: Hougton-Mifflin, p. 109.
4 Conroy, Pat. 1972. *The Water is Wide.* Boston: Houghton Mifflin, p. 115.
5 Conroy, Pat. 1972. *The Water is Wide.* Boston: Houghton Mifflin, p. 250.
6 Miguel Barnet. 1968. *Autobiography of a Runaway Slave.* New York: Pantheon Books.
7 Rickford, John R. 2006. "African American Vernacular English: Roots and branches." In Janina Brutt-Griffler and Catherine Evans Davies, eds., *English and Ethnicity.* New York: Palgrave Macmillan, pp. 259–276.
8 See Patricia Jones-Jackson. 1987. *When Roots Die: Endangered Traditions on the Sea Islands.* Athens, GA: U of Georgia Press; and Laura Tanna. 1988. *Jamaican Folk Tales and Oral Histories.* World Mosaic Press.
9 See Rickford, John R. 1986. "Riddling and lying: Participation and Performance." In Joshua A Fishman, ed., *The Fergusonian Impact, vol. 2: Sociolinguistics and the Sociology of Language.* Mouton: The Hague, p. 271
10 Samuel Dyssli, quote in Peter Wood. 1974. *Black Majority.* New York: Alfred A. Knopf, p. 132.
11 https://scafricanamerican.com/honorees/frieda-mitchell/.
12 Septima Clark was honored by having a new $1 coin minted for her by the U.S. Mint in February 2021: https://www.postandcourier.com/news/us-mint-produces-collectible-coin-honoring-south-carolina-educator-activist-septima-clark/article_fa4c3fd0-6191-11eb-9284-17b193960841.html
13 From a bio in the Stanford Martin Luther King, Jr. Research and Education Institute. https://kinginstitute.stanford.edu/encyclopedia/clark-septima-poinsette
14 Blake, J. Herman and Ervin R. Simmons. 2008. "A Daufuskie Island Lad in an Academic Community: An Extraordinary Journey of Personal Transformation." *Journal of College and Character* X.1: 14.
15 See her *Gullah Home Cooking the Daufuskie Way.* 2003. University of North Carolina Press, and other books.
16 Reported in *The Beaufort Gazette* https://www.islandpacket.com/news/local/community/beaufort-news/article126080574.html

13 Rosa Parks at Stanford

In February 1990, we brought Rosa Parks to Stanford. She was the first of two civil rights icons I would get to meet and record in 1990, the other being Dennis Brutus of South Africa.

The idea to invite Rosa Parks originally came from Matthew McLeod, one of the three student Resident Assistants (Eric Loh and Ashley Ryan were the others) which whom Angela and I worked as Resident Fellows in Arroyo House, one of the Stanford dormitories. At first, I thought it was a pipe dream—she was too legendary a figure, unlikely to have the time to visit us, and probably costing more than the modest annual budget a 90-student dorm received from Residential Education for programming. But we wrote her assistant Elaine Steele in November 1989, and to our surprise, it turned out that Rosa Parks was already planning to be in California in February and was willing to add Stanford to her itinerary.

The next challenge was raising the money for the visit, which we achieved by writing the residence staff of other dormitories, the Associated Students of Stanford University, the Undergraduate Scholars Program, Residential Education and other sources. Then began the planning for the visit itself.

In the end we decided on three main events:

1. A press conference in the morning of Sunday February 18, shortly after Rosa Parks arrived.
2. A reception in the evening of February 18, for all Arroyo residents and all donors.
3. A "Thank you Rosa Parks" program in Memorial Auditorium on Monday February 19 (Presidents' Day holiday).

As it turned out, the press conference provided the best opportunity to hear from Mrs. Parks about her refusal to give up her seat in the "Colored" section of a bus in 1955, the historic event that sparked the Montgomery, Alabama bus boycott, brought the Rev. Martin Luther King Jr. to national attention and energized the Civil Rights movement.

When she arrived Sunday morning, Mrs. Parks spent about half an hour in our Residence Fellow (RF) cottage next to the dormitory, enjoying a cup of tea, relaxing, talking with each of our children, Shiyama, Russell, Anakela and Luke,

DOI: 10.4324/9781003204305-13

Figure 13.1 At Arroyo House reception for Rosa Parks, Stanford, February 18, 1990. Seated: Rosa Parks. Standing: L to R: John R. Rickford, Angela Rickford, Eric Loh, Ashley Ryan, Matt McLeod, Elaine Steele (asst. to Mrs. Parks).

and taking photos with them. Given that she had no children of her own, I was impressed by the ease with which she interacted with our adolescents, aged 16, 14 and 12 at the time, and played with our youngest, Luke, who was only 5. In fact, he grabbed some toys and jumped into her lap. Angela moved to take him out of her lap, but Rosa Parks insisted, "Leave him alone," apparently enjoying it all. I had to pinch myself to believe that this huge figure in the Civil Rights Movement was actually in our humble RF apartment, mingling so freely with my family. The fact that she had been active with the *youth* of the NAACP, as I learned in the press conference half an hour later, came as no surprise.

Most people did not know that Rosa Parks loved young people, as we discovered on this visit. But Douglas Brinkley wrote about this in his 2000 biography, finding evidence for it in her involvement with the Youth Group:[1]

> In 1949, she became adviser to the informal NAACP Youth Group that grew into the organization's official Youth Council in 1953. Childless and far from her nieces and nephews in Detroit, she adopted her neighborhood's youngsters as her own, serving as a sort of special aunt or guidance counselor. Never did Parks seem happier or more at ease than when reading passages from Uncle Tom's Cabin to a gaggle of wide-eyed ten-year-olds or organizing spelling bees at the local church for ambitious high schoolers ... As E.D. Nixon later recalled: "Kids just love Mrs. Parks to death."

The press conference that took place in the Arroyo lounge adjacent to our cottage attracted less than a dozen reporters from local newspapers. But for those who came, it was invaluable. Mrs. Parks, 77 years old at the time, had a lucid memory, and shared with us several details about segregation on the buses that we had not known before.

Mrs. Parks first noted that although born in Tuskegee, Alabama (February 4, 1913), she began school in a rural area nearby in Montgomery County:

> And we lived under complete legal and social, racial segregation. That was considered the way of life. Even though we were considered free. But we still were not free to get the proper education and the employment that would give us a real living wage. And all parts of our lives were completely segregated based on the signs that said either "white only." Or some said "colored." It was always a very oppressive and humiliating way of life.

She went on to say that at the time she was arrested on the bus, December 1, 1955,

> I was on my way home from work, boarded a bus, not with the intention of getting arrested, but only to go home and take care of … the workshop for the NAACP Youth Council, the National Association for the Advancement of Colored People, because I was the senior advisor. I was also the secretary of the senior branch of the NAACP and we were preparing to get out the written notices for the coming up election. So December was going to be a very, very busy month for me, even if I had not been arrested. I was working as a tailor's assistant in a downtown department store, and of course work was always heavy and people are shopping for their Christmas, uh, clothing.

Note first of all that she didn't give up her seat because she was "tired," as often suggested. She was politically active in the NAACP, especially its Youth Council, which she helped to found. She and her husband Raymond had been increasingly sickened by the rapes and murders of black women by white men, and by the false accusations of rape of white women that were lodged against black men (e.g. The Scottsboro Boys of 1931), and had fought to get justice in both kinds of cases.[2] And although she didn't mention that or the fact that she had gone to a 1955 workshop in the Highlander Folk School in Tennessee—a place that was a "site of leadership training for southern civil rights activists," run by Septima Clark (see Chapter 12), Esau Jenkins and Bernice Robinson,[3] it is clear that she was politically conscious, outraged by social injustice and prepared to challenge segregation if provoked.

When Rosa Parks boarded the bus on that fateful day in 1955, she noticed that the driver was the same one who had evicted her in 1943 or so for refusing to leave the bus after she had paid her fare and re-enter the bus from the back entrance, rather than walking to the back through the white section. That was one of several provocations, beyond segregated seating itself, that black passengers were forced to endure, depending on the whims of individual drivers.

For instance, bus drivers would often drive off just as black people were about to board the bus from the back, making them run to catch up with it. The driver might do it again, having a laugh at black people's expense. The youth with whom she worked also told her that drivers sometimes

> wouldn't pick them up, or if they were on the bus wouldn't let them off at the stop that they wanted to get off, and they took them somewhere [sometimes ten to twelve blocks further, according to Raymond Parks[4]] and they'd have to walk back. These abuses only increased their anger and frustration at their second-class status.

On this particular day, Rosa Parks finally felt she had had enough. She was seated in the first row of the black section of the bus, but:

> a few white people loaded the bus and finished filling up the seats in the very front, and … I didn't notice that there was a man standing, and when the driver noticed him standing, he wanted the four of us [in the black section, which could be moved back to accommodate white passengers if needed] to stand up for this man to have a seat. In keeping with racial segregation, there would be three vacant seats … and we would have to vacate. And then four people would be standing or either leaving the bus. And I chose to not stand up after the other three reluctantly did so. And that was when he told me that if I didn't stand, he was going to have me arrested. And I agreed with him that that's what he should do—so he *may* do that. And he did have two police-men to come on the bus and place me under arrest. And I was taken to jail … The evening was just—had gone completely out of what I had planned. But I WAS willing to face whatever consequences I had to, to let it be known that I did not feel I was being treated fairly as a passenger and a person. And I did not see where, as he said, "Y'all make it light on, light on yourselves and let me have those seats." I couldn't see where it was making light on any of us to comply with that type of treatment.

After being fingerprinted and bailed out, Rosa Parks returned to her home "to dis-cuss … whether it would be feasible at all for me to use my arrest as a test case to challenge racial segregation on the buses. So my family and me agreed that we would do whatever was necessary … to end racial segregation on the buses by law."

One of the questions raised at the press conference was whether "Claudette Colvin, the 15-year-old who was arrested on March 2nd, 1955 for refusing to give up HER seat in the back of the bus, was … a member of the NAACP Youth Council." Also why her case, nine months earlier than Rosa Parks', was not con-sidered the first significant challenge to racial segregation. Rosa Parks said that she knew Claudette's family, including her great-grandfather and her mother, but not Claudette, who joined Parks' Youth Council *after* her arrest. She said that she was very upset about the arrest and police manhandling of this "child." However, the judge at Colvin's May 6, 1955 trial dropped the charge of violating the seg-regation law, as Parks noted, and charged her only with resisting arrest. So it was not a good case for challenging the segregation law.

There were other factors too, that made Rosa Parks a better candidate to challenge segregation than Colvin, although Parks continued to support Colvin even when others (like E. D. Nixon, President of the Birmingham NAACP) did not. There was, for instance, the fact that as a teenager, who later became pregnant, Claudette was considered a weaker candidate for the first serious challenge to segregation than the older, better known Rosa Parks. Jo Ann Robinson, a major figure in the Montgomery Bus Boycott, put it this way:[5] "Mrs. Parks was a medium-sized, cultured mulatto woman, a civic and religious worker; quiet, unassuming, and pleasant in manner and appearance; dignified and reserved; of high morals and a strong character."

A similar point recurs in Brinkley's biography of Parks,[6] for instance on page 22, in the fact that "one of her maternal great grandfathers, James Percival ... was a white Scotch Irishman" (shades of my maternal great-grandfather, a Scotsman named Henry Wilson), and on the same page, that "Early on Rosa McCauley [Rosa Parks' maiden name] learned she was not a full Negro, but of mixed blood, a mulatto." On page 38, the author notes that her grandfather was "so light-skinned that he was often mistaken for Caucasian," and that she was initially uninterested in the advances of Raymond Parks, who would later become her husband, "because she had 'an aversion' to light-skinned blacks." Finally, on pages 48–51 Brinkley discusses her admiration for Walter Francis White, executive secretary of the NAACP responsible for many challenges to racial segregation. Born an enslaved person, he was "extremely light-skinned" and was often mistaken for white. But she "admired ... Walter White for choosing not to pass as white, for not being ashamed to pass as Negro."

Mrs. Parks also talked about the mass meeting that was held in the Holt Street Baptist Church on the day of her trial, December 5. It attracted 15,000 people, although the church would hold only 5,000, the others following the proceedings on loudspeakers outdoors. Black people, honoring her heroic stand, had already stayed off the buses in large numbers, and

> when the vote was put before the group of the action to take, without any prompting, they unanimously voted to stay off the buses until changes were made for the better, and we would no longer have to be mistreated or arrested on the buses because of the seating.

This was the start of the Montgomery Bus Boycott, and at that meeting, Rev. Martin Luther King Jr., relatively unknown up to that point, was chosen as the Chairman and spokesperson for the Montgomery Improvement Association that organized the Boycott.

Another question that was asked, by Tim Thomas of the *Unity* newspaper in Oakland, was why had men gotten a lot of the glory in the aftermath of Mrs. Parks defiant action: "What about the role of women, black women in particular, in the Civil Rights Movement?" Mrs. Parks remarked they *were* active in the movement, that the majority were young girls and women:

With the Montgomery bus protest itself, even though the spokesperson was a man, Dr. King and other members of the clergy ... women did a lot of work. The leaflets that were prepared, that were sent out, over the city about my arrest, [were done by] Miss Jo Ann Robinson who was on the faculty of the Alabama State College at that time. And there were several who worked and she stayed up all night and I guess others did too.

This accords with the report of Jo Ann Robinson herself.[7] Not only did *she* have the idea of writing and duplicating thousands of pamphlets, but after staying up all night, she called various members of the Women's Political Council and got them to assist in the distribution of "tens of thousands of leaflets" to numerous sites around the city—crucial to the success of the Montgomery Bus Boycott on Monday, the day of Rosa Parks' trial. This was a far cry from the chauvinism that E. D. Nixon had once expressed, in saying that "Women don't need to be nowhere but in the kitchen."[8] Septima Clark, mentioned in the Sea Island chapter, had similarly expressed the view that most men in the Southern Christian Leadership Conference "didn't respect women too much." She singled out the Rev. Martin Luther King Jr., as being different, as believing that "black women had a place in the movement."[9]

Another question that was asked, by Mario Dianda of the *Peninsula Times Tribune*, was about the similarities and differences Rosa Parks saw between what was happening in the U.S. in the fifties, and what was happening in South Africa in 1990. The major difference Mrs. Parks saw was that in the U.S., "We were the minority, and in South Africa, the blacks were always in the majority being ruled by some very oppressive whites." But she also saw similarities between black people struggling for the right to vote in the 1950s, and a similar struggle in 1990 in South Africa. Nelson Mandela had just been released from prison, she noted, but "They still do not have a vote – a free vote and they're still being killed and maimed by the policemen." It was not until April 1994 that blacks and non-whites first had the right to vote in a South African general election, electing Mandela President. It should be noted that in 1985 Rosa Parks took part in a protest in front of the South African embassy in Washington D.C. She held up a big sign proclaiming "Freedom, YES, Apartheid, NO."

I asked two questions. The first was whether she had had any second thoughts and whether other people had said anything to her after she refused to give up her seat and the bus driver went to get the cops. Her reply was that she had no second thoughts at all, clarifying that the time had come to stand up to discrimination:

Well, no one approached me or said anything to me at all. There were some ... conversations between a few people, and a number of blacks did get off the bus. And some of them asked—when the driver was standing in the front door of the bus, did ask—they did ask him for a transfer. *But I didn't have any second thoughts or wasn't hesitant at all, about taking the stand that I did.*

My second question was the final question of day. Noting that one child had equated her with Abraham Lincoln, I wondered about how her teachers had dealt with the paradox of extolling freedom on the one hand and defending slavery and segregation on the other. In her answer, she first noted that her mother "was a teacher in the rural schools, and I don't remember her ever justifying segregation in any way–and I was one of her students for a while. But she believed in freedom and equality and justice for all people."

When she went to the Montgomery Industrial School for Girls from the age of 11, however, the principal and faculty were all white women from the North, but all the 250 or 300 students were black. Their primary focus was on "the fundamentals of education and discipline … domestic science, geography and some history" without "any very serious and deep discussions on the history and heritage of blacks." However, she did remember one particular point made by the principal, Miss Alice White:

> The only thing I can remember is Miss White saying once when they were discussing Africa, was that in a way slavery was a blessing because it helped to civilize us and make us who were former, I mean who were descendants of slaves, intelligent, to be in the United States, and getting the education. And I'm sure she meant well [everyone laughs], but she herself didn't know, she herself didn't know anything about the, the dawn of civilization being in Egypt, and Africa and all that.

What was striking about her answer was not only that she rejected Miss White's rationalization about the benefits of slavery, but also that she embraced the alternative analysis, that civilization had originated in Egypt and Africa. Rosa Parks was clearly *au courant* with modern scholarship.

The reception for Mrs. Parks on the evening of February 18 was a wonderful celebratory affair, allowing students from Arroyo, and faculty and staff from all the organizations who had contributed to the cost of her visit, to meet her in person and to have their Rosa Parks postcards autographed. The photo and the autographed illustration below are from that reception.

The grand event of Mrs. Parks' visit, however, was to be the February 19, 1990 (Presidents' Day) session in Memorial Auditorium. Entitled, "Thank You, Sister Rosa Parks," it provided an opportunity for over 1,700 people to see this legendary figure. It certainly allowed us to celebrate her achievements, as singers from the Stanford Gospel Choir sang, and the KS Rappers (including its Dyper Posse, from East Palo Alto) danced, while the words of the 1989 song "Sister Rosa" by the Neville Brothers blared from the auditoriums' voluminous loudspeakers:

> December 1, 1955
> Our freedom movement came alive
> And because of Sister Rosa, you know
> We don't ride on the back of the bus no more …
> Thank you, Miss Rosa, you are the spark
> That started our freedom movement
> Thank you, Sister Rosa Parks

Figure 13.2 Illustration of Rosa Parks, autographed to "The Rickford Family" 2/18/90.

In my introductory speech, I first welcomed Mrs. Rosa Parks, noting that she honored us with her presence:

> You are a part of history, and this day and place will become a part of the personal history and family lore of each of us, to be passed on to **our** children and grandchildren. "Rosa Parks?" we'll say, "Yeah I know her! I remember that day back in 1990, when I saw and heard her **myself**. Thank you, Sister Rosa Parks!

I then went on to explain *why* this gracious woman, who had celebrated her 77th birthday two weeks earlier, deserved three cheers:

> The first cheer is for her role as the mother of the modern Civil Rights movement in Americas, which led to significant strides towards equal opportunity and justice for African Americans …

My second cheer [is because] her defiance on that bus, and her work in the NAACP before and after her arrest, unite her with people everywhere who risk ridicule and danger to life and limb in their struggles for equal opportunity and justice. We think immediately of the students in Tiananmen Square in China, of Walter Rodney in Guyana, ... of Nelson Mandela in South Africa and many others whose names we will never know.

My third and final cheer is for the model Mrs. Parks provides to each of us, in our individual lives, when we see or hear wrong things, and in the deep recesses of our minds struggle with the decision of whether to speak out against them or keep silent, and anonymous, and unthreatened ... For while few of us will be giants like Martin Luther King Jr and Nelson Mandela, we will **all** have opportunities to take a stand at some points in our lives ... As we walk the tightrope of indecision about whether to act in cases like these, the quiet example of Mrs. Parks can help us calm the butterflies in our stomachs, and do the right thing. ...

And now, please join me in three cheers for Mrs Parks!

I don't have copies of the remarks of the other speakers that day. But they were too many, and each of them, like the KS Rappers and me too, went on longer than they should have. Speakers included Rachel Bagby from the King Papers Project, History Professor Kennell Jackson, Shana Bhadbury, Eric Loh, Matt McLeod and Jim Lyons, Dean of Student Affairs.

By the time Rosa Parks went to the podium, where I was hoping for an address of 15 to 30 minutes recapitulating the key points about her 1955 arrest similar to what she had given us at the press conference the day before, she spoke for only about five minutes. She said she was glad she was still able to "spread the word" and would continue to do so, regardless of what obstacles she faced, and she hoped that "I can always be a person who is strong enough and spiritual enough to have faith and to carry the message wherever I am."[10] She also noted that it was important to encourage young people to excel, and that our program had great potential for "carrying out the quest for freedom and equality the world over."[11]

However, explaining that she had a plane to catch, she said that she might tell us more about the historic events that preceded and followed her refusal to yield her seat on the bus when she came back to visit us again. Then she sat down. Flabbergasted, especially because we could easily have arranged for a later flight if we had known this was a problem, I brought the program to a close. Rosa Parks died on October 24, 2005. Neither we nor anyone else was ever able to bring her to Stanford again.

We received many thanks and commendations for the event, including favorable reports from many of the local newspapers, and a letter from Stanford's president, Don Kennedy, who said that the "Thank You Rosa Parks event has drawn enthusiastic praise from everyone to whom I have talked. And those who seem most knowledgeable about the event have told me that you and the Arroyans provided really extraordinary Leadership." We also got a short note from a local person, Emily Berman, who said, "I had the good fortune to attend the Rosa Parks program this past Monday with my 2 children. Thank you so much for publicizing it in the *Mercury News*." But we also received a complaint from Steven Fama of San Francisco who was disappointed by the brevity of Mrs. Parks' remarks.

To some extent the shortcomings of that huge program reminded me of the time I attempted to organize a big inter-high school event in 1966 but forgot to ensure that I had a take-up reel for the film that was supposed to be the main activity. (See Chapter 6.) That event had the fortunate result that it introduced me to Angela, my future wife. There were certainly plusses to this much more consequential event at Stanford two dozen years later, among which was the rare opportunity it gave hundreds to see and hear and celebrate Rosa Parks, a giant of a historical figure. But the minuses were important for me to learn from. We should have *started* the program with her, we should have put fewer items on the agenda, regardless of the ardor with which people clamored to be included and we should have given them shorter, stricter speaking and performance times.

Figure 13.3 Actress Adilah Barnes, Angela and me outside the Rosa Parks African American Theme House, Stevenson College, the University of California, Santa Cruz, April 28, 2019.

In any case, we came to value the initial press conference rather than the Memorial Auditorium program as the most important and revealing part of Rosa Parks' visit. We were happy that it was covered in the local newspapers,[12] and are delighted that a recording (with a transcript) of that 45-minute event is available through the Stanford library for everyone to hear and enjoy (https://purl.stanford .edu/fn571cx4601). Hopefully it will remain so long after we have passed on.

About 20 years after Rosa Parks came to Stanford, my alma mater, the University of California, Santa Cruz created a special house to honor her: the Rosa Parks African American Theme House.[13] What's more, it's in Stevenson College, the college I attended. It's Casa Septima, the Seventh House, and with its striking red, black and green colors[14] (the colors of the Pan-African Flag that "represent people of the African Diaspora and … symbolize black liberation"[15]) it differs strikingly from the other Stevenson houses around it. In 2019 Adilah Barnes (actress and UCSC/Cowell College alumna), Angela and I visited and took some pictures in front of it.

Notes

1 Douglas Brinkley. *Rosa Parks: A Life*. New York: Penguin, p. 71.
2 Jeanne Theoharris. 2013. *The Rebellious Life of Mrs. Rosa Parks*. Boston, MA: Beacon Press, chapters 1 and 2.
3 https://kinginstitute.stanford.edu/encyclopedia/highlander-folk-school
4 Quoted in Jeanne Theoharris. 2013. *The Rebellious Life of Mrs. Rosa Parks*. Boston, MA: Beacon Press, p. 113.
5 From an account by Jo Ann Robinson in David J. Garrow, ed. 1957. *The Montgomery Bus Boycott and the Women Who Made It: The Memoir of Jo Ann Gibson Robinson*. U of Tennessee Press. Reprinted in Manning Marable and Leith Mullins, eds. 2000. *Let Nobody Turn Us Around: An African American Anthology*. Rowman & Littlefield, p. 379.
6 Douglas Brinkley. *Rosa Parks: A Life*. New York: Penguin, pp. 22, 38, 48–51.
7 "Excerpts from Jo Ann Robinson's account of the Boycott" in Manning Marable and Leith Mullins, eds. 2000. *Let Nobody Turn Us Around: An African American Anthology*. Rowman & Littlefield, pp. 378–385.
8 Douglas Brinkley. *Rosa Parks: A Life*. New York: Penguin, p. 51.
9 From a bio in the Stanford Martin Luther King, Jr. Research and Education Institute. https://kinginstitute.stanford.edu/encyclopedia/clark-septima-poinsette
10 Mary Ann Seawell, "Rosa Parks, 77, still 'spreads the word'." *Stanford Report*, Feb, 21, 1990.
11 Jenna Johnson, "Parks recalls fight for freedom." *The Stanford Daily*, Feb 20, 1990.
12 Mario Danda, "Parks recalls historic act of defiance." *Peninsula Times Tribune* Feb 19, 1990, B-1, B-3.
13 https://news.ucsc.edu/2013/02/rpaath.html
14 https://housing.ucsc.edu/rpaath/
15 https://www.csusm.edu/bsc/pan-afflag.html

14 Stanford in Oxford—David Dabydeen and Dennis Brutus

In the summer of 1990 I took my first trip to England, the land I had been taught to regard as the colonial "mother country." The visit brought me closer to the lines of empire and domination that help define my family heritage. The occasion was an eight-week study abroad program at the Stanford Overseas Center in Oxford. Stanford Professor David Abernethy and I had created the program, on the theme "Britain in the Third World: The Third World in Britain."

The idea was to use coursework, guest lectures and field trips to help students explore three historically significant migrations of peoples: from Britain to the rest of the world as the Empire expanded (17–19th c.); from Africa and Asia to the Americas, especially the Caribbean—to serve the economic needs of British colonies (17th–19th c.); and from Britain's colonies and former colonies, part of the "Third World," to Britain itself (1940s to the present). The program attracted the most ethnically diverse groups of students (African Americans, East Indians and Indo-Americans, other Asians as well as whites) the Stanford in Oxford program had ever seen. David Abernethy taught a course on "Colonialism and Nationalism," and I taught a course on "English Transplanted, English Transformed: English Pidgins and Creoles." Ultimately, the Oxford program proved as formative for me as it did for many of our students.

The trip led to reconnections with people I hadn't seen for years, and I learned much about the British colonizing experience that had shaped both my forebears and myself. The field trips were especially illuminating. I remember standing outside the shipyards in Bristol—where many of the ships so crucial to colonial expansion and the slave trade were built—and thinking about their voyages to Africa to pick up enslaved persons, from there to the Caribbean and the US with their cargoes of terrified, uprooted human beings, consigned to lives of bondage and oppression, and back to Bristol, carrying colonial products like sugar and tobacco for the colonizers to profit from and enjoy. It boggled the mind and pained the soul.

Our visit to the Georgian House in Bristol was intense. Built around 1790 for John Pinney, a wealthy sugar merchant and slave plantation owner, the house included an exhibition about slavery and sugar plantations. Pinney owned several plantations on Nevis, in the Caribbean, enslaving about 275 people who produced sugar and rum to be shipped to Bristol and London. My paternal grandmother's

DOI: 10.4324/9781003204305-14

Figure 14.1 Students, faculty & staff from the Stanford in Oxford program, England, summer 1990. Prof. Abernethy & myself right front.

father, Harry Davis, came to Guyana with two brothers in the late 19th century from St. Kitts/Nevis after their father died. He may well have been a descendant of one of the enslaved persons who toiled on Pinney's plantations to make Pinney one of the wealthiest people in Bristol.

But it was the program's guest lecturers that made the greatest impact on me. One of these, Guyanese writer **David Dabydeen**, took me back to my youth and my Guyanese upbringing. Dabydeen is an Indo-Guyanese who migrated to England at the age of 13. I taught him English/Literature for a year when he was about 12. At the time I was a junior master at Queen's College, the same high school I'd attended before leaving for university, an unusual arrangement. Dabydeen impressed me even then as a gifted writer, and I confess that one of his short stories was so stunning that I doubted he had written it himself. As I joked with him about it decades later, "I didn't know you would turn out to be David Dabydeen, the famous scholar and writer!"

By 1990, when he participated in our Stanford in Oxford program, Dabydeen was Director of the Center for Caribbean Studies at the University of Warwick. He'd already published *Slave Song* (1984), his first collection of poetry, which won the Commonwealth Poetry Prize, and *Coolie Odyssey* (1988). He'd also written several books on Caribbean and/or Black British literature, including *A Reader's Guide to West Indian and Black British Literature* (1987*),* the focus of his four-week course in our summer program.

Figure 14.2 David Dabydeen 1955-. (Courtesy University of Warwick, Press and Media Relations).

Dabydeen's *Slave Song* dealt with African enslaved people and East Indian indentured laborers, the two main groups of color in my ancestry. His "Song of the Creole Gang Women," dealing with descendants of East Indian laborers (his ancestors), captures many of the questions of power that have shaped my identity and research. This excerpt is from the lamentations of one of the women featured in the poem.

First verse of "Song of the Creole Gang Women" by David Dabydeen

1st Woman
Wuk, nuttin bu wuk
Maan, noon and night nuttin bu wuk
Booker own me patacake
Booker own me pickni.
Pain, nuttin bu pain
Waan million tous'ne acre cane.
O since me baan—juk! juk! juk! juk! juk!
So sun in me eye like taan
So Booker saach deep in me flesh

Kase Booker own me rass
An Booker own me cutlass—
Bu me dun cuss … Gaad let me na cuss no mo!
English gloss (JRR) of first verse of "Song of the Creole Gang Women"
Work, nothing but work
Morning, noon and night nothing but work
Booker owns my vagina
Booker owns my child/children.
Pain, nothing but pain.
One million thousand acres of cane.
O since I was born—jab! jab! jab! jab! jab!
That's how the sun is like thorns in my eye
That's how Bookers searches deep in my flesh
Because Booker owns my ass
And Booker owns my cutlass [machete]--
But I'm done cursing … God don't let me curse anymore!

This poem, like others in *Slave Song*, is written in Guyanese Creole English. It shows how English was transformed into pidgin and creole varieties when transported to Africa, the Caribbean and elsewhere, a process that mirrors my own identity transformation as I migrated to the US.

The poem bewails the endlessness and pain of the work of the sugar-estate laborer. It recalls the eloquent words (down to the endless *cutlass* or machete) I recorded from Granny, a 58-year-old retired East Indian sugar cane field worker, when doing field research in Cane Walk, Guyana in the 1970s. Here is an excerpt from that recording:[1]

Somtaim yuh wuk, wuk, how de wuk
ha-haard ya, how de wuk soo hard, yuhz throw dung yuhself a de
bank an yuh se, "Laad, ah wen dis kutlis ah go kum out a me
aan? E bettuh me dead, befo me ah live!"
English gloss (JRR)
Sometimes you work and work, because the work
is har-a-ard here. The work is so hard you throw yourself down on the
ground and say, "Lord, when will this cutlass come out of my
hand? It's better for me to die, than live like this!"

Returning to Dabydeen's poem, note the reference to "Bookers," the conglomerate of sugar estates and related industries (sugar cane production, engineering, shipping, shopkeeping, spirits) that was started by Josiah, George and Richard Booker in 1833. This consortium dominated the lives of laborers. In 1976 the company was nationalized and became the Guyana Sugar Corporation. Both Enmore and Albion, the plantations on which my white great grandparents worked, as engineer and manager respectively, were Booker plantations.

My paternal great grandmother Parvadi, an indentured servant, would have been subject to the sexual desire of the Bookers manager,[2] Walter Howell

Rickford, without the legitimizing benefit of marriage or full responsibility for any children that resulted. Some have argued that for "allowing" my paternal grandfather Donald Howell and his brother Geoffrey Howell to keep the Rickford name, and for covering the cost of their secondary education, Walter Howell deserves credit. Maybe. But that is a fraction of the more substantial credit that belongs to Parvadi and her East Indian husband for raising and caring for those two Rickford sons, day in and day out along with their joint daughter Alice Ann Mariaye [Marimutha].

What of my Scottish Bookers ancestor who worked at the Enmore plantation, Henry Wilson? The name of the woman who bore two children for him—my maternal grandmother Rosina Wilson (1867–1953), and her sister Margaret— is unknown. This mystery woman, a colored woman from Barbados, does not appear to have worked on a Booker's plantation. But our efforts to find a marriage certificate for Henry Wilson, or a birth certificate or christening record for Rosina or Margaret that would reveal *her* name, have been unsuccessful, despite the fact that we've devoted significant time and expense to the enterprise. We've begun to speculate that Henry Wilson may *never* have married her, leaving her in the same boat as Parvadi. To grant her the dignity and respect she deserves, I have given her the pseudonym Cleopatra.

There is a third Booker's executive in our family history, Michael Norsworthy, who married my eldest sister, June, in 1961 (see Figure 4.1). That was a different time and milieu, or course, than the 19th century in which Henry Wilson and Walter Howell Rickford operated. Michael, unlike the other Bookers men in our lineage, did the right thing, and in fact he has been helpful to me in my efforts to get more information about Henry Wilson and our elusive great grandmother of color. He is writing an autobiography that will discuss, among other things, his work with Bookers in Guyana and around the world.

Another influential figure who talked to us during the Summer 1990 Stanford in Oxford program was the poet **Dennis Brutus** of South Africa. He first gave a guest lecture to our group. But he also did a recorded interview recapitulating some of the key points of that lecture. Brutus's guest lecture introduced me to South Africa and its abhorrent system of racial oppression—apartheid. The interview I did with him after his lecture was even more wrenching.

Brutus was a central figure in the anti-apartheid movement. He campaigned vigorously against racism in sports and was instrumental in getting South Africa banned from the Olympics from 1964 to 1992. He had also worked with Nelson Mandela and Walter Sisulu to call for a new constitution in 1961. For these and other activities, he'd been imprisoned in a cell on Robben Island next to Mandela. He is also regarded as one of Africa's most accomplished modern poets.

As if Brutus and his record were not daunting enough, 1990 was also a momentous *year*. In one of the most improbable events of recent history, Mandela had been freed from prison in South Africa on February 11, 1990 after serving 27 years of his life sentence. Characteristically, Brutus wrote a poem about Mandela's release in March 1990, which he shared with us at the Stanford Center in Oxford:

Figure 14.3 Dennis Brutus (1924–2009), speaking at Kresge auditorium, Stanford
        University, about "Apartheid: A Poet's Resistance," October 16, 1985
        (Courtesy: Stanford News Service).

Yes, Mandela, some of us
we admit embarrassedly
wept to see you step free
so erectly, so elegantly
shrug off the prisoned years,
a blanket cobwebbed of pain and grime.
behind, the island's seasand,
harsh, white and treacherous
ahead, jagged rocks and krantzes ["rocky ledges" in Afrikaans]
bladed crevices of racism and deceit.
In the salt island air
you swung your hammer, grimly, stoic
facing the dim path of interminable years,
now, vision blurred with tears
we see you step out to our salutes
bearing out burdens of hope and fears
and impress your radiance
on the grey morning air.

Brutus was also "colored" in South Africa's fine-grained racial system, somewhat
like I was in Guyana's racial system. And he had gained a distinction in English
from Fort Hare University (BA 1946), as I had in Sociolinguistics at UC Santa
Cruz in 1971. I also wrote poetry in high school and at university and began

Figure 14.4 Dennis Brutus, about to give his guest lecture to the Stanford in Oxford group, after my introduction, August 31, 1990.

UCSC with an initial focus in English literature. Even with several connections and similarities between us, his huge accomplishments and fame left me nervous.

My nervousness showed in how often I repeated myself when I first began the interview,[3] accompanied by Stanford undergraduate Aimee Allison, then an undergraduate in the Stanford at Oxford summer program.[4]

Brutus explained that after graduating from Fort Hare University, he began teaching at Paterson High School, the same school he'd attended as a youth. But in 1960, he "got into a lot of trouble." This was after the Sharpeville Massacre of March 21, 1960, when "people were becoming much more politically active." He became associated with the banned African National Congress (ANC), the main party fighting against apartheid. But he also was the President of the South African Non-Racial Olympic Committee (SANROC). As he explained:

DB: I was in continual confrontation with the white Olympic committee, which said they were for whites only. And in fact, my forming a Non-Racial Olympic Committee was a scandal. Because they said, "Look, we are the Olympic committee. And you can't have another Olympic Committee." And I said, "Well, too bad. If you will admit blacks, fine. But if you're not gonna admit blacks, we're gonna have to form our own Olympic Committee." (JRR: Right.) Yeah. So here we were, forming a Non-Racial Olympic Committee in opposition to the racial Olympic committee. Of course, it got me into trouble, as a teacher, working for a government school, I got several warnings that I had to stop my political activity. And I continued, and eventually I was dismissed. It was inevitable.

At the same time, he was asked by Walter Sisulu and Nelson Mandela to organize a convention of the colored section of the population, parallel to the African section and the Asian section, to seek a new constitution in South Africa. He did organize a convention in Malmesbury, Cape Town, but it became a crime for him to attend *any* meetings. When he defiantly went to a SANROC meeting, in May of 1963, he was arrested by the South African Secret Police. He was released on bail, but he was confined to Johannesburg, and was under house arrest. Defiant still, he tried to attend the 1963 meeting of the International Olympic Committee held in Baden-Baden, Germany, getting there via Swaziland and Mozambique. However, officials in Mozambique, then under Portuguese rule, arrested him and returned him to the South African Secret Police.

Then follows some of the grimmest parts of his interview, which reveal the barbarity of the South African police:

DB: And they were there in plain clothes, but they showed me their guns, under their armpits. The next day they took me to Johannesburg, and they said, "Well, we're not gonna handcuff you, because we hope you try to escape. This will give us an excuse to kill you." So, there was no handcuff. Well, notwithstanding that, because I was back in South Africa, and nobody was aware that I was back, I decided to make a second escape attempt. In Johannesburg, about 5 o'clock in the afternoon, as we pulled up at the police station where I was going to be jailed, … McClain Square. And so I made a second dash, for safety, freedom, assuming they wouldn't shoot in the crowd—

JRR: Right.

DB: —at five o'clock in the afternoon. *I was wrong.* And I was shot in the back, at close range. Bullet entered my back, came out of my chest. And I kept running, for a while. Then stopped. And then the guy who shot me, his name was Helberg, an elderly gentleman with grey hair, he came up to me, and I said, "Hey, I've been shot!"

And he said, "I know. I shot you."

But the assumption that the police wouldn't shoot at him in a crowd was wrong. After the Sharpeville Massacre of 1960, where police shot into a crowd of about 7,000 protestors, killing 69 and injuring another 180, there could be no question about the ruthlessness of the South African police.

Luckily for Brutus, the bullet just missed his heart. He lay on the ground in a pool of blood, with a collapsed lung, using a handkerchief to plug the hole in his chest. When someone called for an ambulance, insult was added to injury:

DB: So the ambulance turns up, and they get out, they take out their stretcher, and come over to me. And they take a look at me, they take their stretcher, put it back in the ambulance, and they drive off.

AA: Hmm. [Incredulous]

DB: So I said to the cops who were guarding me, "Hey I need that ambulance! You know, what's happened?" And I remember Helberg saying, "Well, ... you know that's an ambulance for whites only. You have to wait for the black ambulance!"

JRR: Segregation even in life and death!

Although South African apartheid had a four-way distinction between white people, colored people, Indians/Asians, and black people, when it came to emergency medical care, the distinction was binary, between those who were white, and those who were not.

Brutus' brother and some associates, I learned, were planning to rescue him from the hospital in which he was held, Coronation. But the chief of the platoon, expecting trouble, was especially vigilant the night of the planned rescue. When the potential rescuers got to the hospital, in a stolen ambulance, they used a ladder to peer into Brutus' room. Realizing he was heavily guarded by armed police, they called off the attempt. Moreover, he was getting a blood transfusion at the time. "So for them to have moved me would have pretty much meant my death at that stage" he pointed out. "I was glad they called it off!"

Brutus said that story that had never been told before our interview. He only learned the full details when he went to prison at Robben Island, and met some of the men who were part of the escape attempt but were subsequently arrested on other charges.

Once out of hospital, Brutus was sentenced to 18 months on Robben Island, in the maximum security section for political prisoners. He was in a cell next to Mandela's, and like him, spent his days doing hard labor, breaking rocks with a hammer. Eventually he was released, but then put under house arrest, before opting, as some other South Africans did, for one-way exile in England:

DB: So my house became a prison, ... and it also became a crime for me to write poetry ... [to] write anything which MIGHT be published ...

JRR: So letters to your wife?

DB: Well that's the one exception. You were allowed letters, to pretty much anybody. But if the person who got your letter showed it to someone else, this constituted publication. And so *they* would go to prison for publishing your letter. And *you* would go to prison for having your letter published. But I only did a year under house arrest. And then I got permission to leave, on what was called an exit permit [in 1966]. Which meant signing an agreement to go to prison if I returned. And I signed that. So in fact, currently I'm investigating whether that agreement is still binding ... So that I'm trying to go back, but I need to know whether—what will happen if I go back. So I have written to the Consul, I didn't get a satisfactory answer, so I've now written to [Frederik Willem] de Klerk [President of South Africa 1989–1994], asking him what is my status.

Years later, in January 2001, de Klerk visited Stanford University, and I sat across the table from him in a small meeting with heads of various programs within the

Center for Comparative Studies in Race and Ethnicity. I was Director of the program in African and African American Studies at the time. I wanted to ask Dennis Brutus' question for him, about whether the exit/exile agreement he had signed with the South African government was still binding.

But of course, by that time it had become irrelevant. Although as a minister in the white minority government of President P.W. Botha, de Klerk had enforced apartheid, when he became President in 1989, he freed Nelson Mandela and negotiated with him to dismantle the system of racial caste and white minority rule. In 1993 he shared the Nobel Peace Prize with Nelson Mandela, and after Mandela became President in a 1994 landslide electoral victory, he was appointed Deputy President, until 1996. Many questions remain about de Klerk's role in abolishing apartheid and participating in the degradation and massacre of people of color in South Africa before and after the rapprochement with Mandela, which was itself strained.

As for Brutus, during his exile he moved to the US and held academic positions in English and African Studies at Northwestern University (1971–1985) and the University of Pittsburgh. Characteristically, the Reagan administration attempted, unsuccessfully, to deport him in 1983. Unbanned by the South African government in 1990, when Mandela was also freed from prison, Brutus was affiliated with the University of KwaZulu-Natal, and received several honorary doctorates and other awards before his death in 2009. He was 85.

In 1996, four years after South Africa was allowed to rejoin the Olympics, Josia Thugwane became the first black South African to win an Olympic Gold Medal, in the men's marathon. He had started running when apartheid was still intact, but in 1988, when non-white people were still denied "access to technical instruction, equipment and running tracks," he was allowed to train with the running team of the coal-mining company where he worked as a janitor.[5] Amazingly, he made the Olympics team, and more amazingly, he won the marathon at the 1996 Olympics in Atlanta, by three seconds, the closest finish in Olympic marathon history. As Nelson Mandela said, Thugwane "reinforced our pride and confidence as a nation."

Reading about and watching videos of Thugwane's historic achievement, and the mass celebrations that followed among South Africans, brought tears to my eyes. Because his victory represented the heights to which black people—indeed all people—could soar, once the chains of racism are severed. But thousands of black, colored and Indian South Africans paid a price for the severing of those chains. Dennis Brutus, whose role in keeping South Africa out of the Olympics from 1962 to 1992 was crucial to Thugwane's gold medal win in 1996, must have been overjoyed by Thugwane's victory, perhaps touching the scars from his near-death shooting 33 years earlier, and thinking that they were worth it.

A September 3, 2020 review by Keith Gottschalk[6] of a new biography of Dennis Brutus[7] notes something Brutus did not mention in his interview with us, that "Repeated beatings, and harrowing assaults, culminated in months of solitary confinement, causing hallucinations and nervous breakdown." It is all the more

Figure 14.5 Josia Thugwane, first Black South African to win Olympic Gold, 1996 (GEORGES GOBET/AFP via Getty Images).

remarkable that Brutus emerged from prison intact, to continue his political activism and his poetry.

I was also pleased that I had recorded Brutus' interview, and that in donating that recording to the Stanford library to make available online to the world, I had helped to preserve the history of his struggle and achievement, in his own words.[8]

I should add that sociolinguists, who regularly make audio recordings with people from all walks of life, in many parts of the world, can undoubtedly make more such records publicly available to preserve the history of people both unknown (like Granny from Cane Walk, Guyana, quoted above) and renown (like Brutus). We have begun to digitize and make such recordings centrally available, for instance in CORAAL—the Corpus of Regional African American Language—and we should do more, making that information more widely known to researchers in all fields. Recently, I used CORAAL recordings along with a group of researchers to show that automatic speech recognition systems used by Amazon, Apple, Google, IBM and Microsoft made many more errors with black speakers (35%) than with white speakers (19%).[9] That is a very different kind of fight than the one Brutus waged, but it ultimately has the same goal, reducing inequality and discrimination.

Finally, David Dabydeen and Dennis Brutus, like John Agard, Grace Nichols, Loretta Ngcobo and other speakers in our 1990 Stanford in Oxford summer program—all exemplify the concept of "The Empire Strikes Back." African Studies in the US and Caribbean Studies in the UK are better programs because of the contributions that Brutus, Dabydeen and other Caribbean and African stalwarts made to them. They represent some of the many Third World immigrants or visitors to the UK, Europe and North America, who have themselves or through their progeny made significant contributions to education, music, medicine, athletics, science, the arts and other fields. Vidur Dindayal has featured *some* of the Guyanese achievers, both in the UK and in the USA/Canada.[10] On a personal note, London-born Nubya Garcia, a 29-year-old tenor saxophonist, granddaughter of my sister June, and daughter of my Guyanese niece Loraine Ayshah Jansen and Souleyman Garcia, British-born but with Trinidadian parents, was the winner of Jazz FM's UK Jazz Act award for 2019. She was also featured in *The New York Times* in August 2020 for "making a big impact on London's buzzing scene" by infusing "jazz with Afro-Caribbean influences."[11] She also made the September 2020 cover of *Jazzwise*, the UK's biggest-selling jazz monthly.[12] And in the April

Figure 14.6 My great-niece Nubya Garcia, performing at Jazz Middelheim Festival, Antwerp, Belgium, August 17, 2019. (Photo by Peter Van Breukelen/ Redferns/Getty Images).

2021 issue of *Ebony*, she was featured as one of "7 Young Jazz Giants You Need to Know."[13] The Third World in Britain indeed.

Notes

1 Rickford, John R. 1987. *Dimensions of a Creole Continuum.* Stanford University Press, p. 163. The extract is written in the modified Cassidy/LePage orthography set out there (pp. 7–9).
2 See Bahadur, Gaiutra. 2013. *Coolie Woman*. University of Chicago Press.
3 Recording available from the Stanford library at https://purl.stanford.edu/cf842sd4281
4 Now founder/president of *She the People*, an organization promoting the political power of women of color.
5 https://mrdivis.wordpress.com/2016/07/10/south-africas-first-black-olympic-gold-medalist/
6 Keith Gottschalk. Sep. 3, 2020. "Book Shines Light on Dennis Brutus, One of South Africa's Most Underrated Poets" in *The Conversation.* https://tinyurl.com/y56gzk4b
7 August, Tyrone. 2020. *Dennis Brutus: The South African Years.* Best Red.
8 It is not the only such recording. There is a 1986 half hour interview with Brutus by Terry Gross of National Public Radio, available from the Library of Congress. And a series of recordings Brutus made at the University of Texas at Austin when he was a visiting professor in1974–75 were the basis of an edited 2011 book by Bernth Lindfors. There may be more, especially in South Africa. All will be invaluable.
9 https://www.nytimes.com/2020/03/23/technology/speech-recognition-bias-apple-amazon-google.html
10 Dindayal, Vidur. 2007. *Guyanese Achievers, UK.* Trafford; and *Guyanese Achievers, USA & Canada* (Trafford 2011).
11 https://www.nytimes.com/2020/08/17/arts/music/nubya-garcia-source.html
12 See also: https://en.wikipedia.org/wiki/Nubya_Garcia
13 https://www.ebony.com/entertainment/7-young-jazz-giants-you-need-to-know/

15 African and African American Studies, Learning Expeditions, Kongo Cosmograms

In 1997, I was invited to direct the *program* in African and African American Studies [AAAS] at Stanford and I held that position for seven years, from 1998 to 2005. In February 2021, Stanford provost Persis Drell and Humanities and Sciences Dean Debra Satz, following petitions from the Black Student Union and the Black Graduate Association, announced that they had accepted a Task Force's recommendation that AAAS should become a *department*.[1]

AAAS was established at Stanford in 1969, recommended by a committee chaired by Professor James L. Gibbs in 1968. Like many African American Studies programs, it followed the assassination of Martin Luther King Jr., in April 1968, which fueled demands from black students for changes in the curriculum and faculty. It was the first ethnic studies program at Stanford, and the first African American Studies program at a private university in the US.

The first Director of AAAS was Professor St. Clair Drake (1969–74). Both he and Gibbs insisted that "Africa" be included in the name of the program. They had both worked in Africa, and wanted to emphasize the important connections between Africa and African America.

One reason I was asked to direct the program was because I had been involved with AAAS for some time. My course on African American Vernacular English [AAVE] was one of the core courses in AAAS (I'd been teaching it since 1980), and I'd been on the Steering Committee for the program for years. An inspiration for my agreeing to direct AAAS was the fact that Sylvia Wynter from Jamaica, the scintillating intellectual who taught me in high school (see Chapter 5), had served as AAAS Director from 1976 to 79. She was followed by Kennell Jackson, Jr. (1980–89). Another motivation was a series of ideas I had for improving the program and increasing enrollment, including creating a AAAS website and expanding the three or four lectures AAAS had each quarter into a credit course with weekly lectures, many of them by visitors from other universities. I asked students to conduct recorded interviews with each lecturer, the interviews themselves providing a potential resource for further research.

I also started a Stanford Oral History Project in East Palo Alto (SOHP-EPA), the nearby black and minority community, and by 2004 we had finished two dozen interviews with former mayors, leaders and other community members. Copies are available in the EPA library and in the Stanford Library. Most importantly,

DOI: 10.4324/9781003204305-15

Figure 15.1 Some of the Black faculty at Stanford, early 1980s. Seated, L to R: Arthur
   B. C. Walker, Sandra Drake, St Clair Drake, Sylvia Wynter. Standing, L to
   R: Ronald Alexander, Ewart Thomas, Clayborne Carson, Condoleezza Rice,
   John Gill, John R. Rickford, Clayton Bates, Kennell Jackson, Jr.

I wanted to initiate a series of Learning Expeditions to places of interest in the
black world, in the US, the Caribbean and West Africa. AAAS received funds
from the President's Fund to facilitate such initiatives. That sealed the deal. I
said "Yes!"

Our first Learning Expedition, in 1999, was to the **Georgia and South Carolina
Sea Islands**, where I had spent an academic quarter during *my* undergraduate
days (see Chapter 12, and Figure 12.1). We *did* go to Daufuskie Island, and I
introduced the Stanford students, staff and faculty to some of my black contacts
from my earlier visits, like Susie Smith, in whose home Angela and I had stayed
in 1972. But the island had changed a lot since then. There was now a Daufuskie
Island *Resort* and dozens of vacation rentals and homes on the island, with many
rich whites. And the number of resident black families had significantly declined.
Not a place to experience Sea Island black culture now, in the sense that was true
decades earlier.

Our base was Penn Center on St. Helena Island, historic because it "is the site
of the former Penn School, one of the country's first schools for formerly enslaved
individuals."[2] It was also where Dr. Martin Luther King Jr. would often meet
with John Lewis and others in the 1960s to plan and strategize, and where Frieda
Mitchell worked, so it was rich in black history. We visited the York W. Bailey
Museum on site, with historical photographs and artifacts, and adjacent Brick
Baptist Church, built by enslaved people in 1855.

It was at Brick Church that pastor Rev. Ervin Greene read to us from *De Good Nyews Bout Jedus Christ Wa Luke Write*, a 1994 translation into Gullah of the *Gospel According to Luke* that he had worked on as lead translator, assisted by Pat Sharpe, other linguists and Gullah speakers. Here is an excerpt from Luke 2:7, the Christmas story in the Gullah translation:[3]

> She hab e boy chile, e fusbon. E wrop um op een clothe wa been teah eenta leetle strip an lay un een a trough, de box weh feed de cow and oda animal. Cause Mary an Joseph beena stay weh de animal sleep. Dey ain't been no room fa dem eenside de bodin house.
>
> "And she brought forth her firstborn son, and wrapped him in swaddling clothes, and laid him in a manger; because there was no room for them in the inn."
>
> (Luke 2:7 King James Version)

As Rev. Greene told us excitedly, a Gullah speaker from Bluffton, S. Carolina confided to him that she kept the Gullah translation and the accompanying tape recording on a bedstand next to her bed. And she used them regularly, because "Dis de firs' time God talk to me the way I talk!"

Following a tip-off from Prof. Herman Blake, whose family is from John's Island, we also had the moving experience of participating in an Usher Anniversary service at St. James African Methodist Episcopal church on John's Island. The melodic incantations of the songs by the ushers of various churches, the spirited (*ring*) *shouts* in which the participants enter and circle the church (usually counter-clockwise) with dance-like movements and rhythmic hand-clapping, represent a powerful ritual, a rich African and African American tradition.[4]

We also visited the Boone Plantation in Charleston, S. Carolina, and were silent and down spirited as we trudged through the dreary former slave houses on the site. Much more animated was our visit to the oldest black-run blacksmith shop (169 years old at the time) in the area. There Philip Simmons, an African American native of Daniel Island, worked for several decades, crafting many of the gates and decorative ironworks around Charleston.[5] Mr. Simmons told us about his craft and career, how he got into blacksmithing from the age of 13, beginning as an apprentice to Peter Simmons, a former enslaved person. It was fascinating, although some students at first grumbled because we went to his shop instead of going to an alligator farm! But Simmons' life and work were much more important. Dr. Lonnie Bunch, creator of the Smithsonian's National Museum of African American History and Culture in Washington, DC, confirmed in a Stanford Community Hour Zoom on March 7, 2021 that the outer framework or filagree of the Museum commemorates the elaborate iron works Phillip Simmons had crafted. The museum has an exhibit on Phillip Simmons to which I plan to donate a copy of the hour-long recorded interview I did with him at the time.

A major highlight of our first Learning Expedition was the *First African Baptist Church*, in Savannah, Georgia (not marked in Figure 8.1, but south of

Daufuskie, on bank of Savannah River). The church had its roots in a congregation founded in 1773, by George Leile, an enslaved person, making it the first black Baptist church in North America. The current building was not constructed until 1859, by people who had been or still were enslaved, working in the evenings and nights.

One of the most fascinating parts of the church is the basement, where there are several dozen holes near the supporting posts, each shaped like a diamond containing a cross. Those holes served two functions. One was to provide breathing space for enslaved people in the underground railroad who were hiding in the four-foot space below the church. The other was to symbolize the *Kongo cosmogram* or belief system, as noted by church Deacon Harry James: "When you look at the holes, they appear to be in the pattern of a diamond. But that is not a diamond. That's an African symbol, a Kongo *cosmogram*!"

I was intrigued by this reference to a Kongo *cosmogram*, and did some more research on it subsequently. Yale professor Robert Farris Thompson, in *Flash of the Spirit* explained that the four points of the *cosmogram* represent the four moments of the sun, rising in the East, moving counter-clockwise to its pinnacle in the North, setting in the West, and returning after its descent below the horizontal *kalunga* line to rise again in the East. The sun's key locales mirror the beliefs of the *baKongo* people in the continuity of life, from birth (East), to the peak of life (North) in the mountain of the living (*ntoto*, above the *kalunga* line), to death (West) and passage through the underworld of the South (*mpemba*, the

Figure 15.2 AAAS Learning Expedition group in First African Baptist Church, Savannah, GA, 1999. In the center in blue shirt is Deacon Harry James who told us about the Kongo *cosmograms* in the basement.

inverted mountain below the *kalunga* line), until one is reincarnated in the East. As Thompson notes,

> The Kongo *yowa* does not signify the crucifixion of Jesus for the salvation of mankind; it signifies the … vision of the circular motion of human souls about the circumference of its intersecting lines. The Kongo cross refers therefore to the everlasting continuity of all righteous men and women.[6]

We were blown away by these symbols and their African connections. But they were also striking because they attest to the presence and influence of enslaved people in Gullah territory from Angola (where the Bakongo or Kongolese people came from), not just Sierra Leone or other countries in West Africa. *Gullah* is often said to be a shortened form of *(An)Gola*.

When I met Robert Farris Thompson some years later and showed him photos of the *cosmograms* in the First African Baptist church, he was amazed at how perfectly they had been preserved, in contrast with others found elsewhere (on the Levi Jordan plantation in Texas, for instance). Note too that the counter-clockwise progression of the sun in the Kongo cosmogram is the same direction in which churchgoers generally moved when doing a *ring shout*!

Our 2000 Learning Expedition was to **Jamaica**, West Indies, and I was assisted in leading it by Dr. Lawford Goddard, professor of Africana Studies at San Francisco State University. The expedition included lectures by local experts (Dr. Velma Pollard and other poets and scholars); a meeting with Governor General Sir Howard Cooke; a guided tour of the impressive National Art Gallery in Kingston; and a daylong trip to Accompong, a historical maroon village in Cockpit Country, St. Elizabeth.

Figure 15.3 One of the many Kongo *cosmograms* in First African Baptist Church, Savannah, Georgia.

But the most astonishing part of the Jamaican Learning Expedition was our visit to National Heroes Park in downtown Kingston. There, in the Monument to Samuel Sharpe, a Baptist Deacon who was hanged for instigating the Christmas rebellion of enslaved people in 1831, there is a huge cross overhead that is usually interpreted to represent his Christian faith. But to do that would be to make the same error of interpreting the diamond-enclosed crosses in the First African Baptist Church as only a Christian symbol.

A bronze plaque within the monument instead guides us to an alternative interpretation. It depicts the symbols as a Kongo *cosmogram* and includes the description of the cross as seen in Thompson's book and with key elements of the Bakongo cycle iterated.

Moreover, there is, for Jamaica as for the Georgia and South Carolina Sea Islands, evidence that significant numbers of enslaved Kongolese people came from the Angola region. In *Roots of Jamaican Culture*, Alleyne 1989 noted that "it seems quite clear that Kumina [the Afro-Jamaican religion] emerged in St.

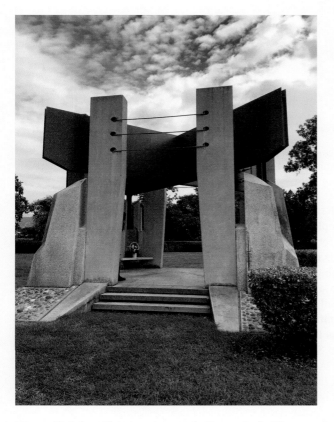

Figure 15.4 Sam Sharpe monument in Heroes Park, Kingston, Jamaica, with a cross-like structure overhead. Photo by Amanda Gooden.

Figure 15.5 Bakongo *cosmogram* and its continuity elements depicted on a plaque at Sam Sharpe's monument, Heroes Park, Kingston, Jamaica.

Thomas [a South Eastern parish of Jamaica] because of the presence there of large numbers of Bantu people from the Congo-Angola area."[7]

It was remarkable for us was to see, in two different geographical locations, the same African elements manifested.

In 2001 our Learning Expedition took us to **Ghana**, West Africa. This expedition benefited from a pre-trip visit by Associate AAAS Director, Dr. Diann McCants, who selected the hotels and planned the itinerary, keepings costs and historical/cultural significance in mind. We had a richer series of lectures by local professors and experts than ever before, supplementing the mandatory course of lectures that we had at Stanford in the preceding quarter.

We were based in Accra, but went northwest into the Asante/Ashanti region to visit a Kente cloth factory, and several shops in which Ashanti wood carvers could be seen practicing their skillful art. We visited an elementary school in Agona Duaka, and were treated to a traditional dance performance by school-aged children. We also paid a visit to the home of a nearby ancestral chief with whom Professor Kennell Jackson, a former AAAS Director, had been acquainted from his field research. And we went to a reception at the home of Kwesi Yankah, a professor at the University of Ghana who had been a visitor at Stanford for a year.

The most moving parts of the Ghana trip were our visit to the Ancestral River Park, where enslaved people headed for the New World had their last bath, and to Cape Coast Castle, where they were confined in dark, insanitary dungeons before exiting through the Door of No Return for the long voyage to the Caribbean and North America. Our expedition members were silent, gripped by the grim realities of the experience, involving in many cases their possible ancestors.

Those three Learning Expeditions were all that we had planned, and for the next two years we had none, our resources depleted. But then Stanford Associate Dean Bob Gregg gave us funds for a final Expedition, in 2003, to Belize, Central America. Vera Grant, the new AAAS Associate Director, was the principal organizer of this trip.

A major focus of the Belize trip, and the winter quarter preparatory course that preceded it, were the Garifuna (plural "Garinagu") descendants of an Antillean Carib people (the Callinago or Kalinago) who mixed with hundreds of African enslaved people in St. Vincent after their ship ran aground in 1675. The Garinagu, sometimes called "Black Caribs" to distinguish them from the "Yellow Caribs," resisted the incursions of European colonizers in the 18th century. But for them, as for other Garinagu, it was a losing battle. In 1796, the British deported them from St. Vincent. They settled along the Central American coast, mainly in Honduras and Belize.[8]

Our Belize tour included a visit to the Garifuna Cultural Museum and a lecture by its founder, Sebastian Cayetano. We sampled Garifuna cuisine and were entertained by a cultural performance that included drumming, singing and dancing. We also had a lecture by anthropologist Joseph Palacio, an authority on the Garifuna, focusing on Garifuna history and Garifuna identity as a blend of Native American and African cultures.

We also enjoyed a reception with Governor General Colville Young. Dr. Young, a linguist whose academic writing on Belize Creole (Kriol) was part of our preparatory reading, discussed Belize Creole and other topics. He also played for us the humorous Mighty Sparrow calypso about the mad woman who crashed the governor's ball and "shake she waist in the Governor face." Here is the first verse, with the official lyrics as in https://genius.com/Mighty-sparrow-governors -ball-lyrics, but sung by Sparrow in Trinidadian Creole English (*ah nevuh see nutten . . . jump de wall, . . . Governuh face* and so on).

[Verse 1]
The governor had a ball, I'd never seen nothing so yet
A mad woman jumped the wall and invade the fête
Prospect with the baton in hand, conducting the police band
He say "The woman shake she waist in the Governor face"

Eve Aird of Sacred Heart College (wife of my former University of Guyana student Chris Aird) gave us a lecture on "Higher Education in Belize." She discussed the struggles faced by community colleges and the University of Belize, due to dwindling financial resources and the difficulties of mediating between English, Spanish, Mayan, Creole and Garifuna languages.

A highlight was our visit to two Mayan archaeological reserves, Cahal Pech and Xunantunich, near the border with Guatemala. We ended that day in Dangriga, a coastal village that boasts the largest proportion of Garifuna/Garinagu in Belize. After dinner, oral historian Eugene Hernandez lectured on "The New Garifuna Village," focusing on recent attempts to achieve economic self-sufficiency through a new fishing cooperative, which we also visited.

In Dangriga, we visited the Holy Family primary school to distribute gifts of school supplies, and toured a factory in which cassava bread, a staple of the Garifuna people and of many Amerindians in Central and South America, was being made with the help of modern mechanization. We also visited a local artist, Benjamin Nicholas, known for his depictions of Garifuna life on life-sized canvases. And we enjoyed a demonstration of drum making by Daytha Rodriguez, and went to a *dabuyaba* (Garifuna healing site) led by Ifasima Efunyemi. Both women made lasting impressions.

After dinner, we were treated to another performance by Garifuna dancers and singers, and, by way of cultural exchange, Stanford acapella singers, J'Leise Springer and Umi Jensen, sang the African American National Anthem ("Lift Every Voice and Sing") and the Polynesian "Song of the Islands" for our Garifuna hosts.

We also had a lecture by spiritual leader Buye Manu, whose extensive account of Garifuna healing practices and traditions, delivered in Garifuna, was translated into English by Ifasima Efunyemi. We then drove to Punta Gorda, the Southernmost big city in Belize. Along the way we were treated to a tour of the Traditional Healer Garden in the Toledo District, led by Victor Cal, a Maya K'ek'chi member, and three members of the "Traditional Healers Association" in the area. We were struck by the different yet comparable approaches to healing through nature and spirituality in the Garifuna and Mayan communities. In the evening, Lucia Ellis, the daughter of Garifuna leader and historian Godsman Ellis, helped us discuss our reactions to all that we had seen and heard.

This final expedition enriched the lives of its participants by extending their readings, transporting them to a part of the world most had never visited, and introducing them to peoples whose rich, multicultural histories and experiences caused them to reflect on their own friendships and relations and academic/professional futures.

In Winter 2004, I taught AAAS 105, "Introduction to African and African American Studies." Clayborne Carson, Professor of History and Director of the Martin Luther King, Jr., Papers Project, normally taught it, but was unavailable that year.

I introduced one element from the "Ethnic and Status Groups" course I had taken with Professor J. Herman Blake at UC Santa Cruz 35 years earlier—an oral family history project. Students had to interview their parents, grandparents and other relatives to track down their family tree and history, relating it to some of the readings and topics for the course, presenting it orally and submitting a written version at the end of the course. As in Blake's course, we had black students, white students, Asian students, and all their oral histories were fascinating.

In addition to this oral history component, we concentrated in one of our twice weekly class meetings, on readings from Marable and Mullings' edited book, *Let Nobody Turn Us Around: An African American Anthology*, with subsections on Slavery and Abolitionism 1789–1861, Reconstruction and Reaction 1861–1915, Plantation to Ghetto 1915–1954, We Shall Overcome 1954–1975 and The Future in the Present, 1975 on.[9]

A third component that occupied the other weekly class meeting was Disciplinary Perspectives. Students read and heard from Stanford faculty members in various disciplines to learn how Africa or African America is studied from different perspectives. Faculty members who participated in 2004 included Professors Harry Elam (Drama), Claybourne Carson (History), Linda Darling-Hammond (Education), Claude Steele (Psychology), Sally Dickson (Public Policy), Roger Peeks (Medicine), David Abernethy (Political Science) and myself (Linguistics).

Overall, I learned as much about black history from this course, as the students did. I had to put in more work on it than the average linguistics course, since many of the readings were unfamiliar. But I felt immensely grateful for and educated about the historical experiences that had shaped my African American brethren and sisteren, whose family I, my wife, our children and grandchildren had joined.

In 2005, my final year as AAAS Director, we had ten graduating majors and eight graduating minors. Minors were popular with our students, since many either double-majored, or did a minor in AAAS and a major in another subject. Mae Jemison, the first female African American astronaut, had majored in Chemical Engineering in 1977, but fulfilled the course requirements for AAAS. She said she did the former for her career, but the latter for her *soul*.

AAAS diploma award ceremonies on Commencement day are always intense emotional events because we offer each student and/or their parent or other relative the opportunity to speak, recognizing, as former AAAS Director Morris Graves put it, that the "accomplishment is not just the student's, but their family and community's as well." At every single AAAS diploma award ceremony I've attended, tears were shed, by moms, dads, students and other attendees.

The most emotional such ceremony I attended was on June 14, 1998, while Morris Graves was still Director. I remember it like yesterday. It was emotional for me to begin with because I had flown in for Stanford graduation ceremonies from Vancouver, WA, where my eldest brother Edward ("Teddy") was in a coma from a stroke, and I would fly back there that same night. But the effect of my own grief, added to the emotional reflections of parent after parent, were amplified when AAAS graduating major Ryan Bathé[10] asked her mom, Clare Bathé, a professional jazz vocalist,[11] to sing "The wind beneath my wings." Both the words and the beautiful way they were rendered brought tears to my eyes, as they did to many of the people in that room.

Figure 15.6 JRR (standing third from right, back row) with his final class of AAAS majors and minors, June 2005.

An extract from The Wind Beneath My Wings

Bette Midler

> Did you ever know that you're my hero
> And everything I would like to be?
> I can fly higher than an eagle
> For you are the wind beneath my wings

To critics of ethnic studies, like businessman and former University of California Regent Ward Connerly, I would contend that AAAS and similar programs and ceremonies are vital for the minds and souls of many of the students who go through the challenges of higher education. It is the wind beneath their wings. And ours as well.

Notes

1 https://news.stanford.edu/today/2021/03/22/departmentalizing-african-african-american-studies-aaas-program/
2 http://www.penncenter.com
3 This version differs in some detail from that in *De Nyew Testament,* the Gullah New Testament that was published by the American Bible Society, New York, in 2005.
4 Samuel A. Floyd, Jr. 2002. Ring Shout! Literary Studies, Historical Studies, and Black Music Inquiry. *Black Music Research Journal 22, Supplement: Best of BMRJ*, 49–70.
5 John Michael Vlach. 1981. *Charleston Blacksmith: The Work of Philip Simmons*. Athens, GA: U. of Georgia Press.

6 Robert Farris Thompson. 1983. *Flash of the Spirit: African and Afro-American Art and Philosophy.* New York: Random House, p. 108. See also Grey Gundaker. 1998. *Signs of Diaspora, Diaspora of Signs*, esp. Oxford University Press, pp. 44–46.

7 Mervyn Alleyne. 1989. *Roots of Jamaican Culture.* London: Pluto Press, p. 92.

8 Godsman Ellis. 1997. *The Garinagu of Belize.* San Ignacio: The Haman Belize.

9 Manning Marable and Leith Mullins, eds. 2000. *Let Nobody Turn Us Around: An African American Anthology.* Lanham, MD: Rowman & Littlefield.

10 Herself an actress, Ryan Bathé is married to actor Sterling Brown (see chapter 16).

11 Jazz vocalist Clare Bathé was a member of the disco group *Machine*, whose 1979 single, "There But for the Grace of God Go I," was listed by *Slate* magazine as the sixth greatest dance song of all time in 2006. She was also the dance and vocal coach in Lena Horne's show "The Lady & Her Music."

16 Ebonics, Rachel Jeantel, Trayvon Martin, Black Lives Matter

During the 1990s, many of the issues of race, identity and language that I had engaged with throughout my career exploded into the public conversation. On December 18, 1996, the Oakland, California school board, resolved to recognize Ebonics—or "ebony phonics" (black dialect)—as the "primary language of African American children." Actually, black dialect (which linguists call African American Vernacular English [AAVE] or African American Language [AAL]) is the primary informal language of many African Americans, *period*.

When and how African Americans wield that dialect can help determine their access to education and employment and can influence the treatment they receive from cops and courts. For example, jurors neither understood nor valued the six-hour testimony of Rachel Jeantel, the prosecution's main witness in the 2013 trial of George Zimmerman for killing Jeantel's friend Trayvon Martin, largely because Jeantel spoke a form of AAVE. Trayvon's murder and the exoneration of Zimmerman sparked "Black Lives Matter," the movement against racist police violence that continues to reverberate as I write these words in 2021.

Let's go back to Oakland's 1996 resolution. Judging from the outrage expressed in the US and elsewhere in the world by many people after the school board's decision, the assertion that Ebonics was the primary language of black children was controversial in itself. But Oakland's *additional* proposal to take Ebonics into account in teaching black children Standard English (SE) was absolutely explosive, especially when it was misinterpreted, as it usually was, as an effort to teach children to speak *in* Ebonics and abandon Standard English.

Anger and derision swirled about the Oakland resolutions in the media and in many public gatherings during that Christmas holiday season. Here is a sample from America Online, a popular platform at the time. (Paulsaxton's comment was one of the rare positive takes, and the most accurate about Oakland's intent):

> This is the dumbest idea to come along in a long time.
>
> (FLGuard, 9/20/96)

> VERY VERY STUPID.
>
> (III Duke, 9/21/96)

DOI: 10.4324/9781003204305-16

The posted summary misrepresents the position of the Oakland Schools. Teachers are not to teach or teach in Ebonics. They are to understand Ebonics as a distinct language in order to assist students to translate the "dialect" in which they were raised into standard English.

(Paulsaxton, 9/21/96)

Ebonics has no dictionary, no text books, no grammar, no rules.

(LewisLaneL 9/23/96)

As a linguist, I knew that most of these diatribes were dead wrong. At least two dictionaries of Black Talk existed at the time, and thousands of articles had been published about the rules of pronunciation and grammar of "AAVE." In fact, in the same year the Ebonics controversy broke, linguist Edgar Schneider reported that "African American English has been the most prominent topic of writings on American English in general, with more than five times as many publications devoted to it than to any other group."[1]

Moreover, most critiques of Ebonics and of the Oakland school board decision ignored the fact that far too few black students in Oakland were succeeding academically when taught by conventional methods. Critics were generally unaware of the pedagogical technique known as "contrastive analysis," an approach designed to help dialect speakers distinguish between their mother tongues and the standard language of school and work. Contrastive analysis had shown success when used to teach students who spoke AAVE and other vernaculars.[2]

It should also be clear: many linguists who are aficionados of Black Talk, including me, have no objection to the teaching of Standard or Mainstream English, and believe that every vernacular speaker who wants to master that variety should be helped to do so. Linguistic versatility is a virtue, and mastering SE in the racist and classist societies in which Black Talkers often live, especially so. Our main dispute is about the *means* of achieving this end. Ignoring or dismissing Black Talk rather than contrasting its regularities with SE to facilitate mastery of the latter often leads to failure, as demonstrated in millions of classrooms in North America, Britain, the Caribbean and Africa.

In many ways, studying and teaching linguistics, and researching and writing about AAVE for more than three decades (it was the first course I taught at Stanford when I joined the faculty in 1980, and I taught it every year) had prepared me to make an expert contribution to discussions of the Oakland resolutions. One former Stanford student who had taken and remembered my AAVE course, was actor Sterling K. Brown,[3] who introduced his 2018 Commencement address at Stanford with these remarks:[4]

President Tessier-Lavigne, thank you so much for sharing those beautiful words with us this morning … I will, from time to time, be slipping into a dialect known as AAVE – for the uninitiated, that is African American Vernacular English. In some sections of the country, they will refer to this dialect as "Ebonics," but here, at Leland Stanford Jr. University, where it was taught to me by Professor John R. Rickford, we call it AAVE.

By 1996 I had come a long way from the wide-eyed novice who landed in New York in 1968 with his suit and gold Guyana tiepin. But for much of December 1996, media outlets were primarily quoting not linguists but prominent figures such as Reverend Jesse Jackson, who called the Ebonics resolutions "an unacceptable surrender, borderlining on disgrace," and writer Toni Morrison, who found the Oakland school board decision "very threatening."

My perspective was strikingly different. My Caribbean background and research had familiarized me with the process of contrasting Creole English ("Me ah go dung deh" or "Ah goin' dung deh") and Standard English ("I am going down there"). I was well aware of the disdain and misinterpretation that efforts to draw on Creole English while teaching Standard English had long generated, even (or especially) in the anglophone Caribbean.

Forty years before the Oakland school board's resolutions, linguist Robert Le Page had proposed in 1955–56 that some Jamaican students might be taught for the first year or two in Creole and then transitioned to Standard English as a "foreign language," a proposal that was lambasted in a Kingston newspaper as "pernicious and insulting." Similarly, a 1977 proposal that Standard English be taught in Trinidad and Tobago elementary schools by comparison and contrast with the local creole elicited widespread controversy and condemnation.[5] While teaching at the University of Guyana from 1974 to 1980 I had taken part in several policy

Figure 16.1 Actor Sterling K. Brown with JRR at Stanford's commencement ceremony, June 17, 2018. In his address he cited my AAVE course. President Marc Tessier-Lavigne, who introduced Brown, is far left.

debates and radio/newspaper discussions in which *any* positive statements about the creole language were misinterpreted as critiques of teaching Standard English. Similar controversies arose over whether to take into account the native creoles of Caribbean immigrant children in Canadian schools.

The first inkling that I might have something to contribute to the public debates over "Ebonics" in the 1990s came when Mary Rhodes Hoover, Professor of Education at Howard University and literacy consultant to the Oakland school district, suggested to Oakland school superintendent Carolyn Getridge that I could help her respond to the barrage of criticism she was receiving for the district's resolutions.

Mary Hoover had received her PhD in Education from Stanford and published several papers and books on AAVE and bidialectal literacy.[6] Moreover, she had lived and worked in East Palo Alto, across from Palo Alto, where I lived—both less than an hour from Oakland. As a UC Santa Cruz undergraduate, I had used her co-authored *Mnemonic Phonics* (1969) to tutor Wilbur Gowder, a black student.

My phone conversation with Getridge went something like this:

CG: Good evening, Professor Rickford. Mary Hoover has told me about you. I wonder whether you might be able to give me some ammunition to fight these critics of our Ebonics resolutions.
JR: A pleasure to hear from you, Ms. Getridge. You're certainly doing some interesting things up in Oakland with African American Vernacular English!
CG: What we'd particularly like from you is evidence from other places in the US that our proposals and resolutions *work*.

I told Getridge about the evidence that comparing and contrasting AAVE with Standard English helps AAVE-speaking children perform better in school than approaches which ignore or castigate AAVE. For example, in 1980 the scholar Hanni Taylor demonstrated that an experimental group of inner-city university students in Chicago who were taught using the "contrastive analysis" method mastered Standard English much more effectively than a control group of students who were taught using traditional English department techniques. Kelly Harris-Wright (now Kelly Wright) also got promising results when she conducted a similar experiment in DeKalb County, Georgia; elementary students there who were taught to switch from "home speech" to "school speech" also performed better than those who were not.[7] Other studies have produced similar findings.

I had a few more phone calls with Superintendent Getridge, and she invited my wife Angela and me to meet with the Reverend Jesse Jackson when he visited Oakland on December 30, 1996 to clarify his understanding of their Ebonics resolutions.

It was not until December 26 that I got a chance to express my views in the media. On that day I published an op-ed in the *San Jose Mercury News* titled, "Ebonics succeeds where traditional methods do not."[8] The same day I appeared on National Public Radio's (NPR) *Talk of the Nation* broadcast on Ebonics. Korva Coleman, the NPR host that day, had me pitted against my former student John

McWhorter, who had completed his Stanford PhD in Linguistics in 1993 with a dissertation on Saramaccan, an English-based creole spoken in Suriname, adjacent to my native Guyana. Our major disagreement was that he felt the differences between AAVE and Standard English were not significant enough to warrant the special measures Oakland was proposing, and I felt they were. On most other linguistic issues, however, we agreed, and, as African Americans and linguists, we responded to callers' questions similarly.

Of course, much of the important grappling over Oakland's Ebonics proclamation occurred behind closed doors. Superintendent Getridge and her colleagues arranged the private, small-group meeting with Reverend Jesse Jackson that December in the hopes that Jackson might revise his negative public stance on the Oakland board's resolutions once he learned more about the academic problems the decrees sought to address. Getridge's team shared with Jackson the concerns of the African American Task Force, whose work had preceded the resolutions. The Task Force found that black students constituted 53% of the students in Oakland, but 71% of those in Special Education and only 37% of those in Gifted and Talented classes. Moreover, the African American grade point average in the district was only 1.8 (or a "C-" average).[9] Jackson immediately related to these dire statistics, noting that many jail and prison inmates were poor readers whom schools had failed.

After hearing the explanations of school officials and experts (Angela and I both spoke—me as a linguist, she as a literacy specialist—as did Getridge and Task Force members), Jackson seemed persuaded that the goal was to improve the education of all Oakland children. But he emphasized that the crucial message—that Oakland administrators valued Standard English and wished to help their students master it—was not being clearly conveyed. Jackson subsequently appeared at a press conference to say he now supported the efforts of the Oakland school board.

Some of the original supporters of the Ebonics proposal wanted him to apologize for having critiqued them initially. Jackson, however, deftly sidestepped the issue. He accused the news media of misrepresenting the board's intention, which, once again, was to more effectively teach Standard English. He also reminded the press that half of all African American youths are born into poverty.

The day I met with Jackson, the late Geoff Nunberg, language commentator on NPR's *Fresh Air*, and a friend of mine, contacted me about getting the Linguistic Society of America (LSA) to weigh in on the Ebonics issue at the society's upcoming meeting. I was on the LSA's executive committee, and could help to draft resolutions and help push them through on short notice. Early in January 1997, the LSA membership overwhelmingly affirmed AAVE or Ebonics as "systematic and rule-governed like all natural speech varieties," and they did this before TV cameras and reporters from several newspapers. The LSA noted the individual and group benefits *both* of preserving one's vernacular speech patterns *and* of acquiring Standard English. Finally, citing evidence from studies of dialect speakers from Sweden, the US and other countries, the LSA recognized the Oakland school board's approach as "linguistically and pedagogically sound."

Beginning that January, and for many months after, I did scores of interviews with news organizations—from *The New York Times* and *The Washington Post* to the *Chronicle of Higher Education* to *Talk of the Nation* to the *Toronto Star*—about AAVE/Ebonics and the Oakland resolutions. It was a hectic time! Following a suggestion by my best friend and Stanford colleague Ewart Thomas, I created a website with the help of Stanford alum Emerson Swan of Cyngnusoft that presented my thinking on AAVE.[10] (I found that reporters would often get the story wrong, even after I had talked to them for an hour or more.)

It took some time for me to adjust to my increasingly public role as an expert on issues relating to AAVE. I was invited to write a commentary ("Suite for Ebony and Phonics") for the December 1997 issue of *Discover,* the popular science magazine. But my first version was rejected with the comment, "You linguists don't know how to write for the general public." I took this as a challenge. Studying the writing style of Stanford neurobiologist Robert Sapolsky, a frequent contributor to the magazine, I submitted a revised draft that was accepted. Since *Discover* gave me copyright, I fielded many requests to reprint this piece.

I honed my ability to address popular audiences by writing a trade book on AAVE, at the invitation of literary agent Noah Lukeman. Bearing in mind my previous experience with *Discover*, I asked my son Russell, a graduate of Howard University and a correspondent with *The Philadelphia Inquirer* at the time, to be co-author. This turned out to be one of the most rewarding collaborative experiences in my scholarly life. The book proposal was rejected by over two dozen publishers, often with the sneering derision Oakland's resolutions had first received. But when it was published by John Wiley in 2000, *Spoken Soul: The Story of Black English* became very popular.[11] The book is often used in university courses on AAVE, American Dialects, Language in the USA or Language and Education.

I also took part in two terrific videos. The first was a video segment on Ebonics on *Nick News* (with Linda Ellerbee) aired in 1997, in which I supported the resolutions, and writer Maya Angelou opposed them, although she has used AAVE in her poems. The second was a 2017 feature film *Talking Black in America* filmed by Neal Hutcheson and Danica Cullinan.[12] I was an Associate Producer, working with executive producer Walt Wolfram, and other experts, including former students of mine, like Renée Blake. The film is extremely popular. In these ways, I've continued to help shape public awareness—and appreciation—of AAVE, a language variety as pervasive and expressive as it is disparaged and denied.

In 2015, I delivered a presidential address at the annual Linguistic Society of America meeting entitled "Language and Linguistics on Trial: Hearing Rachel Jeantel (and Other Vernacular Speakers) in the Courtroom and Beyond." Jeantel was a good friend of Trayvon Martin, the young man who was fatally shot by George Zimmerman while Martin was visiting his father's home in Sanford, Florida, on February 26, 2012. Just a few weeks earlier, the teenagers (Jeantel and Martin) had turned 18 and 17, respectively. Zimmerman, a neighborhood watch captain, was 28. Suspicious of Martin, who was returning to the gated complex after going to buy some Skittles and juice, Zimmerman called the police, who cautioned him not to follow Martin. He did so anyway. An altercation ensued, and Zimmerman shot Martin dead.

In some respects, the case is reminiscent of the infamous murder of 14-year-old Emmett Till, the Chicago boy who was visiting relatives in Mississippi in August 1955 when he went to the store to buy bubble gum. No one could testify to the savage beating and killing of Emmett Till except Roy Bryant and J. W. Milan, the two white men who brutally murdered the youth for allegedly breaching the racial etiquette of the Jim Crow South. They shamelessly confessed to the crime in *Look* magazine on January 24, 1956. By contrast, Jeantel had been talking to Martin by cell phone until moments before he was killed. In Zimmerman's 2013 murder trial, therefore, she was considered the star witness, and testified for nearly six hours.

Jeantel, however, spoke in a deep variety of AAVE. Her style of speech was castigated on social media, and most jurors in the trial found her difficult to understand. One juror told CNN that she found Jeantel hard to understand "a lot of the times," and not credible. In the end, Jeantel's testimony, the closest thing we will ever have to Martin telling his own story in court, was ignored in deliberations among the six jurors, and "played no role whatsoever" in their not-guilty verdict.[13] In protest against that acquittal, the activists Alicia Garza, Patrisse Cullors and Opal Tometi launched the "Black Lives Matter" slogan, which evolved into a powerful national and international movement.[14] Of course, *all* lives matter. The slogan emphasizes that black lives *do* matter, in the face of discriminatory violence against black people by police and vigilantes, many of whom were—and are—frequently exonerated.[15] Recall the 1969 UCSC play "Justifiable Homicide" cited in Chapter 9, based on real events in San Francisco.

In a 2016 article in the journal *Language*, Stanford graduate student Sharese King and I noted that there were other cases in which AAVE-speaking defendants

Figure 16.2a Witness Rachel Jeantel gives her testimony to the defense during George Zimmerman's trial in Sanford, Florida, June 26, 2013 (Photo by Jacob Langston-Pool/Getty Images).

Figure 16.2b A cardboard photo-realistic figure of Trayvon Martin, as a crowd gathered to protest in Manhattan, July 14, 2013 (Shutterstock).

Figure 16.2c George Zimmerman arrives in court at the Seminole County courthouse for a hearing in Sanford, Florida, December 11, 2012 (Photo by Joe Burbank/ Orlando Sentinel/Tribune News Service via Getty Images).

or witnesses posed comprehension challenges for speakers of other American English dialects.[16] One of the earliest examples we could find was a 1960s case from East Palo Alto (near Palo Alto and Stanford) in which Young Beartracks was sentenced to five years to life for the second degree murder of Chicago Eddie.[17] The jurors in the trial complained that "the greater part of the testimony had been incomprehensible to them" (one wonders how they agreed on a verdict under such circumstances), and the prosecutor maintained that it would have been easier if witnesses had spoken a foreign language and he could have used a competent interpreter.[18]

Legal professionals, like so many other members of the public, often assume that AAVE is an arbitrary or haphazard method of communication. In our 2016 article, King and I excerpted samples of Jeantel's speech (taken from nearly 15 hours of her testimony, pretrial depositions and TV appearances) to show that the language she uses is systematic and governed by rules. For example, Jeantel used most of the grammatical markers of AAVE, like stressed *BIN* ("been") to express the fact that a state began or an action happened a long time ago:

"I BIN knew I was the last person to talk to Trayvon." (deposition 3/13/2013)

She also used invariant *be* to signal a habitual action:

"That's where his headset *be* at." (testimony, 6/26/2013)

This short excerpt from courtroom testimony, which shows that Trayvon was running *away* from Zimmerman rather than following or stalking him, as Zimmerman claimed, allows us to discuss other AAVE features:

Excerpt from Courtroom Testimony of Rachel Jeantel (RJ), day 1 (Prosecutor Bernie de la Rionda (BR) questioning), as recorded by the court reporter (CR) and annotated by us [Ø = zero is/are copula, or zero possessive or plural -s]

RJ: He said he Ø from—he—I asked him where he Ø at. An he told me he Ø at the back of his daddy Ø fiancée Ø house, like in the area where his daddy fiancée—by his daddy Ø fiancée Ø house. Like—I said, "Oh, you better keep running." *He said, naw, he lost him.*

BR: Okay. Let me stop you a second. This—this lady [the Court Reporter] has got to take everything down, so you make sure you're—Okay. So after he said he lost him, what happened then?

RJ: And he say he—, his daddy Ø fiancée Ø house is, and I told him "*Keep running.*" *He—and he said, "Naw," he'll just walk faster.* I'm like, "Oh oh." And I—I ain't complain, 'cause he was breathing hard, so I understand why. Soo

BR: What—what happened after that?

RJ: And then, second Ø later—ah—Trayvon come and say, "Oh, shit!"

CR: [Unintelligible—requesting clarification] "Second later?"
RJ: A couple second Ø later, Trayvon come and say, "Oh, shit!"

Note how frequently Rachel omits *is* or *are* or their contracted forms (e.g. he*'s* or they*'re)*, the forms linguists call copulas because they connect a subject and what is said about the subject (its predicate): "he Ø at the back ..." Rachel actually omits *is* and are 77% of the time. That rate is similar to the omission rate of black teenagers Foxy and Tinky (70% omission) at the ages of 16 and 20. (Foxy and Tinky were part of an earlier linguistic study I did in East Palo Alto with Faye McNair-Knox.)

Moreover, Rachel follows the grammatical restriction that *is* and *are* appear "without restriction" when they come at the end of a clause,[19] as shown by the sentence-final **is** in: "he Ø by—um—the area that his daddy Ø house **is**." In various other ways Rachel's Miami-based AAVE is systematic, following the grammatical rules of black dialect as studied elsewhere. It was absolutely *not* "the blather of an idiot," as one commentator ignorantly and cruelly claimed on social media.

Could these and other linguistic differences between Jeantel's speech and the dialects of her jurors (there were no African Americans on the jury) have been enough to make her unintelligible to them, especially given the reportedly poor acoustics in the large courtroom used for the Zimmerman trial? Sharese and I both thought that the answer to this was yes.

This was reinforced by a subsequent 2019 study in which I was involved, which revealed racial disparities in the automated speech recognition (ASR) systems used by five of the biggest computer companies—Apple, IBM, Google, Amazon and Microsoft—that employ such systems to convert speech to text. For white speaker samples, the ASR systems' average word error rate was 19%, while for black speakers the ASR systems made almost *twice* as many (35%) errors.[20]

But as my colleague Sharese King and I also observed, negative attitudes toward AAVE, compounded by outright racism, also undermined Jeantel's comprehension and credibility in the minds of the jurors. There is much scholarly evidence to support this, but the following observation by developmental psychologist Lois Bloom puts it quite succinctly:[21]

> Jeantel's speech patterns, because they are associated with poor African Americans, were perceived by many, including the people who mattered most, the jurors, as unintelligent, and worse, evidence that she was not credible.

Almost four years after the exoneration of George Zimmerman for the murder of Trayvon Martin, Angela and I got to meet Jeantel after exchanging emails with Rod Vereen, the attorney who helped her through the ordeal of the trial. In April 2017 we joined Jeantel and members of her "Village," the circle of caretakers that had supported her educationally and emotionally, at a gathering in a Miami restaurant. I was both excited and apprehensive about meeting her. I feared that having been castigated by so many strangers in the court of public opinion, she might

Figure 16.3 Sharese King and JRR after receiving the award at the annual Linguistic Society of America meeting in Austin, TX., January 7, 2017, for Best Paper in *Language*, 2016. Courtesy of Allyson Reed for the LSA.

not trust me to tutor her in reading. The trial had exposed, in a painful fashion, her weaknesses in this area. Of course, many of her Miami peers also struggled with literacy. At the 94 percent black Norland Senior High School she attended, only 12 to 23 percent of students, between 2010 and 2012, performed at grade level on the Comprehensive Assessment test in reading.

But Jeantel readily agreed to keep in contact, and I tutored her regularly in reading via FaceTime and Skype from June 2017 to June 2020, sometimes with the help of Angela, an expert in the teaching of literacy. I continued this for three years because of a conviction that scholars have an obligation to help the members of the community they study.[22] I share the deep concern of journalist Nikole Hannah Jones that "hundreds of school districts across the nation have become increasingly segregated after being released from court-ordered integration."[23] Literacy has been one of the major casualties of that trend, partly because the funding and resources necessary for first-rate instruction remain concentrated in majority-white districts.

My work also increasingly focused on fighting linguistic prejudice, achieving equality in education, developing versatility in vernacular speakers and promoting justice. In the summer of 1917 Angela and I spent three weeks at the Rockefeller Foundation Bellagio Center in Italy gaining international perspectives as over a dozen scholar-activists took part in a Thematic Residency on "Youth as Agents of Transformative Change." I also gave a keynote talk at the 20th International Congress of Linguists held in Cape Town, South Africa in July 2018 on "Language Variation & Versatility by Social Class & Race in

Figure 16.4 Rachel Jeantel seated between her Haitian aunt Marie François, my wife
        Angela, and Dorothy Bendross-Mindingall, Miami school board member.
        Standing second from right is attorney Rod Vereen, Rachel's counsel. Our
        first meeting, Miami, Florida, April 13, 2017.

Communities, Schools & Courts," and a plenary presentation on "How can linguistics contribute to life, liberty and the pursuit of happiness, including criminal justice?" at the Georgetown University Round Table on Language and
Linguistics, Washington D.C., in 2019. I also introduced a new class at Stanford,
"Tryna Make a Difference," featuring lectures by some of the leading figures
nationwide who discussed dialect differences and their implications for criminal
justice. And I submitted depositions on two court cases involving the language
of black defendants.

   At a major sociolinguistics conference held at New York University in 2018,
my former student Renée Blake invited Jeantel to come and meet some of her
students. To our delight, Jeantel accepted. Just before I delivered the keynote
address, Jeantel also read a striking poem she had written. I will share just the first
and last stanzas as a reminder to me, and all of us, of the deep pain that prejudice
and injustice, in language as in life, leave in their wake.

Figure 16.5 Some of the scholars at the three-week Rockefeller session on Youth as Agents of Transformative Change, in Bellagio, Italy, summer 2017. L to R: Anna Penido (Brazil), Khary Lazarre-White (NY), Mrinal Dasgupta (India, UK), Aya Chebbi (Tunisia), Ananya Kabir (India, UK), Princess Laurentien van Oranje-Nassau (Netherlands), JRR and Angela (Guyana, California).

Sadly a young soul had to die by Rachel Jeantel (excerpts)
My mindset everyday is,
"I Defeated Yesterday, I Elevate Today, I Control Tomorrow."
I said this every day to the point it became a routine. You see,
behind this smile, I am a Black woman
who Society feels threatened by
and perceives as ghetto. They don't know
we feel pain just like anyone else. They ask
what do we want? In other words, "Why
can't you shut the hell up and accept the way things are,
accepting that society will never truly view you as equal?"
…
Sadly a young soul had to die
for me to open my eyes.

Notes

1 Edgar W. Schneider. 1996. Introduction: Research trends in the study of American English. In Edward W. Schneider, ed., *Focus on the USA*. Amsterdam: John Benjamins, pp. 1–13.

2   See John and Russell Rickford. 2000. *Spoken Soul: The Story of Back English*. New York: Wiley, pp. 176–178.

3   Sterling K. Brown has acted in *The People v. O.J. Simpson*, *This is Us*, and *Black Panther*, inter alia. He has won Emmys and a Golden Globe award. He was one of *Time* magazine's 100 Most Influential People of 2018.

4   For the full text of his remarks, see https://news.stanford.edu/2018/06/17/2018-com mencement-speech-stanford-alumnus-sterling-k-brown/

5   Lawrence C. Carrington, and C. Borely. 1977. *The Language Arts Syllabus 1975: Comment and Counter-Comment*. University of the West Indies, St. Augustine, Trinidad and Tobago, Multi-Media Production Centre.

6   See, for instance, Hoover, Mary C. 1978. Community attitudes toward Black English. *Language in Society* 7.1: 65–87.

7   Kelly Harris-Wright. 1999. Enhancing bidialectalism in urban African American students. In C. T. Adger, D. Christian and O. Taylor, ed., *Making the Connection*. Washington, DC: Center for Applied Linguistics/Delta, pp. 53–60.

8   A longer version than was published in the *Mercury* appears on the Ebonics writings section of my web page: http://johnrickford.com

9   For these and other statistics and for lots of other articles about the issues, see *Rethinking Schools* 12.1, fall 1997, or the book version, *The Real Ebonics Debate*, ed. by Theresa Perry and Lisa Delpit, Beacon Press, 1998.

10   My writings on the Ebonics issue are still on the website he created, http://johnrickford .com.

11   The term *Spoken Soul* came from author Claude Brown, in The Language of Soul, *Esquire*, April 1968: 88. 160–161.

12   https://www.talkingblackinamerica.org

13   According to Juror Maddy, in Lisa Bloom. 2014. *Suspicion Nation: The Inside Story of. the Trayvon Martin Injustics and Why we Continue to Repeat It*, Counterpoint, Berkeley, CA: Counterpoint, p. 148.

14   https://www.nationalgeographic.com/history/2020/07/alicia-garza-co-founded-black -lives-matter-why-future-hopeful/

15   See Judith Degen, Daisy Leigh, Brandon Waldon, and Zion Mengesha. 2020. "A Linguistic Perspective: The Harmful Effects of Responding 'All Lives Matter' to 'Black Lives Matter'." http://alpslab.stanford.edu//blog.html

16   Rickford, John R. and Sharese King. 2016. Language and Linguistics on Trial: Hearing Rachel Jeantel (and Other Vernacular Speakers) in the Courtroom and Beyond. *Language* 92.4: 948–988. (Best Paper in *Language* award, 2016.)

17   For the extensive research that led us to Swett 1969 and many other cases involving AAVE and the legal system, we are indebted to Carra Rentie, a Stanford undergraduate major in Linguistics who went on to do a Stanford J.D. and is now a practicing lawyer.

18   Swett, Daniel H. 1969. Cultural Bias in the American legal system. *Law & Society Review*, 4: 99.

19   Labov, William. 1969. Contraction, Deletion, and Inherent Variability of the English Copula. *Language* 45.4: 715–762.

20   A. Koenecke, A. Nam, E. Lake, J. Nudell, M. Quartey, Z. Mengesha, C. Toups, J. R. Rickford, D Jurafsky, and S Goel. April 7, 2020. Racial disparities in automated speech recognition. *PNAS* (*Proceedings of the National Academy of Sciences*) 117.114. 10.1073/pnas.1915768117

21   Lisa Bloom. 2014. *Suspicion Nation: The Inside Story of the Trayvon Martin Injustics and Why we Continue to Repeat It*, Berkeley, CA: Counterpoint, p. 133.

22   I had to stop tutoring in July 2020, because I underwent surgery. But tutoring thereafter was taken over by two NYU students recommended by Prof. Renée Blake: Raina Carroll and Ky Malone. From Rachel's reports, they are doing a great job.

23   In *Pro Publica*, December 19, 2014.

Epilogue: The gift of Love

This memoir chronicles my upbringing in Guyana, South America, and the major transformations that accompanied my coming to America to study in 1968: switching from literature to linguistics, and from a colored identity to a black one. In closing, I want to note how these transformations have been extended in the love of our four children, Shiyama, Russell, Anakela and Luke. I'll also note who were the main mentors who influenced their development, as Blake, Keesing and Labov did mine (Chapters 9, 11, 12).

First of all, as examples throughout this book demonstrate, switching to linguistics did not deprive me of my love of literature, especially poetry. My children inherited the poetic muse too. The following poem, from Cornell professor/activist **Russell**,[1] written many years ago, reflects his love for me and the joy we shared flying kites in his youth. It is a tender account of a moment that transcends place and time. Indeed, it recalls my own father's meticulous crafting of kites for his children and the exuberance of flying them with him on Easter Monday (Chapter 10):

Runner-Up By Russell John Rickford

I raced my father
him in dashiki, cracking
sandaled feet
corduroys
smelled like old books
when he caught
me in piano hands
dragon-green eyes
laughing
through his beard
scraping me
breathless
until we went flying again
us together
below impatient kites.

The second poem is from our poet/writing tutor son **Luke**,[2] schooled by Harvard Professor Helen Vendler and by the late Irish poet and Stanford professor Eavan Boland, his staunchest supporters. It radiates with love for his mom Angela on her birthday in 2005:

Sweet Dreams By Luke Marshall Rickford

smell of wheat and cut grass
yellow stripes of light across
a road somewhere far off

buckled in the back seat
nose against glass
i watched the thin white arms

of windmills turning
slowly in the dry heat.
rows of cool green lettuce

and impersonal cows
passed us by. You were up front
with your shades on,

singing along to the radio:
"i will always love you."
when night came i fell asleep

with my head on a pillow
made out of the sweatshirt
you'd been wearing.

After working in the field of mental health as a Clinical Art Therapist, **Anakela** chose to shift her focus from providing psychotherapy to emotionally disturbed and developmentally delayed children, to rearing her own three beloved children as a full-time mom. But until she had her second child, the mentorship of her Spelman College art teacher, Arturo Lindsay, and her Loyola Marymount University marriage and family therapy instructor, Paige Asawa, inspired her as she worked for about ten years as a Clinical Art Therapist.

This is love of the transformative kind, providing cathartic, emotive expression, solace and therapeutic counseling to children and adults in need, many of them from underserved black and Hispanic communities. Because of confidentiality restrictions, I will not name the institutions and clinics where she worked, but I was impressed by the effective, restorative strategies art therapy afforded her clients, such as memory boxes for coping with grief. The reparative effect of emoting through art was also used for recovery from other traumatic experiences, and was employed by Anakela and other Loyola Marymount students during a trip in 2007 to Baton Rouge, Louisiana, to assist survivors of Hurricane

Katrina, mostly black.[3] How I wish that Guyana had similar therapies for those needing it!

Overall, emigrating to the USA has been bountiful for our family. And I hope readers would agree that we've contributed to the understanding and enhancement of the black experience in America in some respects, in return. But being black in America also has its downsides. We've had to struggle against the prejudices of *some* of our children's teachers, and we always had the nagging fear that the tendency of police to shoot and kill people of color might affect *our* family or friends. In Chapter 7 I noted that the police in Guyana threatened, but didn't shoot John Agard, after neighbors misinterpreted our juvenile antics as those of would-be thieves. In Chapter 9, by contrast, I discussed acting at UCSC in *Justifiable Homicide*, a play based on a San Francisco incident in which a cop shot a black man dead but was absolved of all responsibility by the courts, in an all too familiar pattern.

On April 20, 2021, we got our first indication that things could be different when Minneapolis policeman Derek Chauvin was found guilty of murder and manslaughter for kneeling on the neck of George Floyd until he died in May 2020, an incident that provoked world-wide protest.[4] But less than a week later another black man, Daunte Wright, 20, was killed by police following a traffic stop just ten miles away.[5] Police in the US "kill far more people than do police in other advanced industrial democracies," and:

> Black women and men and American Indian and Alaska Native women and men are significantly more likely than white women and men to be killed by police. Latino men are also more likely to be killed by police than are white men.[6]

On our daughter **Shiyama's** 46th birthday, June 2, 2019, Miles Hall, the 23-year-old son of her black college friends, Scott and Taun Hall, was shot dead by police in Walnut Creek, California. We had met Miles and his parents at an earlier party in Shiyama and Neale's home.

Apparently, Miles was having a schizophrenic mental health episode on June 2, but in the words of the Halls,

> the Walnut Creek police responded to our call for help … with lethal force. On a sunny afternoon in our quiet neighborhood, the Walnut Creek Police shot and killed Miles within a block from our home before making any efforts to de-escalate the situation.[7]

Shiyama, a Public Affairs Director at Kaiser who had been most influenced by race theorist Kimberlé Williams Crenshaw while doing her J.D. at UCLA Law School, sprang into action, fighting for justice, love in public. Writing to friends of Scott and Taun in June 27, 2019, she noted that:

> The video of Miles' horrific last moments in the reckless hands of Walnut Creek police officers was released two days ago … I had to will myself to watch it, and it took until the wee hours of the morning to do so.

This was a gross miscarriage of justice and a violation of human rights and humanity. Miles was not running at police officers, as they'd claimed. He was running off to the side, away from them, terrified and trying to get home to his respite and a place of comfort.

Immediately after beanbags were fired, bullets were fired—with no tasers or de-escalation strategies used at any point. A rookie cop with 1 year of experience fired at Miles, along with … an officer with four years' experience …

I'm incensed by this disgusting display of police brutality. I would like to do something about this, rather than just stand by and be saddened and sickened.

The action she *did* take was to cofound FOSATH (= Friends of Scott, Alexis and Taun Hall) a grassroots organization, later a Facebook group, to lobby for justice. The group began attending monthly Walnut Creek City Council meetings en masse, created yard signs and lobbied the DA to press criminal charges. Today FOSATH has swollen from 8 to 525 members, and State Assembly member Rebecca Bauer-Kahan, District 16 has introduced AB 988—the Miles Hall Lifeline Act—to create a new 988 phone line to provide a better response for individuals in crisis who need help from mental health professionals rather than untrained police.[8]

In September 2020 the city of Walnut Creek agreed to pay $4 million to the Taun family to settle a lawsuit by civil rights attorney John Burris, but it did not admit to liability or fault by City employees. On May 7, 2021 as this memoir was being finalized, the Contra Costa District attorney's office announced that the two

Figure 17.1 "Justice for Miles Hall" yard sign amid Angela's roses, in our Palo Alto driveway, May 2021.

police officers who shot Miles Hall will *not* face charges, a decision that made national news headlines on CNN and NBC. Nevertheless, the Hall family and FOSATH are not about to give up the fight. They held a rally on the same day. The Hall family and FOSATH plan to lobby the California attorney general to review the local district attorney's investigation of the case.

As the cases of Trayvon Martin (Chapter 16) and so many others testify, the lives of people of color *do* matter, and we need justice. In the words of Cornel West, "justice is what love looks like in public, just like tenderness is what love feels like in private."[9]

On a more hopeful note, I'd like to end this memoir by pointing to two positive developments, and they are both Stanford-related.

The first is that Stanford linguistics professor Dan Jurafsky and Psychology professor Jennifer Eberhardt, along with other researchers from Linguistics, Psychology and Computer Science, have been studying body camera footage from the Oakland Police Department for years to understand and improve police-community relations. One important finding so far, shared with the police, is that officers use less respectful language with black than with white community members,[10] and this can lead to more negative outcomes. The project has now expanded to include body cam footage from other police departments, the language of community members, and researchers outside Stanford as well. There is good reason to believe this massive project will yield results that will help these and other police departments and save lives.

For the second positive development, I need to share another poem, written by our son Luke when he was a teenager:

Potential By Luke M. Rickford

The most beautiful sound I ever heard
Was purer than the preacher's word
Clearer than the dawnsong of any blackbird
It resurrected my soul.
The most joyous thing I was ever told
Was more wonderful than whole mines of gold
Deeper in meaning than the Dead Sea Scrolls
It chilled my hot blood cold.
The greatest day I was blessed to see
Was far far dearer, more sacred to me
Than the morning the slaves found out they were free
For that was beyond my control …

I asked a young Black girl
Dare she dream
Of being our country's president
And though her response may seem self-evident
It was the sweetest Yes
I've known.

Figure 17.2 Vice President Kamala Harris takes the Oath of Office on the platform of
the US Capitol during the 59th Presidential Inauguration, January 20, 2021.
(Photo by Biksu Tong, Shutterstock.)

That dream (appropriately gender sensitive, since *all* US presidents and vice-presidents until then had been *male*) is closer to reality than when Luke wrote it about 20 years ago. Because in 2021 we now have Kamala Harris as Vice President, the first woman, and the first person of African and East Indian heritage to fill this role. Her dad was Stanford Professor Donald Harris, originally from Jamaica, and her mother was Shyamala Gopalan, originally from India, and a leading cancer researcher who earned her PhD from the University of California Berkeley. Kamala was born in Oakland and raised in the San Francisco Bay area. As Harris herself notes in her autobiography, in words that resonate with me because I too was an immigrant, and the Vice President's words recall both public (justice) and private (tenderness) love:[11]

> My mother was expected to return to India after she completed her degree …
> But fate had other plans. She and my father met and fell in love at Berkeley
> while participating in the civil rights movement. Her marriage—and her decision to stay in the United States—were the ultimate acts of self-determination
> and love.

Notes

1 Russell's influences at Columbia include dissertation members Eric Foner and Manning
Marable, among others. In addition to *Betty Shabazz* (2005), he single-authored *We Are*

an African People: Independent Education, Black Power and the Radical Imagination (Oxford, 2019) and edited *Beyond Boundaries: The Manning Marable Reader* (Routledge, 2011). He has also been extensively involved in struggles for justice, from teaching in prison to fighting for workers' rights.

2 Four of Luke's poems appear in *Falling Hard: 100 Love Poems by Teenagers*, ed. by Betsy Franco, Cambridge: Candlewick Press, 2008.

3 https://www.dailynews.com/2007/10/05/healing-after-the-hurricane/#

4 https://www.bbc.com/news/world-us-canada-56818766

5 https://www.cnn.com/2021/04/13/us/daunte-wright-family-reaction/index.html

6 Edwards Frank, Hedwig Lee and Michael Esposito. 2019. "Risk of being killed by police use of force in the United States by age, race-ethnicity, and sex." *PNAS* 116.34: 16973–16978. https://www.pnas.org/content/116/34/16793

7 https://www.justiceformileshall.org/miles

8 https://leginfo.legislature.ca.gov/faces/billStatusClient.xhtml?bill_id=202120220AB988

9 Documented by Takim Williams as having been best contextualized by Cornel West in a 2011 Howard University speech: https://www.traffickinginstitute.org/incontext-cornel-west/

10 https://news.stanford.edu/2017/06/05/cops-speak-less-respectfully-black-community-members/. See also Rob Voigt, Nicholas P. Camp, Vinodkumar Prabhakaran, William L. Hamilton, Rebecca C. Hetey, Camilla M. Griffiths, David Jurgens, Dan Jurafsky, and Jennifer L. Eberhardt. 2017. "Language from police body camera footage shows racial disparities in officer respect." *PNAS* (=*Proceedings of the National Academy of Sciences*) June 20, 2017 114 (25) 6521–6526.

11 Kamala Harris. 1920. *The Truths We Hold. An American Journey*. New York: Penguin Books, p. 5.

Index

Note: References in italics and bold refer to figures and tables respectively, and references following "n" refer to endnotes.

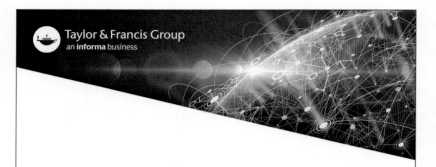

For Product Safety Concerns and Information please contact our
EU representative GPSR@taylorandfrancis.com Taylor & Francis
Verlag GmbH, Kaufingerstraße 24, 80331 München, Germany